THE REFERENCE SHELF   VOLUME 45 NUMBER 2

THE PERFORMING ARTS
IN AMERICA

EDITED BY
DIANA REISCHE

THE H. W. WILSON COMPANY
NEW YORK   1973

THE REFERENCE SHELF

The books in this series contain reprints of articles, excerpts from books, and addresses on current issues and social trends in the United States and other countries. There are six separately bound numbers in each volume, all of which are generally published in the same calendar year. One number is a collection of recent speeches; each of the others is devoted to a single subject and gives background information and discussion from various points of view, concluding with a comprehensive bibliography. Books in the series may be purchased individually or on subscription.

Library of Congress Cataloging in Publication Data

Reische, Diana L   comp.
   The performing arts in America.

   (The Reference shelf, v. 45, no. 2)
   Bibliography: p.
   1. Performing arts--United States.   I. Title.
II. Series.
PN1582.U6R4   790.2'0973   73-7542
ISBN 0-8242-0505-7

PREFACE

Several years ago a study commissioned by the Twentieth Century Fund found that only 3 percent of the American public ever attends a live cultural performance in a given year. Further, it found that this 3 percent who went to theater, opera, symphonies were much alike: fairly young, professional, and above average in income. It is well to keep these figures in mind when considering the state of the performing arts in the United States, for the vast majority of Americans, evidently, do not see live theater, attend the opera, watch ballet or modern dance, or hear musicians perform in person.

All this does not signify, however, that 97 percent of the American public is culture starved. Far from it. The revolution that has taken place in our century in the arts is that a performance which in the past was inevitably "live" can now be recorded and filmed, taped and televised. It is not even necessary to go somewhere to see it if there is a television set in the house. Moreover, records and tape cassettes can be bought and played at home or in the car. Radio broadcasts music that only the rich once heard. Television washes over tens of millions every day. In fact, a top-rated popular TV program is seen on a single Saturday night by more people than attend all the plays on Broadway in a year.

The discussion, then, is about two kinds of performing arts: live performances such as theater, dance, opera, pop concerts, night club acts, symphonic music—anything that either succeeds or fails before one's eyes without possibility of editing or dubbing or refilming to tone up and smooth off the performance's rough edges; and recorded and filmed performances such as movies, recordings, most television. The dividing line is not always firm between the two forms, but the concept is useful for purposes of discussion.

3

One of the authors quoted in this book refers to theater as a handicraft industry in the machine age. It is an apt image, and explains much of the economic dilemma faced by virtually all live performing arts. No one has devised a way of machine-tooling a new play or opera. To hone it to whatever perfection it will achieve before it goes before an audience is all tinkering and "hand" work.

Each performance of a ballet or an opera or a play depends, too, on the mood and talent of each performer, the dexterity of the stagehands, the imagination of the director. The exact mood and shading of tonight's performance won't be there tomorrow, for even the difference in the audience affects how performers feel. It is costly, very costly, furthermore, to mount highly polished live performances.

While there are certain shared problems and joys in all the performing arts, live performances have special pitfalls and frailties not necessarily shared by recorded ones. Too, there are economic strengths available to film, television, and recordings not generally available to live performances —unless they can be filmed for subsequent showings.

What, then, is the state of the performing arts in the United States today? Several approaches to the question are possible, and each is only that, for the question requires several different kinds of answer. One approach is in terms of mechanics and economics—spaces available, cultural centers, and methods of financing. These aspects of the arts are discussed in the first section of this compilation. Again, the difference between live performances and mass-media performances stands out sharply—for the economics of the two are quite different.

Although the money involved and the place the performance is presented are vital to the survival and effectiveness of a performing troupe, they tell little about the quality of the performance. Is it vital? creative? Does it touch people's lives? Does it expand the audiences' perceptions? Who is superb in this field and who is merely popular? Here one enters the realm of personal taste and criticism. As much as possible, this book attempts to avoid these enticing but complex questions and rather to survey in general terms the health of each of the separate art forms. Individual authors, of course, have made some of their own judgments, but the compiler's effort has been to include articles that illuminate the state of each art form.

For convenience, after Section I the book is divided into sections according to generally accepted types of performances—for instance, theater, film, opera, and dance. It must be kept in mind, however, that one of the strong trends in the arts is a melting of traditional lines as one art form spills over and enriches another. Full-length movies are now often simply films of pop music festivals. Ballet is on television. Films are made especially for television.

Talented performers and creators slip easily from one form of expression to another. Jerome Robbins, to name one, has been equally successful as a choreographer for hit Broadway musicals and as a creator of classical ballet set to Chopin and Bach. Leonard Bernstein, also highly successful on Broadway, gave music lessons on television to children, with the New York Philharmonic on hand to demonstrate.

Physical theater itself is changing as architects explore new methods of making a single building flexible enough to accommodate classical theater, repertory explorations, and perhaps even musical events. Libraries and museums are opening their doors to music ensembles and dance groups.

Another clearly perceived trend in all forms of the performing arts is a loosening of previous strictures and conventions. Language that would have been unacceptable on the stage or on film a decade ago is no longer so. Popular songs have lyrics that would have rendered them unbroadcastable a decade ago—yet today they are on radio regularly. Nudity is frequent in films. Sexual practices and deviations that weren't even mentioned in polite company are now frequent topics of popular films, theater, dance. Great permissiveness is the rule in all the arts, with most forms of censorship either altogether absent or much weakened.

One's personal attitude on the new permissiveness, then, might well shape one's answer to a question about the state of the performing arts. Or the answer might equally well depend on where one lives. In the great cities there is live theater, symphony music, several television channels, and a selection of movie theaters, indicating a time of enormous artistic activity for America. The feast from which to choose in a city like New York is so great that even the most assiduous attender cannot see a third of what is available. For those who live elsewhere, however, the picture is spottier. There is fine regional theater and dance in some sections, none in others. Even the broad range of film shown in cities such as San Francisco and Chicago may not be available in smaller communities.

Yet, because of the recorded arts—film, records, television—a rich smorgasbord of the arts is available to most Americans. It is not as much as everyone might wish but still an array that would have been envied by kings of old.

The editor wishes to thank the publishers and authors who have permitted reuse of their material in this book.

DIANA REISCHE

April 1973

A NOTE TO THE READER

For further information on the arts in America, the reader is referred to *American Culture in the Sixties*, edited by Vineta Colby (Reference Shelf, volume 36, number 1), published in 1964.

CONTENTS

II. THEATER IN THE SEVENTIES

III. OPERA AND DANCE—THE ELEGANT ARTS

IV. MUSIC: POPULAR AND CLASSICAL

DISTRIBUTION OF THE EXPENDITURE DOLLAR, BY ART FORM

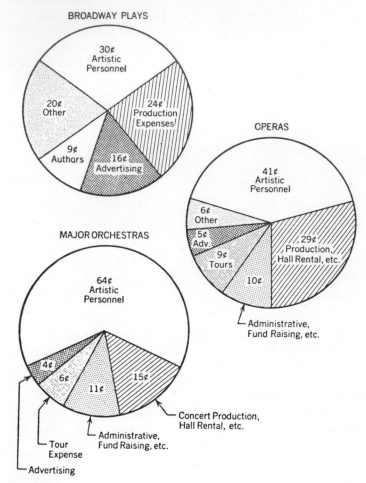

BROADWAY PLAYS

30¢ Artistic Personnel

24¢ Production Expenses

20¢ Other

9¢ Authors

16¢ Advertising

OPERAS

41¢ Artistic Personnel

6¢ Other

5¢ Adv.

9¢ Tours

29¢ Production, Hall Rental, etc.

10¢

Administrative, Fund Raising, etc.

MAJOR ORCHESTRAS

64¢ Artistic Personnel

4¢

6¢

11¢

15¢

Concert Production, Hall Rental, etc.

Administrative, Fund Raising, etc.

Tour Expense

Advertising

Figure VI-1 from Baumol, W. J. and Bowen, W. G. *Performing Arts: The Economic Dilemma.* © 1966 by Twentieth Century Fund, New York. p 144. Reprinted by permission.

I. THE BUSINESS SIDE OF THE ARTS

EDITOR'S INTRODUCTION

In a money-free world a talented writer would create an innovative play, a creative director would assemble a gifted cast, and the ideal space would be available at the right time to offer a showcase for this consummate work of art. In our less-than-perfect world overriding considerations of money, talent, money, space, and again money intrude. The costs of elegant art forms such as opera, symphony, and classical ballet are high and still climbing. Experience over the years has shown that ticket prices cannot be raised to a point where they always cover true costs. Hence there is the need for subsidies—from the rich, from business, from government—to keep repertory and experimental theaters running, opera companies from disbanding, and musicians from striking.

In this section many disparate aspects of the business of the arts are explored. Each performing art has its own particular constellation of economic factors. Some of these specifics are treated in subsequent sections on individual forms of the performing arts. This section offers both an overview of the economics of the performing arts and some of the specific considerations that enter into programming and booking performances.

The first article, by the writer Martin Mayer, explores the economics of the major performing arts. Mr. Mayer is the author of a Twentieth Century Fund study, *Bricks and Mortar and the Performing Arts*. One increasing source of support for the arts is corporate treasuries, as is shown in a second article, by New York *Times* critic Howard Taubman. Even more heartening to many in the arts is the new and growing role of the Federal Government in shoring up financially wobbly performing groups. The article "Government Help Is Increasing" discusses proposed Federal figures for fiscal year 1974 and notes that, with the national bicentennial approaching, additional Federal help can be expected.

The two articles which follow explore the delicacies of programming that will attract audiences, not lose too much money, and still not outrage the critics. One deals with an old performing hall in Brooklyn that is enjoying an artistic renaissance under creative direction. The other discusses a cultural center built alongside a New Jersey parkway. A basic truth in booking performances, as both places have found, is that it is absolutely impossible to please everybody. The next article illustrates this point. Alan Rich takes vigorous exception to the idea expressed by the management of the New Jersey cultural center that programming must reflect majority tastes. Not so, argues Rich. If that happened, most "good" companies would have to go out of business. This age-old argument will not be settled soon to anyone's satisfaction.

The last three articles survey other dimensions of the complicated business of financing the arts and finding a suitable place to present their varied wares. Martin Mayer, a peripatetic observer of the arts, discusses the economics of recording classical music. He notes that American orchestras are making almost no recordings because of the high costs, whereas London orchestras record regularly but are about to be underbid by Eastern Europeans. There follows a how-to article aimed at individuals who seek guidelines for starting a local arts council as a means of strengthening the performing arts. The final article discusses the great changes that are occurring in the kinds of buildings (or spaces) being designed for changing art forms. As the arts merge and experiment, old theater designs are not always adaptable. Designers are seeking spaces that are flexible enough to accommodate several different kinds of performances. In addition, places that in the past did not feature performances—museums, most notably—are opening their doors to music, dance, film, and theater.

THE BUSINESS OF CULTURE [1]

John Crosby's lovely Santa Fe Opera ... [opened] as usual in July, with seven productions, four of them new and one of the four a world premiere. But the decision to go ahead in 1970 was more of a gamble than the bankers who must advance the money ordinarily like, and nobody is guaranteeing that there will be a Santa Fe season in 1971. The Metropolitan Opera is "looking into an income gap" of little less than $5 million next year. The New York City Opera needed contributions of $1.5 million (including those from sponsors in Los Angeles for the brief season there) to keep afloat this year; and the Chicago Lyric last autumn saw its season deficit rise above $1 million for the first time.

Last May [1969], the management consulting firm of McKinsey and Company reported to the presidents of the Big Five orchestras (Boston, Chicago, Cleveland, New York, and Philadelphia) that their total annual operating deficit, which had been $2.9 million in 1963-64 and $5.7 million in 1967-68, could be projected conservatively at $7.9 million in 1971-72. These orchestras earn nearly two thirds of their costs in box-office receipts, record royalties, and such. Most lesser symphony orchestras are proportionately much worse off; some, indeed, are technically bankrupt, and are borrowing to pay this year's expenses, planning to repay in the spring when next year's subscription revenue arrives.

Ballet, until recently a coterie affair in America, has finally achieved here the broad popular appeal it has always known in Europe, with four major touring companies employed virtually all year long (New York City Ballet, City

[1] From "Where the Dollars Go," article by Martin Mayer, music critic and author of a Twentieth Century Fund study entitled *Bricks and Mortar and the Performing Arts* and of several other books. *Saturday Review*. 53:22-4. F. 28, '70. Copyright © 1970 by Saturday Review, Inc. First appeared in *Saturday Review* February 28, 1970. Used with permission of Saturday Review, Inc. and of the author.

Center Joffrey Ballet, [American] Ballet Theatre, and National Ballet of Canada). With its small orchestras and low-paid dancers, ballet is an inexpensive art form next to opera and symphony, yet the four ballet companies, despite their vastly expanded box office, among them showed an operating loss of well over $2 million in 1969.

Only the regional repertory theaters are still free from multidigit deficits, and their time, clearly, is coming: The two largest enterprises, the Guthrie Theatre in Minneapolis and the Lincoln Center Repertory Theater in New York, are already on the beach, gasping for money. Like the symphony orchestras a decade ago, the repertory theaters in smaller cities are sustained financially by the willingness of their employees to accept psychic income in lieu of decent salaries. With increasing numbers of theater companies securing permanent housing in arts centers, actors will soon be asking why they must work for half (or even one third) the income of the musicians in the orchestras next door. At heart, the actor is just as *petit bourgeois* as the musician, and as the cigar makers and printers proved long ago it's the skilled *petits bourgeois* who build the toughest union.

The arts seem cursed by their own success: The greater attention paid to them, the more money they use. Worse yet, the condition is inevitable and irreversible. The problem in its simplest terms is the artist's inability to improve his economic productivity. Since Carnegie Hall was built eighty years ago, the average American industrial worker has more than quintupled his productivity—that is, aided by machinery, he produces more than five times as much per man-hour as he produced in the 1890s—and the farmer's productivity has gone out of sight. But an orchestra playing to a full house at Carnegie performs precisely the same services that its great-grandfather did when old Andy's friends were in the audience. If the musicians of the orchestra are to maintain their income relative to that of industrial workers, the seats at Carnegie must sell for five times as much in constant dollars. This trend is by no means confined to the arts: Educational, legal, and to a lesser extent medical and domestic services—even storekeeping—are subject to similar relative inflation. As William J. Baumol and William G. Bowen of Princeton put it in their study *Performing Arts: The Economic Dilemma,* the unit costs of labor-intensive services necessarily rise in an economy where wage rates are pegged to the productivity of capital-intensive manufacturing.

To some degree, a few of the art forms have been able to take advantage of changing technology to improve their productivity, if "productivity" can be defined as the numbers of people who enjoy contact with the performance. Recordings and movie use of material, for example, have made possible the continuing and ever more expensive production of Broadway musicals (the Metropolitan Opera, supposedly so wasteful, mounts new opera productions far more elaborate than anything on Broadway for about one third the cost of launching a new musical). Records have also helped the balance sheets of two symphony orchestras, The New York and the Philadelphia; and complicated interaction with film and television has kept the legitimate theater from feeling the full effects of union wage-scales.

Other performing groups have been able to reach larger audiences through expansion of traditional activities—by touring or "running out" to serve additional communities, by lengthening seasons, by increasing the number and variety of performances for school children, by moving to larger halls and theaters, or simply by selling more seats through more professional promotion and manipulation of the subscription series device. Especially in the eastern half of the country, the rapid growth of new summer festivals has enabled orchestras—and, surprisingly, ballet companies—to play to larger audiences for longer seasons.

Such activities—plus higher ticket prices—have generated substantially greater income for the performing groups, and the increasing cash flow is beginning to produce side benefits in the form of better management. Not the least of the handicaps the arts have been carrying is incompetent business leadership. Among the horror stories of recent seasons were the near-catastrophic depletion of the Chicago Symphony endowment fund after management contracted for renovation of the concert hall on the basis of a conditional gift, which the orchestra board later rejected; the total loss of control over production expenses at the Metropolitan Opera in its first year at Lincoln Center; the payment of large consulting fees by the Saratoga Performing Arts Center to prominent New Yorkers, some of whom never even bothered to visit Saratoga; the expenditure of the promotion budget for the entire first year before Ottawa's National Arts Center opened its doors.

These situations were ultimately remedied: The director general of the Ottawa center took over the public relations department himself, Saratoga and Chicago got new general managers, the Met hired a skilled corporate comptroller from the oil industry. Elsewhere, management failures produced more lasting trouble. In Atlanta, the umbrella organization producing for the new Memorial Arts Center collapsed under a hail of bouncing checks. One of the nation's more prominent repertory theaters dissolved when accounting failed to explain the deficits satisfactorily. A new manager arriving in the offices of a medium-sized symphony found that his predecessor had absconded with some tens of thousands of dollars; he then learned that the board didn't want to take action because prosecution might hurt the orchestra's image.

Improvements in management practice will slow the movement of the arts on the road toward insolvency. Ford Foundation internship programs and American Symphony Orchestra League training efforts have already increased the supply of young managers who know at least something about what they are supposed to be doing. The University of California at Los Angeles has begun the construction of an academic program leading to a degree in arts management. And salaries are rising, increasing the prospects of attracting and holding people of talent.

But after all the possible economies within management are deducted from the cost side of the ledger, and all the probable revenue increases from higher priced tickets or bigger audiences are added to the income side, the future balance sheet for the performing arts still tilts alarmingly toward Loss. Even if a company's operating revenues can be made to rise as fast as costs, deficits rise, too. From 1964 to 1969 the Metropolitan Opera's earned revenues rose a little more rapidly than its costs—96.6 per cent for revenues, 95.5 per cent for costs. As a result, the operating loss increased by "only" 94 per cent, from $1.8 million to $3.5 million.

Disaster Is Nearer Than You Think

It is highly unlikely—almost unimaginable—that private giving can continue to pay off the constantly rising deficits of the performing groups. Disaster is much nearer than outsiders seem to realize for a number of institutions, some of them world famous. Corporate contributions, on the rise recently under the leadership of the Business Committee for the Arts, cannot be expected to increase during the profits squeeze of the next eighteen months and may very well decline. Most large individual contributions have been in the form of stocks, thanks to a provision in the tax code that permits the full market value of donated property to be taken as a deduction from taxable income—even though that market value includes a hefty profit on which the owner has paid no taxes. (This provision is one of the loopholes through which some millionaires have entirely escaped income taxes, and for a while last summer Congress seemed ready to kill the deduction; if it had, it would also have killed a lot of orchestras at one blow.) ...

Fickle fashion directs the attention of the rich to do-goodery in the slums, while labor disputes in the arts diminish the psychic rewards of giving. Ultimately, the tragedy of the Metropolitan Opera strike may turn out to have been the late-afternoon encounter of board members and artists at the Drake Hotel, where the directors discovered, apparently for the first time, that the singers and dancers and musicians were not always grateful for the efforts of the board in raising the money to help pay their salaries.

Federal aid to the arts has been, of course, very substantial. Most of the money given to performing groups comes from the rich, the larger corporations, and the foundations —and at least half that total is in fact a Government contribution through operation of the tax laws. In European countries, such contributions are not deductible from taxable income, and government appropriations for arts support can be seen as a centralization of help given here on an utterly decentralized basis. Except in the case of opera, which is massively supported by government grants in Europe (enabling opera houses there to bid against the Met for the services of the superstars), the figures are often comparable. The London Symphony Orchestra, for example, receives about 16 per cent of its total income from the British Arts Council, which probably is somewhat less than the proportion of the total income of American orchestras attributable to taxes forgone by the Treasury.

Nevertheless, as President Nixon recognized in his message to Congress requesting an increase to $40 million for the annual funding of the National Foundation on the Arts and Humanities, Federal support to the performing arts will have to be lifted substantially in the next few years if our institutions are to survive, let alone prosper. We have gone further along the productivity road than have our European contemporaries, and our unit costs for services are thus relatively higher. W. McNeil Lowry, Ford Foundation vice president and founder of its arts program, has commented glumly that the need (including rescue of drowning art museums) is closer to $160 million a year. Even if the President's figure is right, he is talking about a necessity rather than a panacea.

It should be remembered that money alone guarantees very little. Government grants have helped London's Covent

Garden to become one of the great opera companies of the world, but they have failed to lift the Paris Opera from its slough of inconsequence, or to remedy the tradition of slap-dash performances in Vienna. Nobody in his right mind would compare the state-supported ballet companies of the Italian opera houses with any of our major dance groups.

Moreover, while right-wing worries about political dom-ination of the arts are clearly ridiculous, there are reasons for concern about the directions Government-sponsored com-mittees might take in awarding grants. Traditionally it has been the experimental company and the avant-garde artists who needed help from organized charity, and many of those who would be involved with Federal aid programs are still living in an older era. There is a real danger that Federal support will be biased toward high-fashion hermeticism and academia, that orchestras playing to annual audiences in the hundreds of thousands will be allowed to wither, while grants are awarded to, say, "exciting" theater groups pre-senting improvised drama in nonsense syllables to audiences of thirty-seven humorless friends. Someone will have to fight to win adoption of the British Arts Council's policy of allo-cating most—by no means all—Government funds to groups that can show substantial public support at the box office.

Federal largesse, moreover, cannot possibly solve the fi-nancial problems of the performing arts. Demands expand to absorb the available resources. In many cities, orchestras and opera companies live by selling season subscriptions made attractive by the occasional appearance of celebrity soloists and singers; aware of their importance to the market-ing operation, the most celebrated of these artists have upped their fees to as much as $10,000 a night. One singer has gone even higher: Last year she demanded from an opera com-pany $7,500 per performance, *after taxes.*

The greatest single gesture of generosity ever made to musical performance was a Ford Foundation grant of $85 million (three times annual box-office receipts) to the nation's symphony orchestras, awarded on a matching basis

for endowment purposes. To date, this munificent gift seems
to have weakened rather than strengthened the orchestras.
The huge figures thrown around in the newspapers and in
campaigns to raise the matching funds stimulated demands
from the musicians much greater than they would otherwise
have made. Of course, the money is now in the bank, and if
things get rough Ford's superbly practical donation will
doubtless allow it to be used as necessary. But actors and
dancers and musicians have been underpaid too long to
permit the institutions that employ them to build a kitty
at their expense.

Immense Capital Investment

An exacerbating element in the attitudes of working artists has been the nation's immense capital investment in
the arts during the last half-dozen years. President Nixon in
his message to Congress estimated that in 1969 alone no less
than $207 million was spent on new theaters and arts cen-
ters. This was at least equal to the total box-office receipts
of all live professional performances above the nightclub
level, and it was something more than five times the total
operating deficit of our four leading ballet companies, six
major opera houses, twelve best nonprofit theaters, and
twenty largest orchestras, all taken together. There is an
American tradition at work here—Andrew Carnegie built
libraries for communities that refused to buy books to put
in them—but it's an unusually stupid one.

A . . . Twentieth Century Fund study, *Bricks, Mortar
and the Performing Arts,* for which I was the reporter and
Roger Stevens was a panel member, examines the ambivalent
effect of the new theaters and arts centers on the performing
groups that occupy them. Unquestionably, the new buildings have strengthened interest in the arts wherever they
have been built, have increased audiences for existing groups,
and have given impetus to formation of new groups. Unquestionably, too, they have increased the costs of operation
for everyone who uses them.

Over the long run, the costs and benefits to the arts from construction projects may come into somewhat better balance than they have yet achieved. The presence of these elephants (usually white) has provoked the interesting idea that theaters and halls should be maintained at public expense, as museums and libraries are. Properly planned, the facilities naturally associated with such centers—especially parking and restaurant facilities which depend for their income on the attractions presented—can be made to contribute to performing expenses.

Kennedy Center in Washington expects considerable revenue from guided tours. In Milwaukee, county government makes up the difference between the revenues of the arts center (including rentals of its ballrooms and restaurant) and the actual costs of operation. In Seattle, Houston, and San Antonio, the performing arts facilities are supported essentially by profits from sports arenas and convention halls in the same complex. Montreal's busy Place des Arts is subsidized by the provincial and local governments; Ottawa's new National Arts Center enjoys a direct grant from the Canadian Parliament. In New York, by contrast, the city government greedily seizes the profits from the Lincoln Center garage (probably about $500,000 a year), even though the garage itself was built without a penny of municipal contribution.

Guaranteed low rentals are a more secure source of subsidy than annual appropriations. The benefits offered by most performing arts groups are overwhelmingly local, and decisions on relative levels of support should surely be as localized as possible. Ideally, the states should provide the necessary help, and it is not impossible that they will: Governor Nelson Rockefeller in his 1970 budget message proposed an $18 million annual appropriation for "aid to cultural institutions" in New York State. (By comparison, all the states together in 1969 provided only $7.6 million.) But the states are hard pressed, and support for such assistance is by no means assured in any legislature. Last September

[1969], on the day the Performing Arts Center opened in Milwaukee, a Wisconsin state legislator told the Milwaukee County executive that if he needed more money for welfare he should cut out the few hundred thousand dollars a year the county spends on the arts: "I grew up," growled Assemblyman Kenneth J. Merkel, "without all that stuff." Whatever its faults, Washington operates on higher levels of sophistication than that.

On the horizon are problems nobody has really thought about. Video recording, pay cable TV, and satellite relay systems, which make transmission costs independent of distances, will eventually bring the world's most talented theater, dance, and opera companies to home screens at low prices. How well local lesser-but-live professional talent will be able to compete is something nobody knows. Among the factors certain to influence the answer are the degree to which the suburban sprawl will further disperse potential audiences, the quality of urban transportation systems, and the heightening or reduction of the fear of going out at night. Meanwhile, President Nixon has asked for $40 million, and the arts need what the President proposes, intelligently administered, just to stay alive. Everyone should give a heave and a ho on Congress for the money that will insure the chance of a future worth planning for. [By fiscal year 1974, the President's request had risen to $80 million.—Ed.]

ARTS GET MORE CORPORATE HELP [2]

Direct corporate support of the arts is likely to climb to $75 million in 1972. In the opinion of officials of the Business Committee for the Arts, such a projection is not wild optimism but based on remarkable development in the last few years.

In the words of Robert O. Anderson, chairman of Atlantic Richfield and of the committee:

[2] From article by Howard Taubman, former *Times* critic-at-large specializing in theater. New York *Times*. p 43. Ja. 10, '72. © 1972 by The New York Times Company. Reprinted by permission.

The past year [1971] provided encouraging evidence that corporate support of the arts will continue to expand rapidly in 1972 and the years ahead. Between 1968 and 1970 corporate philanthropic contributions to the arts increased 24 per cent—from $45 million to $56 million, according to a nationwide survey conducted by Touche Ross & Company, in behalf of the Business Committee for the Arts.

Eighteen per cent of the corporations said they would give more in 1972 than they had in 1970 and plan to increase their giving in subsequent years. Sixty-eight per cent said that they would contribute at least as much in 1972 as they had in 1970. Since 1965, when total corporate philanthropic contributions to the arts were only $22 million annually, they have increased 160 per cent.

The aim of business supporters of the arts is to match the performance record American industry made in gifts to higher education. From a few million given to colleges and universities just after World War II, business support has risen to hundreds of millions. . . .

But total corporate giving to education in 1970 declined 9.3 per cent, according to the 1970 *Survey of Corporation Support of Higher Education* just issued by the Council for Financial Aid to Education. Campus turmoil and financial chaos have not gone unnoticed in corporate board rooms. . . .

What business will do specifically in 1972 will be along the lines of its support in recent years—that is, it will contribute to the maintenance and operating funds of museums, symphony orchestras, opera companies, dance companies and theater groups. It will also make substantial commitments to the wide dissemination of the arts as Texaco has done in its sponsorship of the Metropolitan Opera broadcasts for many years and as Mobil Oil has done with "Masterpiece Theater" on National Education Television.

According to G. A. McLellan, president of the Business Committee for the Arts, and his staff, business is on the lookout for fresh, exciting projects to support. When the Aluminum Company of America was told that last year's stunning exhibit at the Museum of Modern Art of the Stein family collection needed support, it came forward with a $100,000 contribution.

The Joseph Schlitz Brewing Company, which has underwritten New York Philharmonic concerts in the parks, intends to bring the orchestra to Milwaukee for a free concert and to send the Milwaukee Symphony to New York.

Some corporations will contribute toward bringing the arts to the educational television network. General Telephone and Electronics is supporting performances by Joan Sutherland, the soprano. The Standard Oil Company (New Jersey) and its principal United States affiliate, the Humble Oil and Refining Company, are helping to make possible twenty programs devoted to performing artists from around the world. CIBA-Geigy is contributing toward a series called "The Restless Earth."

Besides direct support, business intends to continue and perhaps increase its indirect support. The big department stores—Macy's, Gimbels and A&S [Abraham & Straus] in New York are typical—have made a practice of devoting advertising space in newspapers to publicize the arts in their communities.

According to Mr. Anderson, "several companies have begun to provide a wide range of free management and fiscal services to arts institutions that are otherwise unable to afford them."

For some of these services, corporations have not attempted to fix a dollar value and have not even listed them in the sums they will allocate to the arts in 1972. One corporation that made a four-figure gift to Lincoln Center [New York] last year accounted for it under "miscellaneous." Business support for the arts, which is indirect or not clearly defined as such, should bring the total corporate commitment in 1972 to well over $80 million.

GOVERNMENT HELP IS INCREASING [3]

The inclusion in President Nixon's 1974 budget of a record $80 million for the arts, more than doubling the amount of the previous year, is a tribute to the combined efforts of national, state and local arts organizations in pushing for Federal support of culture.

The proposals, which supporters expect Congress to approve, are even more noticeable when they are placed against the background of large-scale fiscal trimming of other Federal programs, particularly in the areas of social services and education. They reflect, spokesmen for national and state arts organizations agreed . . . President Nixon's awareness of the plight of the arts in America and a recognition that support for the arts has become a glamorous political issue. Others see it as motivated by the approaching Bicentennial of 1976, toward which the arts are expected to make a major contribution. The Administration request specifically notes, "in 1974, emphasis will be placed on projects leading up to the Bicentennial."

The enlarged Federal arts proposal parallels the increased budgetary emphasis on the arts in New York State, which has been warmly supported by Governor [Nelson] Rockefeller. It was understood that, in informal conversations with the President, the governor had urged continued support for national arts programs. . . . [In January 1973] Governor Rockefeller proposed a $15 million arts budget for fiscal 1974, $2 million more than in the previous year, and subsequently asked for an additional $5 million in his "deficiency budget" for 1972-73 for the State Council on the Arts "to alleviate the mounting fiscal crisis" in nonprofit arts organizations.

Nancy Hanks, chairman of the National Endowment for the Arts, which will distribute the proposed [Federal] funds, said . . . [on January 30] that her organization would receive

[3] From "Nixon's $80-Million Aid for Arts Is Hailed" by George Gent, cultural news reporter. New York *Times.* p 26. Ja. 31, '73. © 1973 by The New York Times Company. Reprinted by permission.

$72.5 million for grants to the nation's cultural organization, as well as to provide assistance to individual performing and creative artists. For direct contribution to state councils of the arts under the Federal-State Partnership program, $8.25 million is being set aside, with each state expected to receive $150,000.

An additional fund of $7.5 million will be provided to encourage cultural organizations in seeking contributions from outside sources.

"We're very pleased at the steady growth of the endowment of the last few years," Miss Hanks said. She noted that the Endowment had nearly doubled its allocation every year since 1970, when the appropriation was for $7 million.

"As far as where the money will go," she declared, "we feel very strongly that we should continue to be responsive to the needs and requests of the people out there."

A similar view was expressed by Amyas Ames, chairman of Lincoln Center for the Performing Arts and head of Partnership for the Arts, a four-year-old nationwide lobbying organization supported by cultural leaders and seeking $200 million annually in Federal support for the arts.

"The news of the President's proposed budget is wonderful," said Mr. Ames. "Step by step he has moved Federal aid for the arts toward levels that will be truly effective." Mr. Ames said Partnership for the Arts and other arts organizations had set a goal of $200 million for the nation's Bicentennial in 1976.

"Our proposal is a real goal," he said, "and one that has gained acceptance in every state, where people on the grassroots level have written to their Congressmen and to the White House expressing their views on the crisis affecting the arts. The President's action recognizes it as a real crisis." . . .

"I think the record of Nancy Hanks and the President in effect doubling the appropriation in the arts each year has been extraordinary and reflects the kind of concerns which have been felt in this state all along," said . . . [Eric] Larrabee [executive director of the New York State Council on the Arts].

BRINGING THE ARTS BACK TO
FLATBUSH AVENUE [4]

From about the time the Dodgers left, some fourteen years ago, the mere mention of Brooklyn conjured up visions of dreary slums—Bedford-Stuyvesant, Green Point, Brownsville. This largest of New York's five boroughs, if it were independent, would rank third in size among the nation's cities. But it has come to be regarded as a region of utter physical and spiritual urban decay.

Thus it may come as news to outsiders, particularly Manhattanites who rarely cross the river, that Brooklyn once more is showing signs of life. Young married couples are moving in and sprucing up depressed old brownstone neighborhoods. Businessmen and civic leaders have organized to fight for the reconstruction of down-at-the-heels public and private facilities. Not the least of the renovations has been the revival of the once prestigious Brooklyn Academy of Music.

During its 114 years, the Academy had been host to such performers as Enrico Caruso, Isadora Duncan and Sarah Bernhardt. But, with time, its bookings had dwindled to a few recitals. Surrounded by rundown hotels, nondescript stores and deteriorating brownstones, it drifted into such obscurity that even taxi drivers didn't know it was still there.

Rejuvenation began in 1967 with the appointment of forty-three-year-old Harvey Lichtenstein, a tall, scholarly-looking native son, who launched a torrent of projects for turning the institution into an urban renewal project unto itself. Realizing that Brooklyn was a fragmented community without a radio or television station, a newspaper . . . or any other cohesive force, Lichtenstein set about trying to attract attention for the Academy to create a focus for local pride.

[4] From article by Phyllis Funke, staff writer. *Wall Street Journal.* p 16. N. 22, '72. Reprinted with permission of The Wall Street Journal.

Toward this end, Lichtenstein sought high-caliber attractions that were not appearing elsewhere in the New York metropolitan area. A former dancer, he turned to the field he knew best, figuring he could get the most for the Academy's money by bringing to Brooklyn modern dance companies that were well recognized but unable—at that time—to find theaters in Manhattan.

Among the names he booked were Merce Cunningham, Alvin Ailey, Paul Taylor, Alwin Nikolais and Martha Graham. He also mixed in a bit of theater, including productions by the renowned Polish director, Jerzy Grotowski, The Living Theater, and the Chelsea Theatre Center, for which the Academy was to become a permanent home.

Lichtenstein also concentrated on attracting and involving those who rarely, if ever, went to any cultural event. This meant recognizing that among Brooklyn's 2.6 million residents were many ethnic groups—Jews, Arabs, Irish, Italians, Scandinavians and Latins from nearly every Central and South American country. It also meant remembering that about a third of the borough was nonwhite and that the average family income was less than in the rest of the city. One approach was ethnic programming. During Lichtenstein's first five years, the Academy presented dancers from Cambodia, acrobats from Iran, Berbers from Morocco, and an Afro-Asian Festival, with dance companies from Senegal and Sierra Leone.

This season [1972-73] by more fully utilizing the Academy's facilities—a 2,200-seat opera house, a 1,200-seat music hall and a 200-seat theater—the ethnic schedule is even broader. The first attraction in this category was the Jewish State Theater of Bucharest, performing in Yiddish. It was followed by the Nuria Espert Company of Spain, with its revolutionary production of García Lorca's *Yerma* in Spanish with simultaneous translation available.

The music calendar lists "Black People's Music" which on various dates presents the gospel choruses of various Brooklyn churches in concerts of new and traditional music;

while the dance calendar features the Jamaican National Dance Company in April.

Because of its success, the Afro-Asian Festival is being repeated, this season spotlighting the Dancers of Mali, the Whirling Dervishes of Turkey and the Darpana Dance Company of India. These and other carefully selected programs are often presented to city schoolchildren, more than 200,000 of whom will be bused to the Academy this season.

Seth Faison, a lifetime Brooklyn resident, former chairman of the Academy's board of directors, and vice president of the Wall Street insurance firm of Johnson & Higgins, says, "If you have an audience of 2,000 kids, of whom 1,500 are black and you present them with a white symphony orchestra playing European music, it is as if you are telling them they don't have a role in culture. But if they see even one or two black artists in a company, at least they can think 'Here is an art form that, if I'm good, I can aspire to.' "

The Academy's desire to make the whole community welcome reaches far beyond ethnic considerations, however. To all youngsters it offers dance classes for $1. And though its top ticket price is only $6.50, "rush" tickets for $2 are available for senior citizens an hour before performances. Some attractions are scheduled for Thursday matinees at 1:00 P.M. so that the elderly can receive their half-fare discount on public transportation and be home before dark. Cut-rates are also in effect for students.

Revitalization is not limited to cultural matters. The Academy also has plans for enhancing its physical appeal. Inside it hopes to turn its upstairs hallway into a ballroom for community functions and experimental theater.

Outside its new spirit seems to have touched just about everything around it. On one side block, an entrepreneur has bought 20 of the 23 brownstones and is renovating them. Another side block, formerly covered by a large warehouse, has been leveled. This has exposed the Academy to full view from Flatbush Avenue, a major thoroughfare, and has made room for a low-priced parking lot which will open shortly.

There are plans for a park, with a cafe and cultural facilities, directly across the street.

Measuring the impact of any cultural institution is necessarily imprecise. The Academy is pleased that its membership has increased to 4,000 from 3,000 in the last couple of years. But it also treasures a letter it received from a second-grader who had just witnessed the Blue Nile Dancers from Ethiopia: "I liked the whole thing. . . . They danced lovely. . . . Please invite me again."

"You look at some of the people and just know they've never been to a performance before," says Lichtenstein. "But you also can see the old standbys. All types of people, from all sorts of backgrounds, thronging together with a special sense of belonging. This is what makes reviving the Academy an exciting, rewarding project."

ON RUNNING A "CULTURAL CENTER" [5]

At the dawn of its fifth season, the Garden State Arts Center [in Holmdel, N.J.] is still trying to solidify its identity. The philosophy of its program is being sifted to make all segments of state residents feel welcome. Solvency, meantime, remains a stranger.

Annual deficits totaling some $1.2 million over the first four seasons have been absorbed in the operating expenses of the New Jersey Highway Authority, which built, owns and operates both the center and the only route to it—the Garden State Parkway.

That jurisdictional arrangement, born of the Authority's legislative mandate, and the use of parkway tolls to help finance the $6.75 million center, originally drew sharp criticism from some state legislators and newspaper editors.

The complaints started close on the heels of the announcement in the mid-sixties of the heady recreational and cultural plans the authority had for 250 of the 350 acres

[5] From "Parkway Arts Center Popularizes Program," by Robert Hanley, metropolitan reporter. New York *Times*. p 55. Ap. 2, '72. © 1972 by The New York Times Company. Reprinted by permission.

purchased near Exit 116 as part of the parkway's right-of-way. Armed with broad development powers, the authority had hoped to set an amphitheater, an art museum, a playhouse, a mirror pool and a ski slope among the red and white pine, the pear trees and the native azalea on Telegraph Hill Park, an old picnic grove about thirty miles south of Newark.

Legislative complaints killed nearly all those facilities in the blueprint stage, according to James P. Gallagher, who resigned as chairman of the Republican party in Middlesex County in mid-1970 to take over the nonsalaried post of Highway Authority chairman. What survived was the heart of the development program, an open-sided amphitheater, snug in a hollow, with five thousand seats and eight columns rising toward an inverted dome roof. Its construction costs ran $5 million above expectations.

And persistent heavier-than-desired expenses remained one of Mr. Gallagher's prime enemies after the 1971 season. . . . [The 1971] deficit, he said, was $350,000, even though traffic to the center provided $200,000 of the parkway's total toll income of $47 million.

Hoping for a $200,000 savings this year, Mr. Gallagher has renegotiated the final year of a five-year contract with the Nederlander Arts Associates—a New York firm that had broad booking and operational power since the amphitheater's opening in 1968. . . . Mr. Gallagher said Nederlander made $300,000 [in 1971] for its "very good services" under a contract that Mr. Gallagher believed was to the Authority's jurisdictional and financial disadvantage.

Nederlander is restricted under the new contract to booking performers and handling musicians and stage hands. And gone now is a provision that gave the company two thirds of the net profits and the Authority one third. That clause on the split worked to the firm's advantage, Mr. Gallagher said, because, under it, such Authority costs as security, public relations, maintenance and a shuttle-bus service did not figure in calculation of net profits. . . .

With the cost cutting and tighter management control, Mr. Gallagher hopes to reach a financial break-even point for the center that former Governor Richard J. Hughes once predicted would become "one of the world's greatest stages."

The other major project consuming most of Mr. Gallagher's energies is a broadening of the Garden State Arts Center Fund. Under it, the center's programming has been stretched beyond the original concept of summer week-nights of ballet and classical- and popular-music concerts, and is aimed now at "new audiences"—Jerseyites of all ages, economic backgrounds and ethnic origins.

"Heritage Festivals" are an integral part of the campaign to draw various ethnic groups to the center. Last year, Irish and Italian groups staged a variety of national programs. "And this year," Mr. Gallagher said . . . [in March 1972] "Scandinavian and Polish organizations in the state are going to take part."

Net proceeds will go to the Arts Center Fund. Different from the center itself, which is financed solely by the Highway Authority and paid admissions, the fund survives solely on private contributions. In 1970, enough money was raised to provide a variety of free entertainment for 80,000 students and senior citizens. . . . Mr. Gallagher said 160,000 were able to partake [in 1971].

Currently, he's in the middle of a campaign to raise $300,000 for free entertainment starting in May [1972] for 500,000 people. The performances are to include live shows for preschoolers in July and August by Bugs Bunny, Charley Brown and other cartoon favorites; ballet, light drama and choruses for older children and teen-agers, including those from disadvantaged areas, and band concerts for the elderly, the blind and disabled veterans on afternoons in May and June.

Some of the $300,000 has already been obtained through the purchase of $1,000 sustaining memberships in the fund by members of the business and professional community throughout the state.

But Mr. Gallagher hopes to realize better than two thirds of the goal on June 10, when the comedian Bob Hope is to entertain at the center. Tickets for the gala benefit, priced at $100, $75 and $50, are being pushed among top state officials and legislators.

Four nights after Mr. Hope's appearance, the center's official season will be opened for the third consecutive summer by the New Jersey Symphony Orchestra, conducted by Henry Lewis. . . .

Tickets for the individual performances are almost the same as they were in 1968, $3.50 to $7.50, with top prices for two or three performances scaled to $8.50. Admission for seats on the sloping lawn around the amphitheater is $2.

The official acknowledged that some patrons had questioned why more classical offerings had not been made.

"Popular artists," he said, "are easier to book and are going to fill up the theater more."

Back in the mid-1960s, the center's initial surveys and brochures on the musical tastes of potential patrons seemed to point to broader acceptance of symphonies, opera and ballet.

But in the opening season in 1968, the Philadelphia Orchestra, with Eugene Ormandy, was outdrawn 2-to-1 by the jazz greats Gerry Mulligan, Dave Brubeck and the late Louis Armstrong, and 3-to-1 by Andy Williams.

And to this day, Mr. Gallagher is quick to acknowledge that "the classical draw is not nearly comparable to the popular draw."

WHOSE TASTE SHOULD DICTATE PROGRAMS? [6]

There was an article in the special New Jersey section of the Sunday *Times* . . . [in May 1972 that] concerned a hassle now going on at the Garden State Arts Center in Holmdel, New Jersey, as to just how much art an arts center can absorb. Seems as how whenever there's art at the center —the New Jersey Symphony Orchestra, say—it costs the management money, and whenever there's a pop music event—is there someone called Melanie, or did I get the name wrong? —the management makes money. By the law of syllogisms, management wants more pop and less art, which is, I suppose, what managements are for.

There is really nothing new in this situation; New Jersey is just now discovering a basic fact of artistic life that promoters in other parts of the country have long since known: the direct ratio between cultural excellence and bankruptcy. It isn't only a summertime phenomenon, of course, but it becomes more painful in the summer because of the great growth in the past years of outdoor-concert centers that can accommodate audiences of twenty thousand and more. Tanglewood, Saratoga, Blossom and others, no matter what high artistic aims may have motivated them at the beginning, have been increasingly forced to bring in pop entertainers during their season to help wipe out deficits. The old-timers may recoil in horror, but nothing can be done if this business of summer music is to turn a profit.

This situation, as I said above, is not new, and yet it turns my tummy whenever it crops up. Of course, more people want pop entertainment than classics, and, by the same reasoning, more people probably want hockey games or roller derbies than pop entertainment. If statistics about the people's taste are to be the criterion for the running of culture in this country, the concert managers and their clients might just as well quit right now. Nothing in the cultural

[6] From "Nothing for Everyone," article by Alan Rich, staff music and dance critic. *New York.* 5:64. Je. 19, '72. Copyright © 1972 by NYM Corp. Reprinted with the permission of *New York* Magazine.

life of this country is going to make any sense if the concept of majority choice is allowed to determine programming. Can you imagine what would be hanging in the Metropolitan Museum if the choice were put to a city-wide referendum?

Furthermore, the Holmdel center was built by the Garden State Parkway Commission, designed to absorb the surplus income from that expensive-to-drive-on parkway so that the tolls can be kept. Thus, this particular concern with profits is all the more incomprehensible. *Arts* Center indeed; Tanglewood should have it so good!

The serious expressive arts constitute an area of interest for an infinitesimal minority of the consumership. That fact should be self-evident, but it obviously isn't to a great many of the people who are in the arts for money. Every attempt to impose a "something for everybody" philosophy on the serious repertory must inevitably result in a degradation of the original art work—and that includes a huge variety of sins currently being perpetrated in the name of culture, from the rash of Strudelkopf's Greatest Hits albums that the record boys are now foisting upon us, through the Day-Glo Mona Lisas now on sale at your local head shop, to the cutesinesses of the classical deejays on radio. It's perfectly true that the arts are accessible to far more people these days than ever before, and this is of course marvelous. But moving the arts out into the market place is not the same as selling them as is to all comers. People like to point to European nations as an object lesson in consumership of the arts, and it is probably safe to say that Mozart and Beethoven *are* more apt to be household names in Vienna, say, than in Montclair. But the difference is not all that vast, and I am sure that there are far more Viennese than not who prefer football to opera.

The real difference between the situation here and abroad is that the arts are supported more sensibly in most other countries, *even though* their minority status is recognized. Obviously, the answer to the New Jersey dilemma, and others like it in each of the . . . [other] states, is for some

outside agency, private, industrial or governmental, to come
up with enough money for the New Jersey Symphony to run
up as big a deficit as it pleases without it bothering anybody.
Pardon me for being cynical for a moment, but I don't think
that is going to happen in this country, and the reason it
isn't going to happen is made perfectly clear in the reasoning
of the New Jersey management: artistic value=cash return.
Even if Congress were to bankroll the Garden State Arts
Center to the tune of a billion a year, that philosophy would
still obtain, because it is what has made America, you should
pardon the expression, great.

THE ECONOMICS OF RECORDING [7]

The press release from Deutsche Grammophon in October [1972] announcing the completion of the tapings that
immortalized the new Metropolitan Opera production of
Carmen, pointed out that these sessions had been the first
full-length standard opera recording in the United States
since 1964. The situation with reference to symphonic recordings is scarcely better: this year American orchestras will
make fewer than a dozen new discs, and only the rash of
"repackagings"—reissues of old recordings in new couplings
or under new titles—will keep the names of American ensembles alive for American record buyers.

Looked at in a vacuum, the reduction of opportunities
for American groups might seem to make sense as part of
an increasingly international cultural world. National tra-
ditions are vital in the performance of most music between
1700 and 1920, and there isn't much American music the
record buyer wants to hear. With the increasing ease of recording wherever the record company wishes—and with the
spread of the record-buying market across the affluent third
of the globe—one might expect the recording directors and

[7] From article by Martin Mayer, music critic for *Esquire* and author of
About Television and other books about the performing arts. *Opera News.*
37:12-15. D. 9, '72. Reprinted by permission.

their engineers to go where performances would be most authentic.

Factors of this sort did operate to restrict opera recordings in America in the 1950s: one of the weaknesses of the Columbia Records-Metropolitan Opera recordings of those days was a lack of fully European ambience, especially in comparison with recordings made in Italy by EMI (Angel), British Decca (London) and RCA. RCA later built a huge studio complex in Rome, in part to make soundtracks for what then looked like a flourishing Italian movie industry but in large part as a place where opera recordings could be made with some of the best orchestral and choral talent in Italy.

Today, elements of musical tradition seem to play no role at all in the choice of recording locale. Philips does George Gershwin discs in Monte Carlo, ABC with great éclat does Beverly Sills singing Italian oddities in Vienna (with a Finnish conductor), and everybody records everything in London. The New York Philharmonic sits virtually unrecorded while Columbia Records, which has the orchestra under contract, flies its conductor Pierre Boulez and its laureate conductor Leonard Bernstein to sessions with British orchestras in London. Donizetti's three queens [*Maria Stuarda, Anna Bolena,* and Elizabeth I (in *Roberto Devereux*)], Verdi's *Lombardi* and *Attila,* Offenbach's *Contes d'Hoffmann,* all are now recorded in Britain, with British orchestras and with an English chorus (*I Lombardi* was done with a Scottish chorus), whose members are by no means always at home in the language they must sing.

There never is but one reason for such illogicalities: money. It's much cheaper to make recordings in England than it is in either Italy or America. The problem in Italy is the insistence by the musicians' union on a high royalty fee for the orchestra on every record sold; the problem in America is a high initial fee, cash on the barrelhead, for playing at the recording session. The DG *Carmen* is authoritatively estimated to have cost more than $250,000.

Lohengrin in 1964, made with the Boston Symphony Orchestra, is known to have cost RCA $170,000, and very nearly convinced the board of the corporate parent to take the company out of the classical music business. The new *Norma* made in London cost less than $60,000.

One can blame these immense disparities on the greed of Italian and American unions, and say they have pushed the price of recording in their territories beyond the possibility of the market to pay. Or one can blame it on the greed of English musicians willing to undercut the going rate in other countries. On the whole, the impartial observer has to lean against the Americans and the Italians—and to note that the dispute is about to become *vieux jeu* ["old hat," irrelevant] anyway, because the "Socialist" musicians of Eastern Europe have begun to scab on their English confreres, making their services available at really rock-bottom prices. It cost EMI less to record Karajan's *Meistersinger* in Dresden than Philips had to pay to record the much shorter and infinitely simpler *Attila* in London.

The economics of recording are by no means open knowledge, but the situation appears to be as follows:

Of the $6 list price of the typical stereo disc, from $1 to $1.25, depending on the internal bookkeeping of the company, the size of its bureaucracy and the elaboration of mechanical production, can be applied to the artistic and basic engineering cost of the recording sessions.

An American sale of 15,000 copies is a first-class result for any symphonic or operatic recording. Occasional recordings do substantially better than 15,000 sales (discs by Van Cliburn, Joan Sutherland or the like may approach 100,000 sales), but the average even of records by well-known artists tends to be somewhat below 15,000. If the artists involved are internationally known, an American record company can hope for perhaps half as many additional sales abroad, usually through foreign licensing arrangements that yield perhaps half a dollar for each record sold. On a successful disc, then, the total revenues allocable to the musical and recording costs will be something less than $20,000.

The major factor in determining these recording costs, even in opera, is the payment to the orchestra. American union contracts governing these matters are complicated and very different from orchestra to orchestra. The basic union contracts call for a weekly salary in return for eight "services" a week, most often four three-hour rehearsals and four two-hour performances. Special provisions govern special events, like tours, broadcasts and recordings.

At most of the major orchestras, recording involves a fee over and above normal salary. The largest fees are paid by the Philadelphia Orchestra: RCA gave that ensemble an exceptionally generous deal to wean it away from its long-standing Columbia affiliation, and management then of necessity agreed to an exceptionally generous contract with the union. The cost to RCA of a three-hour recording session with the Philadelphia Orchestra is apparently $13,000. The conductor's fee, and payments to soloists, singers and chorus, if any, must come on top of that.

For this price, assuming that the orchestra has already rehearsed for public performance the works to be recorded, the record company is permitted to take one hour of finished tape. (If the orchestra has to learn or relearn the works for recording purposes, the maximum permissible finished product from a session is twenty minutes. For obvious reasons, such sessions never happen any more in America where name orchestras are involved. Newell Jenkins, however, recently recorded a Rossini opera in New York with a free-lance ensemble, working under the twenty-minute maximum; his cost projection for a three-disc album is now $85,000.) In fact, however, even the Philadelphia and Ormandy, which are two extremely efficient institutions, cannot produce a full hour of finished product from a three-hour session, and something between thirty and forty minutes is what the recording directors actually expect. At best, then, three sessions, at $39,000, are needed to produce two discs. It will be noted that the cost for the orchestra alone—$19,500 for a rather short record and more for a longer one—eats up the total revenues allocable to music from a successful sale. This is why RCA's contract with the Philadelphia will not be renewed at the present rates when it expires.

Other orchestras are less expensive. Some of them have arrangements with the musicians' union which permit the substitution of a recording session for a performance, at no additional fee. Under these circumstances, an orchestra that had committed itself to a certain number of weeks of employment for the men, and has no prospect of extending its season of public performances to meet the guarantee, may wish to offer the orchestra to a record company at a reduced rate. Though the figures are not public, the Chicago Symphony probably costs British Decca (London Records) only about $8,000 a session. Even at that price, Georg Solti fears that Decca has been losing money on most of his Chicago recordings.

In London, by contrast, the best of the British orchestras —the London Symphony—can still be bought for about $2,500 per session. Most of what the LSO records, including all the operas, the orchestra learns for recording purposes, and British like American union rules restrict the total product of a session to twenty minutes. This restriction turns out to be unimportant, because an orchestra that has to rehearse from scratch before it can record does not produce twenty minutes of finished tape from a three-hour session: fifteen minutes is more like it. Still, the total orchestra cost runs from $7,500 to $10,000 for a single disc, and at that price a record company may even be able to make a little money— on a successful disc. And the quality, both musical and technical, is often superb.

But the golden age of English recording may be passing. Inflation has hit Britain even harder than it hit the United States. The cost of making records in London and its environs has risen by roughly 25 percent during the last eighteen months, and shows no signs of stabilizing. Meanwhile, representatives of Czech musical organizations have been leaving their calling cards around New York, pointing out that the Prague orchestras all work for the state, the state is willing to schedule them for recordings by American and Western European companies, and an extra payment that amounts to only a few dollars a session per man will (perforce) satisfy the local, government-controlled union. In Eastern Europe the union rules permit payment not by the session but by the minute of finished tape.

On a lower level of quality, minor-league West German orchestras, which may be beefed up by moonlighters from the radio orchestras or the better permanent ensembles, can be hired for as little as $1,500 to play, say, accompaniments to two long-forgotten Romantic Revival piano concertos. The men have never seen the music when they arrive in the morning, but by the time the sun sets they will have completed the recording of two concertos. This is undoubtedly better than nothing, on both sides; but it is not *much* better than nothing, and it leaves the bemused record critic wondering whether the pieces would sound better if more care had been taken in their preparation.

A major source of subsidy in the recording of American orchestras has been the board of directors of the orchestra itself. For years, the Utah Symphony has worked with Vanguard, and before that with Westminster, on a basis whereby the orchestra is paid by its own management, which then receives a larger-than-usual royalty per sale. Maurice Abravanel has made interesting recordings with this orchestra, and Vanguard tries to keep all its records in print (unlike some other record companies one could name), so the red ink on the orchestra's books is probably no more extensive than it would have been if those "services" had been taken for additional concerts. Cincinnati's deal with American Decca, on similar terms, was a disaster for both sides, however: the record company did not even get back its out-of-pocket costs for engineering and equipment.

The increasing costs of music and recordings are not really avoidable (though . . . [in March 1972], in a series of bloody negotiating sessions at New York's Hotel Warwick, the record companies convinced the American Federation of Musicians to sign off without an increase until at least 1974). It is the same problem that affects education, medicine and law—where it is represented by, respectively, more crowded classrooms, higher hospital bills and an overwhelmed court system. The wages of people who work in service industries, as Professors Baumol and Bowen pointed out some years ago in their book *Performing Arts: The Economic Dilemma,* rise as much as the wages of people who work in manufacturing industries—but the productivity of people who produce goods rises with their wages. Thus the costs of services go up much faster than the costs of things.

In the record business this "dilemma" is made much sharper by an inevitable decline in demand. As the head of one of the classical divisions put it, "Operas don't *hit* any more, the way they did." The potential market for the Reiner-Risë Stevens *Carmen* included almost everyone with an LP machine and an interest in *Carmen.* Today, the great majority of those interested in *Carmen* already own a convenient album that is technically at least as good as their equipment. The task of the DG merchandisers will be to convince these people that they need another *Carmen,* and that's a much harder job than selling the first one. Moreover, records turn out to be surprisingly price-elastic, to use economists' jargon: reduced prices do increase the sales of a recording (hence all of today's three-for-two boxes and the like), while premium prices do reduce sales considerably. In short, there is no way DG can get back its investment in *Carmen*: the recording has to be seen as a public relations investment for the company.

Fortunately, managements judge classical divisions by their total profitability, not by the results on any one recording, and discs by popular soloists cost much less to make, sell at the same price (how odd that is, when you think about it) and make profits to help pay for the recording of operas and concerts. Moreover, the record company classical divisions have lost their fear of being vulgar, a word which after all means "popular." Those "Best Of" and "More Top Hits By" Bach things that make the fastidious wince are ways to sell again, to a new audience, recordings originally made for the "straight" market. They help pay the costs to an increasingly important degree. Company managements are being educated, slowly, to see that a record that pays for itself after five years and three repackagings is ultimately as much a money-maker as the record that amortizes its costs over only two years. If marketing can be placed at the service of art, maybe the record companies will be able to continue working in England—if not, for the foreseeable future, in America.

WORKING WITH FOUNDATIONS: HOW TO START A LOCAL ARTS COUNCIL [8]

One of the least publicized programs of the Johnson Administration was the establishment of a National Foundation on the Arts and Humanities in 1965. One of its major roles was to serve as a stimulus to the creation of arts councils on the state level, which in turn could encourage the establishment of community arts councils. It was criticized as inadequate, for only $5 million a year was allocated to it. The program was expanded under the Nixon Administration to more actively stimulate development of the arts in communities throughout the nation. Forty million dollars were requested for 1970-71 to back up the current Administration's intent.

The National Foundation on the Arts and Humanities is really an umbrella over five groups: the National Endowment for the Arts, the National Endowment for the Humanities, the National Council on the Arts, the National Council on the Humanities, and the Federal Council on the

[8] From article by Donald J. Sager, public library administrator. *Wilson Library Bulletin* 45:744-9. Ap. '71. Reprinted by permission.

Arts and Humanities. The Foundation was established as an independent agency in the Executive Branch of Government on September 29, 1965, with the overall purpose to develop and promote a national policy of support for the humanities and arts. Some of the groups are advisory or coordinative; some are active in Federal grants programs. The group which concerns us directly at the community level is the National Endowment for the Arts. This group provides direct grants to states' arts councils and programs.

It permitted many communities their first opportunity to participate in the arts. Funds for each state are divided evenly, with each state receiving slightly more than $30,000 in fiscal 1969. States wishing to participate in the grant program are required to establish and maintain an arts commission or council, and to at least match the Federal grant. Arts councils have been formed in every state and in four US territories. In their first year of operation, 1967, many of the councils devoted their funds toward surveys of the arts in their respective states, which should be a basic source of information in developing cooperative regional programs. The following year, the development of local arts councils was initiated. Some 715 projects developed by the local councils were funded in fiscal 1969.

The states' arts councils function at the state level, similar to the National Endowment for the Arts. They plan, survey, coordinate and stimulate creativity and interest in all facets of the arts in their state. Grants are given to individuals, groups, or organizations. They may range from support of newly established local arts councils, grants to museums, orchestras, libraries, galleries and theaters, seed money for local arts festivals, financial aid to state writers or artists. The structure of these councils usually consists of a panel of private citizens prominent in the state and interested or involved in the arts, who are appointed by the governor, and a professional director and staff. The funds available at the state level are limited; nevertheless, it is a beginning. For many states, it was the first time their state legislatures ever regularly budgeted support for the arts. The Federal grant of $1.7 million in fiscal 1969 stimulated forty-five state legislatures and three territories to appropriate four times that amount. A total of $7.633 million was appropriated by the states and territories for the year ending June 30, 1970.

Many of the states are using the funds to take on tour strong professional programs located in the large metropolitan centers. Traveling art exhibits, concert tours, and drama are thus being extended into rural areas. Cultural activities are being publicized through state art newsletters and general news releases. Some states are offering consultant services to amateur groups, to raise their level of quality. Finding new sources of financial support is another area being mined in some states. Awards for achievement are also being provided to encourage support and development of the arts. Many of these programs are being carried out through the local councils.

Role of the Library

The establishment and organization of community arts councils is where more leadership is presently needed, and where libraries can take an active role. There is no current estimate of how many community arts councils exist, but the number and the extent of their program is limited. In 1967, the Associated Councils of the Arts estimated there were only three hundred local arts councils. The organization and funding of these councils vary widely. They may serve a region, a county, or just a community. Like the National Endowment on the Arts, and the state arts councils, the local arts councils have as their main purpose the stimulation and development of interest in the arts and culture. Locally they work to develop artistic and cultural activities in their communities.

A typical arts council publishes a newsletter listing area cultural events. It aids in publicizing the programs of area cultural groups such as local musical ensembles, choirs, art exhibits, little theater, dance, and literary activities. It may sponsor arts festivals or arrange for tours with the state arts councils. It may establish centralized ticket-selling facilities, and engage in fund raising for producing groups, as a United Fund for the arts. The program may be extensive enough eventually to merit a professional staff and lead to the construction of a civic art center.

In fact, one of the most encouraging facets of the Federal and state program is the chain reaction that started at the local level. The Associated Councils of the Arts estimated that $14 million in private funds were collected in 1969 to finance arts programs initiated by local arts councils.

If the community or area does not already have a council established, the library can play a major role in stimulating local interest in the arts by initiating such a council. It is one of the most effective cooperative techniques in fine arts development.

Getting Started

One of the best sources of information on how to get started is *Arts in the City: Organizing and Programming Community Arts Councils,* by Ralph Burgard, published by the Associated Councils of Arts. The Associated Councils of Arts, formerly the Arts Councils of America, was founded in 1960 as a federation of community and state councils, and is a primary source of information. The ACA's chief role is to serve as a clearinghouse. It is a service organization, and does not make grants. It is non-profit, supported by its member councils and through foundation grants. It offers a national consultant service available to all state arts councils and any community arts council serving populations over 250,000. Its magazine, *Cultural Affairs,* should also be a basic item in any library's collection (Arts Councils of America, 1564 Broadway, New York, N.Y. 10036). Included in each issue are articles on major art programs, recent grants, reports on state and local arts programs.

The best source of assistance for the majority of communities will be the director of the state arts council. He should be equipped to explain the most successful organizing methods, provide technical asssistance, and advise . . . on which projects a council might be able to undertake successfully. [The local librarian] would be expected to have the community contacts, and know who should be involved in the organization.

Even if your community does not have any producing arts groups, [the librarian] should be in the position to know who is always borrowing music, art, or drama materials, the teachers who are involved with extra-curricular programs, plays, or concerts, and the literary groups. These persons have the interest and may have the potential to serve as the basis for an arts council in your community.

Generally the organization of most local arts councils consists of a board of twenty-one members, with chairman, secretary, and treasurer. Membership in the council is composed of active groups (such as musical ensembles) who are involved with creative production and are generally not supported by taxes, and associate members, who are certainly involved with the arts, but not generally in a producing capacity. Libraries usually fall into the latter category. If the council is to serve a region, county, or city, geographic representation should be kept in mind. If the library has meeting space, it might serve as the location for organizing.

What Kind of Programs?

Let us assume you have decided to initiate a local arts council, talked with the director of the state arts council, gained his advice, and got him to attend your organizing meeting. The first question to arise might be the sort of program which would be suitable for your community.

One of the best books on program and potential is *The Arts at the Grass Roots,* edited by Bruce Cutler (University of Kansas Press, 1968). It reports on the first Kansas Conference on the Arts, which involved five hundred delegates representing ninety Kansas communities. Besides covering the nitty-gritty of governing boards and fund raising, it reports on cultural exchange programs, techniques for booking musical attractions, audience development, starting community theaters, organizing and running sales and rental art galleries, and programming in dance and creative writing. When you read about Parsons, Kansas, which manages to get performances by the Kansas City Philharmonic, and Emporia, which has persons like Hans Conried in *Absence of a Cello* for its community theater, and modern dance at Paola, an art gallery in Medicine Lodge, then you can begin to understand the potential of the arts council movement for your community.

A word of warning is called for here. Cultural programming of any excellence and development of the arts in your community will not be achieved with grants from state arts councils. All any local council can and should expect, at least at the start, is advice and perhaps a small amount of seed money. The local council must do the work, and will have to raise most of the money.

To determine just how much work and time is involved, and how libraries in particular are involved, it may be valuable to take the experience of one such council. Lorain County, just outside of Cleveland, Ohio, has a population of 275,000 people. Located in the county is Oberlin College, which has a noted conservatory of music and an art museum. A community college is located in one of the cities. The county has seven library systems, two amateur theater groups, and an assortment of choral and musical ensembles, one small orchestra, and small groups of writers, poets, and artists meeting in the communities.

In 1967, invitations were issued to organizations and individuals known to be interested in the arts by a number of persons in the county who had attended a statewide conference of the Ohio Arts Council, where they learned of the program of the National Endowment for the Arts. The local organizational meeting drew representatives from a wide variety of producing groups, libraries, and other agencies. A formal organization was established, with a board and officers. Two projects were decided upon at the start: a bi-monthly calendar of cultural events in the county, and a program directory of musical groups, speakers on cultural topics, artists willing to exhibit their works, dance and film sources.

The libraries agreed to serve as clearinghouses for information on local programs and activities. Surprisingly, it was learned that most of the cultural groups at the local level simply did not plan two months ahead, and formal arrangements for time, place, dates, and box office were established often at the last minute. With the prospect of wider publicity, however, many of the groups had greater incentive to plan better. Unknowingly, many groups scheduled programs for the same evenings, often appealing to the same limited audience. A Twentieth Century Fund study on the arts in 1966 revealed that only 3 percent of the public ever attends a live cultural performance in the course of any year, and these individuals are almost exclusively from the same socio-economic group—fairly young, professional, and with more than average income. The arts calendar allowed many producing groups to learn for the first time where duplications in dates or overlap occurred. It made clear how better scheduling could increase audience potential appreciably. Many of the organizations which were lethargic were further stimulated when they saw what other groups were doing. Total cultural programs offered in the county rose 30 percent in two years as choirs, libraries, dramatic, film, and art groups were stimulated.

The calendar also revealed gaps in cultural opportunities. Little programming for children or older persons was available in the county. The lack of cultural events for children was particularly tragic, since the arts council felt strongly motivated to develop audiences, and the sooner a child had the opportunity to see a concert or play, or see quality film or art, the greater the likelihood he would develop a taste for the arts. Several institutions, including one of the libraries, greatly expanded their programming as a result. Going beyond story hours, a children's marionette theater was established, children's art shows and exchanges were scheduled, fine arts film series established, creative drama and children's concerts arranged. The calendar showed that virtually no cultural events were scheduled in the county during the summer, on the premise that vacations reduced the potential audience. After analyzing this rationale, the council thought it unlikely that all 275,000 in the county would depart en masse for three months out of the year, and so decided to plan a modest summer arts festival.

The public libraries also cooperated with other agencies and groups in the council in preparing a program bureau or file. They served as clearinghouses, once again, did much of the duplicating and clerical work, and functioned as meeting places for many of the communities and sources of cultural information. Some of the producing groups, in the process, learned that their libraries could provide things like scores and librettos, recordings, plays for reading, costume and set-design information.

Cultural calendars and program directories are part of the regular program of many library systems, it is true, and probably could have been prepared without an arts council. But it is doubtful that it would have attracted as much interest and brought so many groups into contact with one another. Libraries must learn that cooperation is a two-way street.

Funds from the Ohio State Arts Council were obtained in 1969 to aid in publicizing and promoting a summer arts festival, which permitted a coordination of programs for the first time, and allowed several performances of the county's small, but excellent, orchestra in other communities. Two evenings with the arts were held, with dinners, followed by performances by several of the county's producing groups. These formed the basis for fund-raising projects to augment the seed money provided by the state. More recently, the state also provided funds for a full-time director during the summer of 1970 to develop and coordinate this year's summer arts festival. But it is still local money and effort that will be the mainstay of the festival.

Plans for the future include establishing a central office to handle clerical routines, public relations, and ticketing for cultural agencies, a youth symphony, cooperative fund raising, and eventually, maybe an arts center.

What's Ahead?

The effectiveness of the arts council movement still remains to be proven, it is true. The experience of one county, or several score, does not indicate an overnight renaissance. Even a successful program for several years will not tell us whether a local community has become more culturally concious. It is too early to tell; it may take a generation before any effect is felt. We simply don't know how to measure success in the arts. Perhaps when more fund drives or levies are proposed involving purely cultural matters, more can be told. . . .

Considering the attention and the billions given to science and technology, encouragement is long overdue for the arts. That encouragement is best provided at the local level.

Theodore Bikel raised the question, "Are we going to create avenues for cultural reaction, or send the nation bowling, for want of anything else?" We shall see.

NEW SPACES FOR NEW ARTS [9]

The museum and theater, as we have known them, are no longer appropriate to the arts as we are coming to know them. If new buildings (or non-buildings) come into being, it is unlikely that they will grow easily out of exist-

[9] From article by Peter Blake and Ellen Perry Berkeley. *Cultural Affairs.* 15:12-18. My. '71. Reprinted by permission. Mr. Blake is editor of the *Architectural Forum* and Ellen Berkeley, one of its senior editors.

ing institutions, which tend to reproduce what they already have. It is also unlikely that many of the new ideas will come from architects, who with rare exception are either unable or unwilling to make the art of architecture serve the needs of another art form. No, new environments for the arts will most probably be "designed"—or defined—by those who are creating the new art forms: the performers, directors, light sculptors, film-makers, sound technicians, psychologists (one was credited on a recent "electric" event), laser specialists, and spectators. Ghetto residents, for example, have the power, usually reserved to the drama critic, to decide whether a performance of street theater will succeed or fail.

A happening, for instance, is programmed to occur in familiar places (a highway, a hotel room, a street corner). The places are usually indeterminate ones—a roadside, a room. In *Fluids,* by Allen Kaprow, blocks of ice were delivered to various locations around the city and meticulously constructed into "buildings"—which then melted. This was intended as a solid comment on an urban society caught in the dilemma of wanting to build monuments for posterity at the same time that it exists on a system of planned obsolescence. Performing the event in twenty places across the city heightened the idea of multiplicity, said Kaprow, which he considered "the very stuff of our spiritual and economic life." The environment—in its everyday and repetitive aspects—was an integral part of the event.

There are other performances for which no facility can be built. The Philharmonic concerts that draw 70,000 persons to the Sheep Meadow in Central Park may lack much in technical quality. Distractions are many, especially at the edges where people ravel away after only a few minutes. Planes pass overhead. But the vitality of these free concerts would be compromised if they were given in a specially constructed arena capable of holding this vast number of people. If some people enjoy a full performance, others stay half as long, enjoying it no less. Perhaps the traditional concert of up to three hours is too rigid; people should be able to drop in and out of a concert the way they sit in the sun on a park bench, or the way they watch television. In street theater, the casual format permits people to participate or pass by, to hang out of their windows or pull back, as they please. There are problems, to be sure—the sight-lines are pretty muddled. But when people on the block begin talking to each other for the first time, and when the children can barely be kept from jumping onto the backs of trucks, it amounts to an experience that one critic called "the very essence of theater."

The multipurpose theater was given a comprehensive look some time back in the New York Public Library's survey, *Contemporary Theatre Architecture,* which was issued to mark the opening of Lincoln Center's Library and Museum of the Performing Arts:

> Theater technicians and architects—the detractors of this form —claim on artistic grounds that such a range [of performance: operas, concerts, ballet, musicals, dramas] is impossible; they mean that the all-purpose theater is a no-purpose theater. Producers and impresarios—its defenders—insist that, for financial reasons, it is usually the only practical answer to the complex needs of the performing arts. Until the theater planners and the architects recognize another solution, the multipurpose proscenium theater will continue to be the work horse and the whipping boy.

This survey of fifty new theaters and performing arts centers, by theater producer Maxwell Silverman, went on to observe that the best solution is the complex of halls, each with its special and limited uses. Most recent centers have included "a large proscenium theater for operas, concerts and musicals; a more intimate theater for drama; and a still smaller, more flexible hall for experimental productions."

The Krannert Center for the Performing Arts, recently opened at the University of Illinois in Champaign-Urbana, carries the complex solution to its extreme. In this $21 million center are a 2,100-seat Great Hall for orchestral and choral music, a 965-seat Festival Hall for musical produc-

tions, a 678-seat Playhouse for theater and dance, a 130-to-
200 seat Studio Theater for experimental performances.
(These different halls share a three-acre site and a common
lobby and scenery shop.) Nevertheless, it was to the university's six-year-old Assembly Hall—a double-saucer structure that can seat up to 17,500 in an arena, or down to
4,200 in a proscenium arrangement—that John Cage and
Lejaren Hill took their startling collaboration HPSCHD
(pronounced Harpsichord) only a month after the Krannert
Center was opened. Richard Kostelanetz, author of *The
Theater of Mixed Means* [Dial Press, 1968] called the work
"one of the great artistic environments of the decade,"
pointing out that Cage will not touch a "theatrical" space,
preferring to use such places as a stockyards pavilion, scene
of an earlier piece. "Who would believe, before Cage arrived," asked Kostelanetz, "that Urbana's Assembly Hall itself could be transformed into a work of art?"

The assembly Hall in Urbana is not only multipurpose,
serving up anything from basketball to Victor Borge, with
the Poznan Choir and the Royal Marines Tattoo thrown
in (not simultaneously, to be sure), it is also *multiform*.
The director of the hall reports that when only the theater quadrant is in use, neither performers nor audience are
aware of the additional parts of the building. For theater
use, a demountable stage is assembled, proscenium masking
is hung, and battens for lights are lowered from the theater
grid. For concert use, an acoustical shell is assembled, with
results that are reported to be highly satisfactory by visiting groups of the caliber of the Philadelphia Orchestra.
The stage or acoustical shell can be installed in three or
four hours, making possible two entirely different uses on
successive days.

Variable Theater

The multiform, or variable, theater has intrigued people
for centuries. Pliny the Elder described a pair of wooden
theaters built in Rome in 52 B.C. The two faced in opposite directions, playing to two different audiences at once,

but could be pivoted on their revolving platforms (often with spectators still in their seats) to form an amphitheater. As our technology advances, the multiform theater will be increasingly explored as a way to make a single hall serve two or more purposes. In part, the multiform idea makes a hall suitable for more than one kind of performance—but the idea is also used to change the relationship between performers and audience within a hall. Prototype for many of today's variable theaters is Walter Gropius' pioneering "Totaltheater," designed for Erwin Piscator in 1927. "The aim of this theater," said Gropius, "is not to assemble a number of ingenious devices. All of these are merely means to attain the supreme goal—*to draw the spectator into the drama*."

Never realized, alas, the theater would have offered the possibility of proscenium, thrust or arena arrangements. As Gropius explained it:

A complete transformation of the building occurs by turning the stage-platform and part of the orchestra through 180 degrees. Then the former proscenium stage becomes a central arena, entirely surrounded by rows of spectators! This can even be done during the play. . . . This attack on the spectator, moving him during the play and unexpectedly shifting the stage area, alters the existing scale of values, presenting to the spectator a new consciousness of space and making him participate in the action.

(This extraordinary conception would also have included projection—from twelve sources—onto the twelve screens stretched around the entire periphery of the theater. The audience could suddenly find itself "in the midst of a raging sea or surrounded by a rapidly advancing multitude." Gropius was far ahead of his time. Forty years ago, he was saying what many are beginning to articulate today: "I am personally of the opinion that light can make the simplest and most effective modern stage setting: upon the neutral space of a darkened stage one can literally build with light.")

Principles of the Totaltheater are evident in one hall of the John F. Kennedy Center for the Performing Arts. Tucked into the top floor is the 510-seat Studio Theater, equipped with a mechanized turntable that lifts and rotates a circular portion of seats-and-stage to create a proscenium, open-thrust, or arena stage. Another small auditorium that is, in some ways, a realization of the Gropius intent is the 525-seat auditorium in Grenoble's Maison de la Culture. A spectator's platform revolves in the center of the hall. Between the audience and a fixed stage at one end of the hall is a ring stage, which is lined with projection screens and also revolves. The first fully mechanized variable theater in this country, the Loeb Drama Center at Harvard, was built in 1960. The forward seats are fixed on two movable platforms which can be rotated 90 degrees and moved to the sides for a thrust stage, or rotated 180 degrees and moved onto the proscenium stage for an arena form. The four elevators under these seats can also be used to change the configuration of the stage.

Not everyone agrees that technology is the answer. Donald Mullin, a critic of many contemporary theaters, suggests that "all the King's pushbuttons cannot make the Loeb Drama Center work as well as any old vaudeville house that cost a third as much." And in a review of Loeb's first three years, it was reported that the tendency at first was "to use its mechanical facilities to their utmost which often distorted productions into technical extravaganzas."

There are simpler ways to achieve flexibility. Men have been trying to build the ideal theater as long as there has been theater. An expanding technology will change some parts of the job, but will not change it altogether. Theater architecture has a quality, elusive and magical, that is both more and less than sightlines and stagehouses. Donald Mullin called that quality a *sense of occasion*.

Within the house the patrons' main interest, when the play is not in progress, is in one another. Theatre-goers . . . seem to have a definite preference for a U-shaped, galleried auditorium. They can see and be seen. There is a glitter about this type of house that is common to no other. It is in the best sense theatrical, and not just because a play is being produced in the building.

(One does not have to agree with Mullin that the U shape is best, in order to appreciate his point.)

A feeling of theatricality is desirable not only in the audience area. Mullin asserts that the

most theatrically oriented piece of architecture still standing is the Paris Opera, in which the audience members themselves are constantly "on stage." The entire ensemble of salons, foyers and stairways is arranged so that the passage of people in many directions and up and down creates a display that is fascinating by itself. Radio City Music Hall and the New York State Theater have this to a lesser degree.

This theatricality suggests a pageantry in which the spectators have become participants. It is another kind of theater, a counterpoint to what is taking place on stage.

Integration of film techniques and live performance has only begun. Buckminster Fuller has designed an elliptical theater which aims to combine "the best of theater and the cinema." This theater project (done with Shoji Sadao) is simply a "double wall, the inner one functioning as a screen, and the cavity between being for equipment, access, and projection space." The 360-degree projection capacity gives tremendous flexibility.

Any illusion desired can be produced on the walls, on the ceiling, and even on the floor. The whole room becomes a "backdrop," and the audience instead of viewing a stage, is right in the center of a micro-world which is the world of the dramatic theater. Previously cumbersome procedures of scene change, entrances and exits, and intermissions are now accomplished by a light switch. The sense of the actor being in, close to, or far away from the audience may be achieved by adjusting the scale to the projected background. Exterior and interior scenes are equally possible and equally convincing.

This is unquestionably one direction of the future.

Modern technology [writes Fuller] allows the creation of purely illusory dramatic effects which liberate the audience-performer relationship from many of its restrictions. Rear-projection screens, electro-luminescent screens, mirror-projection images can all give the illusion of objects and space, often more vividly than "real" objects and "real" space. Because depth is an illusion, backstage areas and even stages themselves are no longer necessary, and actors move about freely, unencumbered by boundaries of any sort.

Undoubtedly aware of the new boundaries that will be pushed back in the coming years, Fuller expresses the hope that this building will be low-cost and disposable.

These are not futuristic improbabilities. Techniques are advancing rapidly. In the small theater of the new Ottawa Arts Center, designed by Fred Lebensold, it will be possible "to surround people with sound, light, and action. We can move up, down, horizontally, diagonally." Discussing future possibilities with Lebensold, Richard Schechner imagines putting projection bays under the floor, and being able "to open great spaces under people, have them sit on air, have space fall all around them, or close in on them." Electronics is "much more flexible and capable than mechanics." And much of this has already been accomplished. In Prague's fantastic Laterna Magika theater, the stage is, in fact, shaped by rear-projection screens that permit instant changes in scenery; front-projection screens that permit live actors to communicate with filmed images of their own selves; and by innumerable other optical and electronic devices that succeed in turning a fairly traditional stage into a dramatic wonderland.

Special Places to Show Films

Just as the theater experience is changing and expanding, so too is the film experience. Film has barely come of age, having long been considered too commercial to be art. The American Film Institute was launched in 1967, some thirty-three years after its British counterpart. And although America has had a major influence on film-making, the John F. Kennedy Center for the Performing Arts was originally designed without facilities for showing film as art, although documentaries *on* art were to be available in the "tourist orientation center." (One of the theaters was subsequently redesigned, at considerable expense, to be suitable for film-showing.) Film is now being enthusiastically embraced by young people; a recent survey of campus arts suggests that film is replacing the traditional theater in interest and attendance. Indeed, aware that film-making is one of the most attractive arts to the young, Ben Schlanger has suggested that every arts center have a laboratory space, a large studio suitable for experimentation in film technique.

With greater attention being paid to the total experience of film art, it is likely that the place for viewing it will become as much a part of the experience as the film itself. Expo '67's Labyrinth was an environment (with maze-like corridors, and spaces and lighting to suggest infinity) in which the approach to the screen areas was an integral part of the total concept. Perhaps nothing less than the whole environment will be the projection surface of the future, with new esthetic theories of simultaneity suggesting layers of images —the real world seen against the projected world, which is seen against another aspect of the real world. Sensory experience in general is moving beyond all former bounds. The young want music as a background to much of their lives, and they want it of an intensity that threatens to puncture the eardrums of anyone over thirty. It is difficult to predict what physical spaces or equipment this music will require—whether it will be played primarily on radios, tape recorders, record players and TV; whether it will find its milieu in discothèques as accompaniment to dancing; or whether it will be staged as intermedia events in various places found or fixed for the occasion. One thing is certain, though. When the keynote address for a conference of the National Council of Churches is a multi-media event—complete with kaleidoscopic colors, electric guitars, recorded newscast, television commercials, and sounds of warplanes—the art form is no longer esoteric. But the art is not standing still long enough to be measured. The uncommitted space is probably the least that one can provide—and the most that one should.

Museums as Theaters

Museums, too, are off and running in several directions. Harley Parker, director of exhibits design at Toronto's Royal Ontario Museum, urges the use of films, still photos, voice tapes, and other devices to help place exhibits in the proper environment. "Museum fatigue is the result of a clash of spaces," he says. "Artifacts are taken from spaces not visually organized, to spaces that are visually organized There is a psychic clash." He also feels that museum visitors read labels entirely too carefully, then look at the objects all too casually. He wants "no labels at all . . . I want to get away from museums organized as books."

Many believe that the whole function of a museum must change. Arnold Rockman urges a new kind of collection for the museum and a new kind of experience for the visitor. "It is time, I think, to close the art palace and open up a new museum—a universal, democratic emporium in which cookie-cutters, paintings, paper tissues, sculptures, movies, garbage cans, beds, advertisements, drill presses, stage sets, cups and television sets may all exist side-by-side in the same esthetic environment, collectively constituting the current anthropology of the city." This new emporium will be a place of new experiences, a "laboratory of expressive communication." It will be more a performance space than an exhibition space. "The museum's most important business now is . . . with the expansion and integration of the processes of seeing, feeling and thinking." Something like this is already happening at the National Collection of Fine Arts in Washington, where visiting children's groups are encouraged to act out what they see. As Nan Robertson reported in the New York *Times,* they "turn into stripes, tin cans, dying Indians and Abraham Lincoln. They look at what appears to be a plain black square of paint and within seconds they feel cold, quiet, or sad."

But if the arts today tend to merge, as theater incorporates more visual qualities and the visual arts incorporate more action and motion, the facilities for the various arts will tend to overlap, too, for the same desiderata run through all the arts. Participation. Confrontation. Involvement. Exploration. The movement is growing steadily to bring art to the people, as a way of bringing people to the arts. Decentralization is motivated by several ideas, one of them simply the reaction against bigness. A writer in the London *Sunday Times*, complaining of the esthetic impoverishment of the hinterland as a few centers amass greater collections, urged that "the nation's treasures be dispersed to smaller galleries around the country, since the large ones are helping rather than staving off the reduction of human beings into processed zombies. It is better to absorb thirty pictures thoroughly, even at the risk of never seeing some of civilization's masterworks, than to totter through innumerable vast treasure-houses with no more—or even less—real response than we can bring to the streets outside."

In what was once a church in Washington, D.C., then a skating rink, and most recently a theater, the Smithsonian Institution opened its Anacostia Neighborhood Museum late in 1967. In a free-to-touch atmosphere, the museum offers numerous exhibits from the Smithsonian (bone collections, pottery shards, a space capsule), locally initiated exhibits, a closed-circuit TV for dramatic fun, art classes—and so on. Contrary to the expectation of critics who thought the museum would be met with indifference in this ghetto community, the reaction has been extraordinary. To quote one young visitor's contribution to the suggestion box: "I suggest this is the most fun I had on earth." In another renovation, a two-story brick warehouse on New York City's Lower East Side became the Whitney Museum's Art Resources Center. The building contains studio workshops for youngsters and their teacher-professionals (in painting, sculpture, and writing), a gallery for works from the Whitney's permanent collection, and classroom space for use by public school teachers. And in New York's Bedford-Stuyvesant district a one-time automobile showroom and poolhall has been made into a

vital segment of the Brooklyn Children's Museum. Built to
a budget of only $40,000 (and to an equally tight time sched-
ule—sixteen weeks for design and construction), MUSE is an
extraordinary architectural event: Its all-glass facade draws
children's curiosity inside, and its long entry tunnel makes
the arrival a game of mystery. Inside, MUSE offers exhibits
to touch, foreign costumes to try on, animals to handle, and
classes in art, music, dance, theater, astronomy (there is a
tiny planetarium), creative writing, and various other subjects in which the community has expressed an interest. It
is sobering to realize that this busy place, only eight blocks
from the main children's museum, draws children who were
previously unknown to the museum staff.

The branch museum and street and traveling theater
have an inherent danger. Some people look upon them as
attempts to impose an alien culture on minority segments of
the society, they look upon efforts to decentralize the arts as
a kind of "cultural imperialism"—a refusal to recognize that
a real culture exists in the ghetto. Playwright/director En-
rique Vargas, who started an improvisational theater workshop in New York doesn't want to bring culture to Harlem.
"There's plenty of culture right here, but there's very little
communication. I want to have traveling troupes of East
Harlemites. The Teatro de Tripas (Gut Theater) is made
up of two street gangs, the East Harlem Thunderbirds and
the 110th Street Bachelors. Their improvisations grew out
of life in East Harlem. That's culture."

Evergreen Review explored the question in an article by
John Lahr:

When Joseph Papp tried to bring his Mobile Theater into
Morningside Park in Harlem in 1964, ghetto youths, obeying their
own territorial imperatives, threw rocks. Four years later, they sit
respectfully through a performance of a black *Hamlet* only to
heave chairs into the empty wooden rows after the performance
or lob beer bottles over the park fence in the darkness. The in-
truder is not merely the white man, but a life-style with its implied
suburban condescension.

Lahr states that "Papp himself questions the efficacy of his Mobile Theater." He quotes Papp as saying, "There was a time when doing Shakespeare seemed all right. It doesn't seem so right now." Papp recalls the black playwright LeRoi Jones [now known as Imamu Amiri Baraka] saying to him, "They don't need *Hamlet*. Give them plays about their lives." And Papp concedes that this may be "partly right; but someone else would have to do that. . . . I wouldn't know what material to do."

Vargas of the Gut Theater knows what to do. He doesn't arrive "with a controlled environment like the Mobile Unit," writes Lahr, "or elaborate machinery (lights, microphones, etc.) which cuts off the *fact* of the streets rather than acknowledging it. If his work is a service, making the community aware of itself and its potential, the theater also respects the public imagination. Vargas never plays a street without casing it for a few days, observing the habits and rhythms of the people. . . ." His theater develops out of a knowledge of their games, and their fantasies. (The children do not play cowboys and Indians here; they play cops and junkies.) Vargas adds, "You've got to know the architecture of the community, what are the conducive kinds of communication. . . . The people around you are a chorus no matter what you think and cannot hear. You must perform *with* them rather than *at* them."

Another early group is the Bread and Puppet Theater, in New York City, which is perhaps most widely known for its anti-war street parades and pageants, but also operates out of its own home on Delancey Street (as well as in the streets). It is involved in a continuously evolving theater that combines dance, sculpture, puppetry, film, music, myth, and ritual. El Teatro Campesino or The Farm Worker's Theater, characterizing itself as "somewhere between Brecht and [the noted Mexican comedian] Cantinflas," began in 1965, in Delano, California, to dramatize the issues of the Delano grape strike. It, too, has gone beyond its early efforts, moving to Del Ray where it has set up El Centro Campesino

Cultural, a cultural center aimed at "overcoming the cultural as well as the economic oppression of the Chicano community."

This movement of art out into the environment at large —murals and poetry appearing on the sides of ordinary tenements, theater playing in unlikely buildings and spaces, photography and film-making relying heavily on the familiar environment, playground sculpture taking form from the junk of empty lots—is a portentous one. Growing out of everyday life, in this way, the arts can have an immediate impact on everyday experience. The Studio Museum, for example, the first art museum to be located in Harlem, is an integral part of its everyday milieu on Fifth Avenue. This is not the Fifth Avenue of the Guggenheim Museum, but the unglamorous part above 125th Street. The museum has a crisp sign at street level amongst the neighborhood stores; its space is one flight up, in what could have been—and was —a factory loft.

It is increasingly apparent that the Black and Puerto Rican and Mexican-American groups, and perhaps others as time goes by, do not want their arts—and lives—defined by other people. The person who comes bearing the gift of Culture is likely to have it returned unopened. This will be hard for the donor to accept, when he is only trying to further an art he personally finds significant, and when he believes that the only thing lying in the way of its whole-hearted acceptance is lack of a building in which to present it. Obviously, better facilities are needed by almost any group, but the facilities that are needed may be a far cry from "museum architecture" or "theater architecture"—or even "architecture"—as we are used to thinking of these.

II. THEATER IN THE SEVENTIES

EDITOR'S INTRODUCTION

Legitimate theater is alive and well in America, though struggling as always for enough money to do new and innovative things. The story is diverse, with both amateurs and professionals extremely active all over the country. The community or campus that does not have at least one amateur acting organization is rare indeed.

In this section, however, the focus is on the professional companies. The opening article offers an excellent survey of theater production during one year (1972). Drama critic Henry Hewes observes that with great consistency the theater productions judged the best by critics were those done by subsidized, or unprofitable, companies. In some cases experimental productions were financed by more conventional productions staged by the same producer. Without some form of subsidy, says Hewes, Broadway will decline to the point where little other than comedies and musicals is offered—the result of the same old conflict mentioned earlier in this book between mass tastes (or what will fill all the seats regularly and thus make a profit) and what the critics and creative people consider significant, important productions.

The next article offers a look backward on the twentieth anniversary of that phenomenon known as off-Broadway. By definition, off-Broadway is theater produced in any theater outside the main theatrical district in New York City and presenting professional productions that are often unconventional, experimental, or low-cost. The off-Broadway record, says Stuart W. Little, is an enviable one that has enriched theater as a whole. "In the best sense, off-Broadway is not defined geographically, nor by the size of its theaters, nor by a set of production conditions. It is best defined by the spirit of amateurism that enables everyone to focus on the artistic goal rather than the commercial consequences." Beyond Broadway and off-Broadway there is, of course, the rest of the country. "Regional Theater—Filling the Vacuum" is a discussion of the repertory theaters in twenty-four cities linked together in the League of Resident Theatres. The author, Thomas Fichandler, is executive director of one such theater, Arena Stage, in Washington, D.C.

In every field there are one or two creative and determined people who seem to succeed where all others stumble. In theater that man today is Joseph Papp, originator of the New York Shakespeare Festival, which brings free Shakespeare to Central Park in summer. Papp is the subject of the next article. He and his group have already enlarged their operations so that Papp productions frequently occupy one or two Broadway theaters and two or three other stages around town while mobile units offer free shows in poor neighborhoods. Now Papp wants to expand on a national scale. His idea is to create an American National Theater Service that could mount and finance productions to enter even small communities throughout the country. Both government and private sources would finance the service. Because of Papp's astounding record of successful productions —and of convincing public officials to do as he wishes—this projection of the future of American theater should be taken very seriously. In March 1973, the New York *Times* reported that Papp's troupe would replace the Lincoln repertory at the Vivian Beaumont Theater. Papp plans to stress new American plays.

Theater is not necessarily a building, as the next article indicates. In summer all the arts move outdoors, and audiences love it. "Setting Plays Where It Happened" describes the enormously successful outdoor historical "plays of American life." The concluding article in this section points up the fact that theater is not only for the past-eighteen set.

Muriel Broadman Lobl surveys the state of children's theater here and abroad and finds the United States missing from the vanguard of innovative children's theater, except for the Little Theater of the Deaf.

SUBSIDIZED THEATER: 1972 [1]

To a greater extent than ever before, the best of the 1971-72 season originated in the steadily enlarging sector of our theater loosely labeled "nonprofit." If we take the Drama Critics Circle voting as an indication of relative value, the proportion . . . [can be seen in the table on page 69].

What is even more significant is that out of some fifteen attempts to transfer a successful work from its nonprofit birthplace to Broadway, only one was financially remunerative in any substantial way. Furthermore, that one, *Two Gentlemen of Verona,* was produced on Broadway under the nonprofit auspices of the New York Shakespeare Festival, which used some of its benefits to move *Sticks and Bones* to Broadway, . . . kept running at a small loss each week.

It should also be pointed out that Roger L. Stevens has operated similarly in bringing two Kennedy Center productions (*Lost in the Stars* and *The Country Girl*) to Broadway. Because the Government gives the Kennedy Center no producing funds, Stevens raised private contributions rather than invested money to create a revolving fund for original productions at the Center. And, like [Joseph] Papp, Stevens has apparently felt that there is justification for using some of that capital to underwrite the showing of the organization's finest products to Broadway audiences. One can argue that the expenditure is important because the contribution helps sustain America's professional theater center. Certainly, if Broadway were to dwindle much further than it has, the whole American theater industry might disintegrate.

[1] From "Theater in '72; the Best Theater of the Season Was Created by Subsidy," article by Henry Hewes, a contributing editor. *Saturday Review.* 55:38-41. Je. 17, '72. Copyright © 1972 by Saturday Review, Inc. First appeared in *Saturday Review* June 17, 1972. Used with permission.

Now it has become apparent that a healthy Broadway needs to offer, each season, a number of such subsidized plays. What remains to be worked out is the means of making this possible. A $5-top ticket price is essential. This will require Broadway theaters to work out a special formula that will make it possible for plays to operate at two thirds their present minimum costs. The building of a committed audience of theatergoers who will support this kind of work will be necessary. The Theatre Development Fund, with a minuscule annual budget of $175,000, has made an admirable beginning in this respect and presumably could, with a much larger budget, develop a corps of theatergoers large enough to guarantee a three-month run to any play it selects.

Why is this subsidy necessary? Because, without it, Broadway will deteriorate from a democratic mixture of entertainment and culture into a small group of theaters offering only comedies and musicals. Certainly, without most of the aforementioned nonprofit institutions' contributions, the season would have been a disaster.

Esthetically it was a strange year, with even the best work being more promising than fully achieved. Yet it was a season in which more good new playwrights than usual emerged. Jason Miller's *That Championship Season, . . .* scheduled to be transferred to a Broadway playhouse in the fall, won this season's Drama Critics Circle Award for the Best Play. The drama offered a deliberately unpleasant but often funny series of altercations between some typical middle-American bigots. Some critics felt that, like the TV series *All in the Family*, it might be giving comfort to theatergoers who shared to some extent the bigotry it purportedly attacked, but all agreed that the play was beautifully performed and that it stunningly caught the flavor of a crassly powerful segment of our society, a segment that is, one hopes, on its last legs.

Trailing Miller by only one point and receiving a Drama Critics Circle Citation was David Rabe (pronounced to rhyme with Abe), who had had his first exposure last May—

Drama Critics Circle Vote

Originating at Nonprofit Institutions	*Points* *
New York Shakespeare Festival *Sticks and Bones* *That Championship Season* *The Basic Training of Pavlo Hummel* *Two Gentlemen of Verona*	113
Chelsea Theater Center *The Screens* *Kaddish*	37
The Royal Shakespeare Company *Old Times*	34
Chichester Festival *Vivat! Vivat Regina!*	11
Royal Court and Arena Stage *Moonchildren*	10
La Mama Experimental Theatre Club *Godspell*	3
Repertory Theater of Lincoln Center *The Ride Across Lake Constance*	2
Negro Ensemble Company *Sty of the Blind Pig*	1
Stratford Festival, Canada *There's One in Every Marriage*	1
Communications Project—The Extension *And They Put Handcuffs on the Flowers*	1
	Total 213

Originating at Commercial Theaters

The Real Inspector Hound	17
Ain't Supposed to Die a Natural Death	9
The Prisoner of Second Avenue	2
Twigs	1
Wise Child	1
	Total 30

* Each of the 21 critics votes for his choice in three categories (Best Play, Best Foreign Play, Best Musical) rating a title as first choice (3 points), second choice (2 points) or third choice (1 point).

too late to be included in the Circle's 1970-71 voting. Rabe's second work, *Sticks and Bones,* was an uneven and often incomprehensible work. Yet it succeeded in doing what no other play about the Vietnam war has done. Uncompromisingly and relentlessly it gave us glimpses of contemporary American society seen with the special vision of a returning soldier. The soldier is welcomed, but his vision is so disturbing that he is asked to commit suicide. The most intense moments of the conflicts between him and his complacent family furnished deeply stirring drama.

There were those who felt that Rabe's earlier play, *The Basic Training of Pavlo Hummel,* was in some respects superior to *Sticks and Bones.* Indeed, a second production of *Hummel* by the Theatre Company of Boston, with Al Pacino playing the title role, strengthened this view because it more strongly focused on the young man who found a false sense of manhood in the army and as a result brought on his own ignominious death in a Saigon brothel.

Miller and Rabe were only two of the many unestablished dramatists to be helped by productions of their works at the New York Shakespeare Festival's Public Theater complex. Equally exciting was Richard Wesley, who came to the Public Theater from Harlem's New Lafayette Theater with *The Black Terror.* This drama about the dilemma of a black militant man and a woman whose love for each other is overridden by the insoluble differences between his rational radicalism and her emotional espousal of the cause, constituted a frightening and moving statement about the potentially tragic present situation.

Perhaps the best writer among this season's crop was Michael Weller, whose *Moonchildren* placed fourth in the voting. In his comedy about college kids inventing ways to protect themselves against involvement in an unsatisfactory environment, Weller proved himself adept at creating imaginative put-on dialogue and characters whose inner lives emerge with subtlety.

Finally, there was David Wiltse, whose *Suggs* was staged at the Repertory Theater of Lincoln Center's Forum Theater. Wiltse's deceptively entertaining comedy about a man trapped and destroyed by the New York City mystique made a sadly true statement about the quality of contemporary New York living.

Although the New York Shakespeare Festival was the greatest single source of theatrical excitement this season, the Chelsea Theater Center of Brooklyn also rose to a new glory. Straining its financial and physical resources, producers Robert Kalfin and Michael David attempted an uncut five-hour production of Jean Genet's *The Screens,* which was voted the Best Foreign Play of the season. Willa Kim's costumes, which won her the Joseph Maharam Award for outstanding costume design, reinforced both Genet's poetry and his humor, but many critics felt that the performance never established a rhythm and that, except for a few striking scenes, the production amounted to little more than an illustrated reading of the text. Yet the size and profundity of the work is overwhelming, as it follows a large cast of characters through an Arab uprising. As in other Genet plays, the task of most of the characters is to be more totally the persons and professions circumstances have made them than people ever are in real life, and in *The Screens* the playwright merges the world of the living with the world of the dead to enlarge the landscape of his considerations. The Chelsea Theater Center has retained the costumes, and *The Screens,* one would hope, will be produced again, perhaps in a shorter version.

The Chelsea also came up with two other ambitious productions, both of which moved to off-Broadway playhouses. One was Allen Ginsberg's *Kaddish,* featuring a remarkably vivid performance by Marilyn Chris, as Ginsberg's psychotic mother, and an interesting use of multiscreen projections by Video Free America. The other was a refreshingly lusty revival of *The Beggar's Opera* in Robert U. Taylor's atmospheric unit set.

As usual, the La Mama Experimental Theater Club offered an eclectic mass of projects, the most impressive of which was Andrei Serban's stunningly pure re-exploration of Euripides' and Seneca's *Medea*. The Judson Poets' Theater and its merry pastor-composer, Al Carmines, busted out with three often-inspired musicals, *Wanted, Joan,* and *A Look at the Fifties,* all of which were spiked by the talent of Lee Guilliat, a singing actress whose intensity and sense of humor perfectly matched those of Carmines. And Robert Wilson, whose *Deafman's Glance* was the rage of Paris last summer, offered *Overture for KA MOUNTAIN AND GUARDenia Terrace,* a beginning of the Byrd Hoffman School of Byrds' next work that required audiences to attend two three-hour sessions, one of which started at 6 A.M.

The Open Theatre also presented a few performances of a "work in progress." Called *The Mutation Show,* it was a constantly interesting extension of the group's technique, and despite its unfinished construction this study of freakishness within socially prescribed norms received the top Obie [i.e., off-Broadway] Award as the Best Theater Piece of the season.

Impressive, too, was the Negro Ensemble Company's production of *Sty of the Blind Pig,* Philip Dean's haunting study of slow-dying black atavisms. And the Company Theatre from Los Angeles brought its *James Joyce Memorial Liquid Theatre* to the basement of the Guggenheim Museum, where it provided a surprisingly pleasant mixture of theater, personal sexual therapy, and audience-involving games.

Some of off-Broadway's more noticeable achievements included the premiere of Tennessee Williams's latest play, *Small Craft Warnings;* an overstretched but nevertheless often very funny lampoon of drama critics, *The Real Inspector Hound* by Tom Stoppard; and Fernando Arrabal's uninhibitedly impassioned effort to dramatize the horror of Spanish prisons, *And They Put Handcuffs on the Flowers.*

On Broadway Melvin Van Peebles impressed some of the critics with *Ain't Supposed to Die a Natural Death,* a raw, strident, and colorful musical describing Harlem life, and followed it with a more good-natured show about a Saturday-night party called *Don't Play Us Cheap*. There was also a "street cantata," *Inner City*, which introduced the fervent Linda Hopkins. And Micki Grant's *Don't Bother Me, I Can't Cope* delighted almost everybody with a series of musical numbers that expressed both the black man's pain at being unjustly treated and the capacity for love and friendship that may give him a spiritual superiority over most of the rest of the population.

Other highlights of the season included Sada Thompson's protean portrayal of four different women in *Twigs;* Aileen Atkins's offhand Elizabeth in *Vivat! Vivat Regina!;* Raul Julia's delightful amorality and Jonelle Allen's impulsive vitality in the dynamic and outrageous *Two Gentlemen of Verona;* Phil Silvers's personal comic style in *A Funny Thing Happened on the Way to the Forum;* the self-intoxicated fun Robert Morse had in drag in *Sugar;* Vincent Gardenia's fiercely absurd delineation of a "benevolent" brother in Neil Simon's inconsequential smash hit *The Prisoner of Second Avenue;* Maureen Stapleton's utterly honest playing of the harassed wife in the revival of *The Country Girl;* and Blythe Danner's fresh beauty in Ellis Rabb's melancholy version of *Twelfth Night* at the Drama Repertory Theater of Lincoln Center. Incidentally, the Center's final production of the season, *The Crucible*, used the stage in a way that indicates the potentiality for more effective future use of its Beaumont Theater.

Finally, one must mention the sensitive staging of Peter Hall and the beautiful setting by John Bury for Harold Pinter's excursion into memory, *Old Times*, as well as the emotional power of, and the thrilling Kurt Weill-Maxwell Anderson score for, *Lost in the Stars*. These highlights were welcome compensations in a generally troublesome and transitional season.

TWENTY YEARS OF OFF-BROADWAY [2]

On the eve of its twentieth birthday what can be said in celebration of off-Broadway? One thing we can say is that off-Broadway is traumatized once again. This time the problem is not only skyrocketing production costs ($50,000 to put on a straight play, $75,000 for a musical) and a ticket price that has been driven well into Broadway range (up to $7.95 or $9.90). It's also the flight of middle-class whites from the city—1.2 million in ten years—that is depriving all New York theater of its core audience. Paul Libin, president of the League of Off-Broadway Theaters, calculates that the diminution of audience has had especially severe repercussions on the volume of projects. Off-Broadway is beating a retreat from the experimentation, encouragement of talent, seriousness, and bold ideas that marked its best years. Those years, it should be said, have left their mark, giving the contemporary stage some of its finest work, supplying the reputations of neglected playwrights, and sending shock waves of new ideas and experimentation into the conventional theater. Yet, almost from the hour of its birth, off-Broadway has feared for its survival.

Historically, off-Broadway can be said to have begun on April 24, 1952, when Tennessee Williams's *Summer and Smoke* with Geraldine Page opened at Circle in the Square to become the first major theatrical success below 42nd Street in thirty years. Up to that moment, the downtown theater groups were not especially conscious of audience. Off-Broadway came into being as a revolt against the over-organization of Broadway. It aimed to provide a showcase for new talent, and Miss Page and the Circle's director José Quintero were the first beneficiaries. Off-Broadway, too, was a place to revive the classics and to reclaim good recent plays that had missed in Broadway productions. (*Summer and Smoke* was a Broadway failure four years earlier.) It was a place where

[2] From article by Stuart W. Little, writer on the arts. *New York.* 5:54-5. Ap. 24, '72. Copyright © 1972 by Stuart W. Little. Reprinted by permission of John Cushman Associates, Inc.

permanent theater could take root and grow. *Summer and Smoke* spanked the breath of life into Circle in the Square, most durable of off-Broadway institutions.

Off-Broadway forged the characters of some of the theater's hardiest spirits: Theodore Mann, T. Edward Hambleton, Joseph Papp, the late David Ross, Joseph Beruh, Max Eisen, Gene Frankel, Richard Barr, Paul Shyre, Robert Hooks, almost all of whom were working twenty years ago and are still identified with off-Broadway. Out of off-Broadway have come some of the theater's only long-lived groups with continuity of artistic policy: the Circle, the Living Theater of Julian Beck and Judith Malina, the Phoenix, the New York Shakespeare Festival, the theater of Richard Barr and Edward Albee. As Quintero years ago said of his newly staked off-Broadway turf, "We have a sense of belonging. We have a base. We're not a migrant pack like Broadway producers." Marginal economic circumstances enabled groups with common artistic goals to come together and cultivate a high sense of theatrical purpose in escape from the confining commercialism of Broadway.

Off-Broadway became the prophetic theater. Operating closer to emerging ideas, more sensitive to shifts in the theatrical barometer, off-Broadway kept several years ahead of the conventional theater and transmitted its discoveries outward and upward into the main body of the theater. With the Living Theater's 1959 production of *The Connection,* off-Broadway led everyone in its starkly realistic examination of dope addiction. Only a year after the first lunch-counter sit-ins in Greensboro, North Carolina, at the beginning of "The Movement," Gene Frankel's production of Genet's *The Blacks* in 1961 bespoke a new militancy that was to galvanize a generation of black actors. Years before protest erupted in the streets black theater took root off-Broadway. In the early sixties, too, the outbreak of satirical reviews such as *The Second City, The Premise,* and *The Establishment* gave off-Broadway a political edge, particularly in relation to Vietnam and civil rights, of which the rest of the theater was blandly innocent. The Living Theater's production of *The Brig* in 1963 created a vibrant early image of military repressiveness, and in 1967 *Fortune and Men's Eyes* bared the inhumanism of prison life, four years before George Jackson and Attica. Several years before the Homophile Societies and Gay Lib went vengefully public, off-Broadway's 1968 production of *The Boys in the Band* offered the frankest view ever of homosexual society.

In its anti-commercialism and in its custodial concern for dramatic literature, off-Broadway became the model for the resident professional theater movement around the country. It even helped set fashions. As Ted Mann has theorized, the whole "leather look" may have originated with the corselets and boots Patricia Zipprodt designed for the Circle's 1960 production of *The Balcony*. In its early stars—Geraldine Page, Colleen Dewhurst, Salome Jens—off-Broadway set new standards of what constituted good looks in a woman. Almost awkwardly tall and not conventionally beautiful, the new off-Broadway stars challenged Broadway's petite tennis-dress prettiness.

In the plays of Beckett, in the ballads to the underworld, Macheath in *The Threepenny Opera,* in Zero Mostel's portrayal of Bloom in *Ulysses in Nighttown,* off-Broadway projected the image of the anti-hero. The new sort of believability in film stars stemmed from off-Broadway stages: Dustin Hoffman, George C. Scott, George Segal, Peter Falk, Estelle Parsons, Liza Minnelli, who made her debut in *Best Foot Forward* on Stage 73 ... [in April 1963].

Theater ideas are absorbed upwards. The new work of off-Broadway's best-known playwriting "find," Edward Albee, has been produced wholly on Broadway beginning with *Who's Afraid of Virginia Woolf?* in October 1962. All his work off-Broadway, with which his name is so closely associated, was done in a fifteen-month period in 1960 and 1961. Talent developed off-Broadway is quickly commandeered; since *Summer and Smoke,* Geraldine Page, despite a few recent tries, has never returned to off-Broadway. A parade of actors, designers, and directors who made it off-Broadway marched to Broadway or films rarely to return to their point of origin. Created as the original notable rock musical first off-off-Broadway and then off-Broadway, *Hair* has traveled around the world. Tom O'Horgan's off-off-Broadway experimentation with music, movement, and visual symbol has resulted in the Broadway superhits *Hair, Lenny,* and *Jesus Christ Superstar.*

The upward infiltration of ideas has enabled some off-Broadway groups to follow in their wake. This season [1971-72] Joseph Papp's Public Theater notably has been successful in placing two productions on Broadway—*Two Gentlemen of Verona* and *Sticks and Bones.* Today the Phoenix Theater, loosened from a particular off-Broadway base, operates out of either Broadway or off-Broadway theaters, depending on the nature of the project. The American Place Theater recently moved into a modern theater plant in the Broadway core area. In September [1972], Circle in the Square will move into a similar office-building theater of 650 seats at 1633 Broadway while retaining its present Bleecker Street home. Plainly, one of the directions in which off-Broadway is moving is Broadway—and not alone because higher ticket prices and an enforced commercialism make it look more and more like Broadway.

Theater groups are always vulnerable to the law of escalating expectations. At the same time, a contrary pull causes theater always to reach back to its innocent sources. The effort to recover the simple non-commercial impetus that enabled authors, actors, and directors to work in simple partnership in the days of off-Broadway's innocence leads one level down to the dimly defined world of off-off-Broadway.

In the wealth of new theater activity Paul Libin sees his theater coming full cycle, his life repeating itself.

Fifteen years ago when I started work in the theater I began on Broadway as a stage manager. But when I wanted to do serious

work in the theater I came off-Broadway and produced *The Crucible* and got my own theater, the Martinique, to put it in. If we
wanted to do something we just went and did it.

Today, serious theater, Libin believes, is disappearing
off-Broadway and appearing off-off-Broadway, even the classical revivals that were once off-Broadway's special province.
For the well-being of off-off-Broadway groups, Libin's wish
for them is not to become too formalized or too highly
organized.

If they do they will start to destroy themselves. These under-
takings can become bogged down in administrative detail. They
will find themselves in administrative circumstances when they
should be in creative circumstances. Off-Broadway can't answer
the labor problems of the theater. Off-off-Broadway can't answer
the problems of off-Broadway.

A degree of amateurism, in the best sense, is the life
spirit of the theater. For years off-Broadway thrived on the
unformalized cooperativeness of groups brought together
for communal goals. In the best sense, off-Broadway is not
defined geographically, nor by the size of its theaters, nor
by a set of production conditions. It is best defined by the
spirit of amateurism that enables everyone to focus on the
artistic goal rather than the commercial consequences. This
is what must survive for the total health of the theater.

Maybe off-Broadway can't go home again. Maybe it can
try a little harder. For many years Circle in the Square has
dealt with the same union sign company to paint the two
sides of its marquee when a new show comes into Bleecker
Street. In the last five years the cost of the complete job
has soared from $150 to $500, and the Circle, automatically,
has gone along. But when *Kaddish,* the present show, came
in, they decided to shop around and found a little Village
signmaker who did the whole job for the old figure of
$150. The regular sign company squawked loudly, and the
union business agent made phone threats, but the Circle
producers were simply delighted to cut free and get back
to the old days.

REGIONAL THEATER: FILLING THE VACUUM [3]

The League of Resident Theaters consists of twenty-six theaters in twenty-four cities in eighteen different states. All members of the League present professional acting companies in series of plays for a minimum of sixteen weeks per season. The resident professional theater movement began about twenty years ago as an effort to fill the cultural vacuum that existed in so many areas of our country. At the time practically the entire live theater was centered in New York City—in a few blocks known as "Broadway." To make it possible for people all over the United States to enjoy and benefit from professional productions of the world's great stage works a few hardy souls, with help from their communities, started theaters in their home towns. These forerunners included geographically widespread theaters such as: the Alley Theater in Houston, Texas; the Barter Theater in Abingdon, Virginia; the Cleveland Playhouse in Cleveland, Ohio; the Actors' Workshop in San Francisco, California; and Arena Stage, . . . in Washington, D.C. Today, in addition to these, Philadelphia, Boston, New Haven, Hartford, Buffalo, Stratford [Connecticut], Baltimore, Louisville, Chicago, Oklahoma City, New York City, Cincinnati, Minneapolis, Seattle, Los Angeles, Milwaukee, San Diego, Detroit, New Orleans and Providence all have theaters serving the needs of their communities.

Not only have the professional resident theaters been growing in number and spreading across the country, but their audiences have been expanding at a rapid rate. The desire for these theaters and the support for them is evidenced by the fact that in the last completed season three million people attended performances at these twenty-six theaters. Despite these outward signs of health, however, the gnawing disease of insolvency threatens almost every one

[3] From article by Thomas Fichandler, executive director of Washington, D.C.'s Arena State. *Cultural Affairs.* 1⊕:43-4. Spring '70. Reprinted by permission.

of these theaters, from the newest to those that have managed to survive for more than two decades.

Most of the expenditures of these theaters is covered by income from sale of tickets. They generally have sunk their roots into their communities and have built up large subscriber audiences. Their audiences, while devoted, are not affluent, which fact of life is recognized by the modest ticket prices that predominate—prices generally only slightly higher than downtown movies and far below Broadway levels. Nor, even if they could, would these theaters wish to drive away their low- and moderate-income audiences by raising ticket prices to those levels. Ticket sales, although the major source of income for the regional theaters, cannot be counted on to cover total outlays. Deficits in past years have been made up largely through individual gifts —usually in small amounts from a large number of givers —and from foundation grants. Business organizations and governmental units have been of very little help.

Two factors have combined to make the outlook for the regional theaters critical. Foundations have begun to shift their grants to other fields and inflation, which has caused costs to rise much more rapidly than income, has widened the gap between expenditures and income. If you think of theater as a handicraft industry in a machine age, you will realize why this trend is inevitable. A manufacturing firm can fight higher wage rates which it has to offer when prices for food, rent, clothing, etc., are rising by substituting machines for men and thereby controlling unit costs. But a theater cannot readily replace its actors with robots. The answer to the questions of how the deficits of these theaters are to be met lies elsewhere.

Actually the regional theaters have been doing a remarkable job of solving their own financial problems. Last season, for example, these twenty-six theaters had a combined operating deficit (before allowing for gifts or grants) in excess of $6 million. Grants and gifts covered all but $1.6 million. However, these uncovered deficits, added to previous years' deficits, left the regional theater with accumulated deficits of just over $5 million. And these deficits have occurred despite the fact that actors, technicians, directors and other staff members in these theaters subsist on extremely meager earnings. Salaries for full-time employees of $50, $60 and $75 a week are common; the average salary for all full-time employees in these theaters, including managing and artistic directors and top actors, was less than $150 a week . . . [in 1969-70]. And for most employees employment is for only part of the year.

The regional theaters have two distinct handicaps in trying to meet their financial problems. First, when people think of theater they tend to mean commercial Broadway theater, where it is possible in the Russian-roulette game that is played there occasionally to make a financial killing. It is not easy to make them understand that the regional theaters are in an entirely different category—that they, like schools, museums and even garbage-collecting, need subsidies to make ends meet. Second, these theaters are johnny-come-latelies to the field of patronage. What individual fortunes there are that are available to support the arts have long since been preempted by the symphony orchestras, opera and ballet. Theaters, therefore, must look to government for substantial aid if they are to survive.

In the hope that the Federal Government through the National Foundation for the Arts and the Humanities may begin to play its vitally needed role in assuring the survival of the performing arts in the United States, the League of Resident Theaters supports extension of the life of the Foundation and urges that at least the $40 million suggested by the President be made available for its functioning in Fiscal Year 1971. [President Nixon has requested $80 million for 1974.—Ed.] It should be clearly understood, however, that $40 million is merely a token amount in relation to the needs of the arts. The Government owes it to the people it represents to see that their lives are enriched by sustaining the arts which are the ultimate expression of a civilized society. For this noble purpose it must provide many times $40 million a year. A modest goal would be to match on a per-capita basis what our northern neighbor, Canada, provides for its arts—this would mean an annual appropriation for the United States of $300 million!

JOE PAPP SEEKS A BIGGER STAGE [4]

American plays in the 1970s may well be simpler and more human than those of the last decade. They may also attract a bigger audience drawn from every region and social class in the country. Or so Joseph Papp predicts.

Papp is the energetic and innovative producer of the New York Shakespeare Festival Public Theater. His organization has two homes: One is a 2,300-seat open-air amphitheater in Central Park where Shakespeare is presented to the public free every summer; the other is a complex of four separate auditoriums housed since 1967 in the former Astor Library on Lafayette Street in downtown Manhattan. At both locations, which are financed partly by public funds and partly by private donations, many people who never have seen a play before are beginning to love live drama. Vibrant productions and the low ticket-prices on Lafayette Street (student tickets sell for as little as $2) are packing them in.

Papp recently turned fifty and is generating ever more plans and ideas. In *Two Gentlemen of Verona,* a rock adaptation of Shakespeare's comedy, Papp has given Broadway its freshest musical of the season. Another Papp production, *Sticks and Bones,* has been so well received at the Public Theater on Lafayette Street that it is being transferred uptown, where it will become Broadway's only serious new American play. David Rabe, the author, was discovered

[4] From article by Stuart W. Little, author of *Off-Broadway: The Prophetic Theater. Saturday Review.* 55:40-4. F. 26, '72. Copyright © 1972 by Saturday Review, Inc. First appeared in *Saturday Review,* February 26, 1972. Used with permission of Saturday Review, Inc. and the author.

by Papp and may well be the best new American play-wright since Edward Albee.

Since the first of 1972, Papp has been trying to clear his desk of all the clutter of production details that accompany success in order to concentrate on what matters to him most: a populist concept of an American national theater.

No one who has watched Papp plan and maneuver over the years would be surprised by this bold ambition, for from small beginnings he has built a major theatrical power base. He was born Joseph Papirofsky of Eastern European parents in Brooklyn in 1921; his father pushed a wheelbarrow through the Williamsburg section. At the public library and at free band concerts, Papp acquired an early love of culture. His first theatrical experience was as an actor; he once toured in a national company of Arthur Miller's *Death of a Salesman*. In the late 1940s he began a career in directing. Brooks Atkinson, the critic for the New York *Times*, panned his first attempts, some one-act plays of Sean O'Casey.

His New York Shakespeare Festival had its origins in a church basement on New York's Lower East Side in 1953 when he organized a workshop. He first took Shakespeare outdoors in 1956 by staging plays in the East River Amphitheater, thus establishing the pattern of free performances that survives to the present. The following summer he moved his stage to Central Park.

Beginning in 1966, Papp established a year-round operation by acquiring a permanent indoor home, the Astor Library. Papp, in financial straits last spring [1971] for the costly renovation, succeeded in selling the building to the city for $2.6 million—its cost plus improvements. Typically, he had turned a narrow escape into a major cultural victory. Now he was ready to fight for a national theater.

His plans have not yet been fully worked out, but Papp envisions setting up, through massive government aid and private funding, the American National Theater Service. Its most important function would be underwriting the financial losses incurred by a national tour of almost any serious play. Papp, moreover, hopes his productions will reach not only those cities with theaters but also small, remote towns that have facilities no grander than a church or a high school auditorium.

Papp's operations in New York already represent on a small scale what his projected American National Theater Service might be able to do for the entire nation. He has taken his Shakespeare productions out into the streets of the five city boroughs in the summer; each street company works out of a mobile unit, a truck that contains all necessary sets, props, and sound equipment and that can be opened up into a small stage. In the winter his actors tour the city schools. Papp has also organized university tours of such one-man shows as Jack MacGowran's dramatic readings from the plays and novels of Samuel Beckett. Joe Papp, in short, has had plenty of experience taking the theater to the people, but now he wants to reach not just New Yorkers but all Americans.

How will the American National Theater Service be funded? For the service's first year, Papp seeks $1 million from the Federal Government and $400,000 from private sources (the first private donor might well be the Rockefeller Foundation, which Papp already has approached). For the second year, an expanded program would require $2 million from the Government and $600,000 from private sources. In its third year Papp's program would be in full operation and ideally would receive an annual Government subsidy of $3 million and an increased amount of private money. When fully operative, the service would not only underwrite tours of plays but also publish scripts and make films. In the near future Papp hopes to be able to present the whole scheme to President Nixon.

Back to the Humanness of Theater

The National Theater Service has been conceived at an opportune historical moment. With the Vietnam War drawing to some kind of close, Papp feels we are at the beginning of a more positive era. The service would assist in the "liberation and purification" of this era's spirit. In the kinds of scripts submitted to him, Papp detects a shift. He senses a growing reaction against the experimental, dehumanized drama of the past decade. Many plays of the 1960s more often assaulted the senses than made sense. Actors moved in restless patterns, produced choral shrieks and moans rather than coherent individual speech, and flung one another about more like angry gymnasts than sensitive, normal human beings.

I think there is a kind of revulsion against the purely formal aspects of art [Papp says], and a need to get back to the humanness of theater. I only know this by reading what is submitted to me. There is less death and negation in the writing. Black playwrights seem to be less angry than they were and more personal. They write about love, about family, about a real-life situation in a bar.

A return to a simpler, more human treatment of fundamental problems, Papp believes, will help the theater to address a broader public.

Papp's recent thinking has obviously been profoundly influenced by his "discovery" of David Rabe, a playwright whose name Papp mentions in the same breath with Eugene O'Neill's. For many years Papp dealt with only one playwright: Shakespeare. Papp's artistic and organizational energies went into developing an American approach to the classic plays. More specifically, he cast blacks and Puerto Ricans in leading Shakespearean roles, sometimes modernized the lines, and even added rock music—all on Shakespeare's own theory that a play must be as you like it. Papp's urbanization of Shakespeare hit a new high with *Two Gentlemen of Verona,* with its joyful rock score, its celebration of love, and its ethnically diverse cast.

Since the acquisition of the Public Theater, Papp has been turning more toward new plays and musicals. He helped create *Hair*, from which his theater still derives substantial royalties. He produced Charles Gordone's *No Place to Be Somebody*, which won the Pulitzer Prize in 1970. These spectacular successes and Papp's openness to new writers and writing brought scripts flooding in. David Rabe's first play, *The Basic Training of Pavlo Hummel*, came in the mail. Although Papp was on the lookout for a play about the war, he had been getting only predictable antiwar preachments.

Rabe's play was different. It had a military setting, to be sure; in the rapid-fire dialogue and long monologue of the first few scenes, Rabe erupted with a magma of military slang, soldierly lore, swear words, and barracks insults. Yet it was more than a routine propagandist diatribe. And the central character was puzzling. "I had a strange feeling when I read the play," Papp recalled. "I didn't have an immediate positive reaction to it. I didn't know who Pavlo was. Was he a Puerto Rican? Was he working-class? It was a peculiar play."

Not quite knowing what to do with the script, Papp put it aside until another director brought it back to his attention. Mel Shapiro, who recently staged *Two Gentlemen of Verona*, arranged for Rabe to meet Papp. From the first Papp was taken with Rabe, a big, sandy-haired man with the build of a football player, who talks slowly and frankly but writes fast and wild for his stage characters. "He was modest and shy and thoughtful," Papp said. "But I felt we were not talking on the same plane. I needed to get a director who could relate to David. I had a feeling only a buddy in the war—and it had to be *that* war—would do."

Papp picked Jeff Bleckner, who had studied with Papp at the Yale Drama School but had not served in Vietnam. At the initial meeting in Papp's office, Bleckner and Rabe, sizing each other up and getting to know each other, carried on the barest of conversations. New playwright and director fast became a firm team—*Pavlo Hummel* opened last May and is still running—and the two men now work together with great mutual respect.

I participated with them in planning the production [Papp said]. While the work was going on, I became more and more interested in the play. I decided to do it as a major production. Things I didn't *see* I began to *hear*. In reading the play, for example, the mother's speech had seemed tedious. But onstage it came alive.

The speech, as it happens, is central to the script. Pavlo Hummel is a strange, blasted character with an uncreated past, a tortured present, and a future he can foresee only as doomed. With mounting desperation but diminishing success, Pavlo labors to make his pride in his uniform compensate for the indifference of his family. Pavlo's brother doesn't bother to stop combing his hair in order to acknowledge Pavlo's return home on leave. Pavlo's mother belittles her son by derisively asking him about his service in the Army, "How do you like being a robot?" Acted-out scenes of violence tumble furiously one upon another: drill-field punishments; scuffles with sadistic buddies who loathe Pavlo's zeal; a battlefield rescue in Vietnam; and, finally, Pavlo's death, which happens when another solider fights with him over a girl in a Saigon whorehouse and throws a grenade at the hero. But in a play studded with such overt brutality there is perhaps no greater crime than the understated neglect by brother and mother. In her long speech Pavlo's mother recites how a woman moving about in a department store finally receives the news of her son's death. The long, involved speech—Pavlo might just as well not be in the room—is designed solely to insulate the mother in advance from the personal pain of her son's probable death in Vietnam. On his first leave Pavlo Hummel has already been given up at home.

Rabe started *Pavlo Hummel* about six months after he returned from Vietnam in January 1967. He then began to write *Sticks and Bones,* a play about a blind Vietnam soldier coming home. These two plays are linked thematically; in both, the soldier's family refuses to comprehend the son's experience of the war. Rabe himself did not perceive the similarities until the second play was finished. He is now writing a third play, *The Orphan* . . . and recognizes that when it is done he will have completed a dramatic trilogy, which was not his original intention.

Papp's main purpose in transferring *Sticks and Bones* to Broadway is to provide a larger and more conspicuous platform for a playwright with important ideas to communicate. Yet the transfer does pose a risk to the life of the play; Broadway audiences often do not respond to dramas that state strong ideas. But he believes a show that can sell out on a Tuesday night in a three-hundred seat theater in downtown New York has enough draw to fill the 799 seats of Broadway's Golden Theater: "It has that kind of push."

"Why Do You Produce Plays?"

Papp will consider the move a success if the production breaks even; his regard for money is respectful if not altogether commercial. At the Public Theater *The Black Terror* is running at a weekly loss of $5,000.

I don't ask myself why we are supporting that play. I think in terms of perpetuating an important work. This is the most important black statement being made today in the theater. Why do you produce plays in the first place? You produce them because they have something to say and you want as many people to hear them as possible.

Richard Wesley's argumentative play is the most eloquent treatment yet staged of the conflict among blacks caused by their attempts to justify the use of violent means to achieve liberation.

I know exactly what plays I want [Papp said of his most vital function—the choice of scripts—a function he reserves to himself]. But you can't order them up. By producing certain playwrights you can attract others. We want those plays that will make an impact on society. I am looking for a kind of simplicity and directness in the writing, a kind of simplicity that David Rabe has, that will reach great numbers of people.

While setting up such criteria, Papp is not turning his back on the kind of avant-garde drama that provided so much theater excitement during the last decade. His small Other Stage at the Public Theater is open to "plays that are important to do, plays that are literary, that are sophisticated, that are probing, that are avant-garde."

But Papp takes a skeptical view of plays that do not relate to the wider problems of society. "I'm impatient with other plays unless they are brilliant. The brilliant play, even if it has no relevance to our times, is always an exception. Then I would drop all requirements, all limitations."

Papp has some further bold schemes. . . . Concerned about the erosion of police morale in New York City that has resulted from public antagonism, he is ambitious to form a gigantic police chorus and see what influence such a singing group might have in altering attitudes. To the same end, he would form a parallel chorus of inmates from the city's penitentiaries. Out of his American National Theater Service, eventually he would like to see emerge a multi-racial acting company. "Then there would be a true national theater. It would not be just an Anglo-Saxon theater. We would have to have actors who speak well. They would be white, black, and Puerto Rican, and would express the true racial makeup of this country. Then we could start to build an audience."

To put these major schemes into effect, Papp has tried to reduce his administrative duties. Much of the load can be taken up by his able coproducer, Bernard Gersten, who is both everywhere Papp is and everywhere Papp cannot be.

Still, it is hard for Papp to relinquish detail. Large or small, most decisions land on his desk. Recently a talented young graphic artist came to Papp at the dragging end of the business day. Willingly adding half an hour to office

time, Papp examined with care a portfolio containing a
number of fresh and detailed drawings of children that
showed a quick eye for their impish curiosity. When Papp,
who was genuinely enthusiastic about the drawings, heard
that a couple of publishers had rejected the artist's ideas,
he turned to Gersten, "Maybe we ought to go into children's book publishing, Bernie." But the artist had come
really to sell Papp on a logo, a typographical symbol for
the New York Shakespeare Festival Public Theater. Papp,
whose theater uses distinctive type faces but has never had
a logo, wasn't really in the market for one.

"You know how long I've been hearing about a logo?"
Papp asked rhetorically. "Twenty years. 'You need a logo.'
People have been saying that for twenty years."

The artist, conscious of losing ground rapidly, switched
to the consumer's survey as defense: "I've shown these to
a number of people and their opinion . . ." Papp interrupted. "You know the most important opinion you can
get on that?" The Public Theater producer, the seasoned
wager of so many public wars to build his theater to its
present position of strength, looked at the artist levelly
for a full four seconds. "Mine," he said.

SETTING PLAYS WHERE IT HAPPENED [5]

In Palo Duro Canyon, Texas . . . onlookers whooped
it up when a lone horseman waving the state flag posed
dramatically on the rim of the canyon. In New Philadelphia, Ohio, they cheered when a note from George
Washington persuaded Chief White Eyes not to ally his
tribe with the British. On Roanoke Island, North Carolina, they roared when the infant Virginia Dare appeared
in her mother's arms. In St. Augustine, Florida, they
groaned when Don Pedro, the devoutly Catholic conquista-
dor, refused to marry the Indian princess Notina.

[5] From "America Onstage." *Newsweek*. 80:86-7. Ag. 28, '72. Copyright
Newsweek, Inc. 1972, reprinted by permission.

To thousands of theatergoers this summer, these episodes out of American history have taken on the immediacy of current events in a series of seven long-running outdoor dramatic spectacles by the veteran American playwright Paul Green. Poster-like as historical reconstructions, frankly inspirational in content and performed mostly by amateurs, Green's "plays of American life" would seem like white elephants if produced on the slick boards of New York or Los Angeles. But they are right at home in the settings the playwright has chosen for them, and their appeal—and longevity—is greater than anything Neil Simon or David Merrick ever dreamed of.

Craggy

In all seven amphitheaters where Green's works are being offered this summer, the place is as much the thing as the play. History lives for the thousand adults and children who flock nightly to see *The Lost Colony,* now in its 32nd season, being played out on precisely the spot where Sir Walter Raleigh founded his short-lived settlement in the New World—the sandy, mosquito-filled shores of Roanoke Island. When Thomas Jefferson agonizes over the Declaration of Independence in *The Common Glory,* now in its 25th season he does so on the lovely banks of Lake Matoaka in Williamsburg, Virginia. The messenger who brings Washington's note to Chief White Eyes in Green's more recent *Trumpet in the Land* can be seen traveling across the same Ohio ravine where the Delawares once roamed. And who can doubt the hardship suffered by the Texas settlers when thunder and lightning (simulated by a blast of dynamite) break against the awesome, craggy walls of Palo Duro Canyon, whose floor is the stage for the seven-year-old production of *Texas?*

Green calls his spectacles "symphonic dramas," since they blend theater, music and dance. In reality, however, they are more like community festivals—blending local enterprise and civil participation. George Mallonee, managing producer of the Civil War saga *Wilderness Road* in Berea, Kentucky, says that "it's terribly important that the community thinks this belongs to them. Fifty per cent of our company is from the Berea area," says Mallonee. "They know the locale and it rubs off on the new people."

Still, to compensate for the high annual turnover in actors, auditions are held on an interstate basis for most productions. They attract mainly acting students who want the experience of a continuous run and who will work for wages that range from $45 to $145 a week. (The most notable alumnus is perhaps Andy Griffith, who played Sir Walter Raleigh on Roanoke Island from 1949 to 1953.) And though the characterizations range from very bad to usually adequate, the period music (chosen by Green), the lively dancing, the lavish use of spectacle—loud battles with Indians, colonists' ships sailing along on unseen trolley tracks—and low ticket-prices are sufficient to maintain sizable audiences summer after summer. "This is theater for the unsophisticated," says Robert Knowles, production coordinator for *The Lost Colony*. These are people who wander into this place not knowing what to expect and have a moving emotional experience."

Struggle

"The purpose of my theater is to tell a good story and to tell it well," the seventy-eight-year-old Green told *Newsweek*'s Sunde Smith. "We don't have stars in my plays, but heroes. A nation is like the people it admires and worships. I'm sure the human race doesn't care about Freud or the sick 'boys in the band.' People yearn for improvement, for betterment. They lean toward the struggle."

Throughout his long and prolific life, Paul Green has been writing about that struggle with missionary zeal. Reared in the farming country of eastern North Carolina, he began writing because "I was so damn lonesome on the farm. I would plow around and around with that mule and the great overhanging sky. So you start talking to yourself and making things up." He wrote his first plays as a student at the University of North Carolina and in 1927 won a Pulitzer Prize for *In Abraham's Bosom*.

An early love of music ("As a kid in church I saw what music did as drama") led in 1934 to his first attempt at "symphonic drama," the unsuccessful *Roll, Sweet Chariot*, then two years later to his antiwar *Johnny Johnson*, for which Kurt Weill wrote one of his best American scores. Several stints as a screenwriter in Hollywood (he wrote many Will Rogers films) gave him plenty of money, but it was not until 1937, when the Roanoke Island Historical Association commissioned him to write *The Lost Colony*, commemorating the 350th anniversary of Virginia Dare's birth, that he found his true métier.

Honing Up

Green is a vigorous man who likes doing outdoor work on his farm outside Chapel Hill, where he lives with his wife, Elizabeth. Early every summer he visits each of the amphitheaters that are putting on his plays, "coming around as humbly as possible" to see what might need "clarifying" or "honing up." He has two more outdoor spectacles in the works—one for Jekyll Island, Georgia, about the millionaire robber barons who made the spot into their private preserve. Above all, he thinks of his works as "shrine dramas," making pilgrims of his audiences who he hopes will come to feel as he does about his heroes. "I've read a lot about them, and gotten to know them," says Green. "I feel as close to Bunyan, Jefferson or Washington as I do to a neighbor."

CHILDREN'S THEATER IN EUROPE AND NORTH AMERICA [6]

Theatre for young people may be an exciting hour or so for the audience, but it can be much besides for the adults

[6] Article by Muriel Broadman Lobl, children's entertainment critic, winner of a 1970 National Cable Television Association award for a program on theater for youth. Text supplied by author. Reprinted by permission. (A condensed version of this article appeared in *Saturday Review*. 55:62-6. S. 9, '72.)

who put the performances together. It can be used for educational purposes, or to convey political propaganda, or to raise the self-image of an ethnic group. It can be a tool for achieving community unity, or for making money, or just for giving kids a good time. In short, many people all over the world are involved with putting on programs for children and for much the same reasons they or others put on shows for mature spectators. However, children's theatre, which is either subsidized or smaller in scale than adult theatre if not subsidized, has one economic advantage over the "Broadway" commercial theatre; putting it in the same class as off- or off-off-Broadway: it can afford to experiment, and even to fail. And as the adult commercial theatre is enriched by non-commercial experimentation, so too it can profit by the work done for children.

Good theatre for children adheres to the same standards as good theatre for anyone else. Only the subject matter, which must be comprehensible to a given age-range, a more sensitive treatment of sex and violence, and the length of the production, which must be geared to a shorter attention span, mark it as being not primarily for the mature.

An unusual opportunity to see examples . . . from several nations was provided . . . [in 1972] when representatives of youth theatres and individual artists met at the Fourth International Congress of ASSITEJ (Association Internationale du Théâtre pour l'Enfance et la Jeunesse, or International Association of Theatre for Children and Youth) first in Montreal and then in Albany [Georgia]. Six hundred delegates from twenty-six lands, every continent but Africa, exchanged information about young people's theatre and saw productions of plays from Russia, Rumania, Canada, and the United States, purported to be typical.

The Central Children's Theatre of Moscow

The Central Children's Theatre of Moscow was the company which aroused most speculation beforehand. Their program opened with a prologue, in which a troupe of players entered the square of a make-believe town of Old Russia, and collected a crowd by performing somersaults and other tricks common to circus folk the world around. The two stories which followed had been adapted into rhymed couplets by Alexander Pushkin in 1831 and were narrated in the Russian. Pushkin called them "The Tale About the Fisherman and the Fish" and "The Tale About the Dead Princess and the Seven Knights," but with minor distortions they were the same Grimm Brothers' "Fisherman and His Wife" and "Snow White and the Seven Dwarfs" our children have always known. The emphasis was on song and movement, with dance-processions of lords or townspeople or buffoons, or linear dances of knights or peasants. The costuming was sumptuously medieval Russian. So was the architecture, of which we got tantalizing glimpses, particularly in the town of the prologue and in the "Fisherman" story, when his hovel became in turn a farmhouse, a mansion, and a palace as the Golden Fish granted the Wife's increasingly unreasonable demands. The staging techniques, although not innovative, were skillfully handled. Set sections were reversed to reveal other scenes, and the Japanese use of a strip of blue cloth to indicate a river was modified by having several parallel strips, each succeeding one held a little higher by the actor at either end, waved with growing violence to demonstrate the waxing fury of the ocean. It was from between these "waves" that the fish appeared—a rod puppet, all gold and glittery and wriggly, and truly magical. In the second play, after "Snow White" was spared by the Tsaritsa's servant, she met the Seven Knights, who invited her to live with them in their tower. There was another magic moment when back at the castle the Stepmother stood before the Mirror in her jewel-encrusted black robes, a spectacularly beautiful personification of royalty and evil, and faced her image, identically clad, which she questioned and plotted with. . . . In scenes as exquisite as Fabergé Easter eggs, the real protagonist was not a character but an enchanted, opulent Slavic culture in which children could believe miracles could happen.

Indicative of the status of children's theatre in the Soviet Union, was the presence in the cast of five of that country's top artists. Three of them bore the proud title "Honored Actor (or Actress) of Russian Federation," and two, "People's Actor (or Actress) of the U.S.S.R."

The staff for this theatre (actors, musicians, technicians, etc.), 350 in all, is larger but typical of the other forty-seven professional theatres in the Soviet Union for eight- to eighteen-year olds. Each of the others also has its own building and permanent company of from fifty to eighty actors. Along with fairy tales, their repertories include contemporary stories and classics from outside, such as *Tom Sawyer* and *Treasure Island*. Classics from Russian literature occupy a prominent place, and first-rate playwrights and composers are commissioned to write the productions. For five- and six-year olds there are 110 permanent professional puppet companies, each in its own theatre, including Sergey Obraztsov's famous Central Puppet Theatre. And all of this completely subsidized.

The leading children's theatre company in the U.S.S.R. was the brainchild of an extraordinary woman, Natalia Sats. When she was eighteen, in 1921 (four years after the October Revolution of 1917), she persuaded officials of the new government to give her a building to start a permanent theatre for children, the first in Russia—and, she claims, in the world. This became the Central Children's Theatre of Moscow. At that time the conviction was strong that to remake the world one must concentrate the best efforts of civilization on the newest generation. It was in this spirit that Isidora Duncan was invited to set up her school of dance in Moscow the same year, 1921. Madame Sats remained as the director of her theatre for eighteen years, during which she became familiar with Prokofiev, who wrote *Peter and the Wolf* for her to narrate, as well as other music dedicated to her. And then in 1939, the era of the Stalin purges, she dropped out of sight and remained in obscurity for the next twenty years. She does not discuss the events of this period or of her personal life, but it is known that in 1945 she founded the first children's Theatre in Kazakhstan in Alma-Ata, in Central Asia, which presented performances both in Kazakh and Russian.

About six or seven years ago, as an experiment, she began a new enterprise for children, since 1969 called the Moscow State Children's Musical Theatre. Her staff of 200 includes a 37-piece orchestra and 50 excellent voices. When she was unable to find enough operas suitable for children, she had them commissioned.

The Ion Creanga Theatre from Bucharest

From Bucharest came the Ion Creanga Theatre with *Tales With Masks,* one of the great delights of the ASSITEJ Congress. Their program began with the same format as the Russian—a group of strolling players appeared, but this time on an empty stage and wearing leotards and rehearsal clothing. With the spectators' permission for them to perform, presto chango! Before it seemed possible they were dressed in national costumes and singing and dancing up a storm. The play proper, in two acts, told the Adventures of Pacala, a folk hero who at birth was cursed by the Fates to fight forever against the vices of Injustice, Theft, Arrogance, Greed, and so on . . . with the strongest weapons of mankind: satire and laughter. No scenery, just some lengths of peasant weaving outlining the sides of the stage, and a handful of props. The scenes were set by moving on some six-foot-high shield-shapes painted with trees or interiors. When reversed, each was discovered to be a huge mask of the vice Pacala had to combat. The mask concealed an actor—the superb Ion Lucien played most of the vices in addition to co-authoring the production, and he knows how to write funny and act funny—and the actor wore a similar face-mask in normal scale, which he removed to reveal his own face with his features covered by a third mask or make-up.

The hilarious episodes were punctuated by folk dances and songs, and the actors changed masks, costumes, and characterizations so often it seemed as if there were a cast of hundreds played by twenty-odd. The direction was inspired. The stage business, which began with the Masks, continued throughout with engaging, unexpected tricks which were right in context and more than mere gimmicks. The acting and mime were on a high level, with as fine a sense of ensemble as I've ever seen. The great fun came through even without a translator, but what came through most strongly was the charm of the cast, who loved what they were doing and loved their audiences and let it all hang out. Their radiance engulfed the spectators like a tidal wave, and they gave us a picture of Rumania through the eyes of a peasant of a past generation—earthy, gutsy, cynical, and so alive.

Masks in drama go back to the Greeks, of course, and many societies even today customarily use masks in ceremonies involving ritual enactment or dance, and from time to time a modern play experiments with them. But I've never seen masks used in quite this way before—first large, to caricature an abstract quality; then reduced, to bring it down to the scale of humanity; and finally life size, to express its embodiment in an individual.

The Ion Creanga Theatre opened in 1965, dedicated solely to performances for children. Although adult theatres had sporadically put on children's shows in Rumania as part of a "family" entertainment tradition going back some sixteen centuries, this was the first time children had a theatre of their own. In seven years, the Ion Creanga has built up a repertory of forty-five plays, broken down by audience age.

Les Jeunes Comédiens du Théâtre du Nouveau Monde

Les Jeunes Comédiens du Théâtre du Nouveau Monde came from Montreal, bringing Molière's Les Fourberies de Scapin. Both the preceding plays had advantages over this one for the non-foreign-language-speaking observer—they had simple plots and stressed action, which made ⌐ mprehension relatively easy. But what made this company unique was its use of puppetry. Normal scale was created by the actors' bodies themselves, and then small hand-puppets appearing over the edge of the booth forced us to readjust our concept of space and distance. This company of four men and two women employ their puppets with telling effect and with their exuberance have found a fascinating way to bring a classic to today's young people.

The company was organized in 1963, and from 1969 on has been doing "collective creations" on an improvisational basis, without being hampered by a formal script. Their 1971-1972 tour of Canada and New England was subsidized by the Canada Council and the Quebec Government's Cultural Affairs Department.

The Little Theatre of the Deaf

The Little Theatre of the Deaf, one of the companies representing the United States, is an offshoot of The National Theatre of the Deaf. The small group—five actors, only one of whom can hear—was drawn from the parent theatre to perform for children. I've always admired them because they present themselves as actors demanding respect for their craft and not as handicapped persons seeking sympathy for a disability. And they *are* artists and they can create exciting theatre which has validity on its own terms.

The strength of this theatre is in the gesture language. A flick of fingers can define a tiger's whiskers. The sweep of an arm can make the sun rise or set. The most mundane expression can be illuminated by a new vision, quickened by a spark of movement that is poetry to the eye and heart. The audience is never in doubt as to what is happening onstage. The one hearing actor doubles as narrator, maintaining a monologue fitted to the action.

A typical program begins with a happy introduction of
the cast to the children—the actors prancing on in as a horse-
drawn coach, or, in the case of the ASSITEJ performance
poking their hands through holes in a shiny curtain and
greeting the spectators. This is followed by an explanation
of the sign and gesture languages, always entertaining to
kids who love being given the inside dope on arcane codes.
Short tales or poems—James Thurber, A. A. Milne, Ogden
Nash, Haiku—and game stories, like the wildly funny "House
That Jack Built" illustrate how the sign and gesture languages are used. The program usually winds up with an im-
provisation period with suggestions being accepted from the
audience as to what the actors should be.

The Little Theatre players share a quality with the Ru-
manians and French-Canadians—joy in performing and the
ability to communicate it. Since only one other theatre for
the deaf exists, and that in Moscow, this kind of theatre was
new to most of the audience. They applauded not only the
skill of the players as technicians but the message that "Deaf
Is Beautiful" too.

The National Theatre of the Deaf, in operation since
1967, was established through the O'Neill Center and started
its child-size theatre a year later, with the assistance of a
grant from the United States Office of Health, Education,
and Welfare. There is a second company now so that more
children can be reached. The National Theatre has been
asked by three foreign governments to help set up theatres
for the deaf in their countries.

Two Minnesota Companies

Everything at the ASSITEJ Congress was enacted by
adult professionals with the exception of two productions,
both of them from Minnesota. These were startlingly similar
in many respects, and not at all alike in others. *Hang On
to Your Head,* a presentation of the Children's Theatre
Company of the Minneapolis Institute of the Arts, was written and directed by John Clark Donahue. There was a small

core of professional actors, but all the rest of the performers were teenage students. Jon Barkla's large set was a work of art—a spiral construction with a hollow center that enabled the actors to enter or exit from several directions, including up and down, and to play on several levels. To augment the dream atmosphere, smoke was used frequently—to blur details, to cloud comings and goings—and lights on the smoke added an eerie, mysterious quality. The cast of over twenty was costumed imaginatively and moved well through the scenes of fantasy that gave us a railway station, a carnival, a Victorian garden, and an American speakeasy, among others. The production was a visual triumph and, for the director, a *tour de force*.

The Children's Theatre deals with original material, created by and for the Company. The Minneapolis Institute of the Arts has been involved with theatre for young people since 1965, offering full seasons of productions in its auditorium, weekday performances for school groups, and a troupe that tours throughout the state and region. A theatre school for teenagers was begun in 1969. The National Endowment for the Arts, Title III, the Urban Arts Program, and a $250,000 grant from the Rockefeller Foundation contribute to the support of the Company.

The other Minnesota company, the Hopkins Eisenhower High School Theatre of Hopkins, a Minneapolis suburb, brought in *The Capture of Sarah Quincey*, also the story of a girl who escaped reality via daydreams. This ten-year old heroine was portrayed in a virtuoso performance by twelve-year-old Kathy Zahorsky.

The script was totally improvised, using an outline supplied by Gary Parker, who was also responsible for the lyrics and musical direction. Tony Steblay's over-all direction acc unted for the excellent pacing.

The Hopkins Eisenhower High School has carried on a special program in children's theatre for more than twenty years. Yearly, about two thousand grade school children are bused in to see plays like *The Emperor's New Clothes* and

Tom Sawyer. Junior high school students are brought in to see plays by Shakespeare as well as productions of *Billy Budd, Mother Courage,* and *Antigone.*

The Academy Theatre of Atlanta

We know how valuable the physical side of a production can be to the creation of good theatre, how important the sets and costumes are and how necessary the lighting. And then along comes a production without any of these to remind us that when it comes down to basics what makes theatre theatre are actors and material. The Academy Theatre of Atlanta, with an integrated cast of ten men and women, brought its Georgia Tour Play into a studio which allowed for none of the advantages a more formal situation would have provided. There were no special lights, no sets—not even any props except for a couple of chairs. The actors wore street clothes, and no makeup. They turned the studio into an everyday high school classroom and themselves from adult actors into students and teachers or townspeople. Yet without help but from their own talent and conviction and a script that was honest and intelligent, they delivered theatre that was as vital, as dynamic as anything else presented to ASSITEJ. Their open-ended probing of interpersonal relations in turmoil as the result of new desegregation practices was both sensitive and incisive. The dialogue, sometimes wry, sometimes stinging, had the ring of truth. The actors would wander through the audience seated on three sides of the small arena stage, addressing a spectator directly and enlarging the cast to take in everyone present as a participant.

The Academy Theatre received a grant from HEW under the Emergency School Assistance Program to prepare and present a play to serve as a resource for schools and communities of Georgia in their first years of school desegregation. In their research, the Academy Theatre found that most groups were either black or white; very few groups outside the schools had joint meetings or participation from blacks and whites together. Many officials expressed concern that this play could ignite a situation which they were keeping cool, or felt that the Academy people were outsiders, or were afraid to make waves. Although two small communities worked with the Academy to some degree in formulating the concepts of the play, the finished product was never performed in either of them—no one in authority there would stick his neck out. The "Georgia Tour Play," as it came to be called, was played widely throughout the state and changes evolved from the audience discussion which followed.

A performance had been scheduled for a Rome high school when a play review appeared in a newspaper criticizing it for being too obvious in its approach to black and white differences, and despite the approval of his staff members, the principal canceled it. However, in Savannah, at a time when the city was tense over a federally-ordered student busing situation, several performances met with positive and enthusiastic response.

A more typical instance in less tense circumstances was a performance in Albany, Georgia, in a black church. No untoward incident occurred and the church people expressed pleasure that the play had brought white people there for the first time.

Subsidizing Children's Theater

Many factors enter into the fact that the Russian and Rumanian governments subsidize children's theatre totally and either include it in the curriculum or officially encourage attendance indicates its value to those who make policy. So far as Les Jeunes Comédiens is concerned, one evident factor was the pride in and desire to encourage the use of French to keep this half of their bilingual culture flourishing. Grants from the Canada Council and the Quebec government's Cultural Affairs Department applied to touring expenses and not company operations, so the group has made a virtue of necessity with ingenuity triumphing over a limited budget. This is a predicament that many Canadian companies share with some of those south of the border.

In the United States several different situations exist simultaneously. Each of the American programs we discussed has been subsidized either by a foundation or a grant from some division of government. This is true even of the Hopkins Eisenhower High School Theatre, for while it does not receive a grant as such, as part of the school system, staff salaries are paid, rehearsal and performing areas are provided without charge, and all kinds of expenses can be absorbed elsewhere instead of showing in a budget. Thus it has been possible to mount good-sized productions without being forced to depend on box office to defray full costs. But the plays which many children see—those for which children are variously estimated to be from 50 to 90 percent of the audience—are developed by commercial producers who operate without any outside financial assistance. The American ASSITEJ programs were not necessarily any more typical of what most young people see than the spectacular "Nutcracker" the New York City Ballet puts on seasonally, or the *Hansel and Gretel* performed sporadically by the Metropolitan Opera, or a very occasional Broadway production such as the Mary Martin *Peter Pan*.

Historically, the settlement houses of the end of the nineteenth century were the first to take performances for children seriously. Not until 1903 was the first professional children's theatre organized in New York City. It survived until 1909. For the next decades the torch of children's theatre was carried by the settlement houses and other noncommercial producers. Many of the problems plaguing theatre for young people stem directly from the Protestant ethic, which for so long has regarded any theatre with suspicion. Only comparatively recently has the value of theatre been recognized by school systems, which frequently prefer established, conventional curricula to experimental programs.

However, the winds of change seem to be stirring up new concepts of theatre for young people. International meetings, such as ASSITEJ, provide for a fertile interchange of ideas. The Federal Government has been expressing its interest through several agencies, and the arts councils of most states concern themselves with at least some aspect of entertainment for children, as do many state and municipal departments of education and recreation. Here and there across the country are children's theatres fortunate enough to have their own buildings, and others operating out of community centers or colleges. And all across the country touring producers shuttle from school auditorium to church basement, bringing plays and musicals, puppetry and dance, mime and opera, to virtually every spot where enough young people can be collected to make up an audience. It's possible that by the time today's children are grown up, children's theatre may also come of age in the United States.

III. OPERA AND DANCE
THE ELEGANT ARTS

EDITOR'S INTRODUCTION

Perhaps no forms of the performing arts attract such loyal and partisan followers as opera and dance. The audience is passionately devoted but, in terms of numbers, a small one. Both forms of expression are expensive to produce, and neither films very well. Both seem consistently to need outside financial help to keep their theater doors open.

The first half of this section deals with opera, which when done very professionally involves huge casts in full costume, a complete orchestra, and highly-paid superstars. Not too surprisingly, it is the most consistently expensive of the live performing arts. Traditionally, the rich in America have subsidized and attended opera, just as in Europe royalty provided patronage. Even so, ticket prices in many places have soared so high that newer and younger audiences are being discouraged. To keep the expensive halls filled, opera managements have relied heavily on traditional, less innovative, productions.

The first article in this section is a broad overview of opera companies in the United States—what they perform, where, and how often. The next article, "Backstage at the Opera," is a behind-the-glamour look at the most famous of our opera companies, the Metropolitan, making clear why opera is such a costly enterprise. Following this is an article describing a more typical company, the Lake George Opera Festival Company, one of the proliferating and popular summer music ensembles.

The second half of this section explores the many phases of dance in the United States. "Directions of the Dance," by Yorick Blumenfeld, is a comprehensive survey of trends in both modern dance and classical ballet. Dance is enjoying a wave of unprecedented popularity, with new companies and schools forming every year. Dance is, in fact, a field in which American groups have become international leaders; two of the six greatest ballet companies in the world are American: the New York City Ballet under George Balanchine and the American Ballet Theater. In the area of modern dance, American companies have set worldwide standards.

A final article, "Seeing Ballet Sideways," by Tobi Tobias, again looks at a performance from the wings, but this time from the performer's point of view. From that perspective one sees not the glamour and the magic but the work and sweat that go into bringing the magic to the audience out front. The particular performance described is a ballet by the New York City Center Joffrey Ballet, but the effort involved could apply equally to an opera, a new theatrical production, or a symphony performance. For, while a great deal is written about the costs of performances, the places, the problems, it is in fact the performers and their talent that the whole thing is about.

OPERA IN THE UNITED STATES, 1971-1972 [1]

If you are the curious type, you will already have glanced at the . . . box score [below]. One part of every survey is, after all, a compilation of statistics, a comparison of figures; an equally important part, though, is the analysis of these figures, the evaluation of conditions and trends. The 1971-72 season made news on both counts. Opera workshops as well as opera companies are headed in new directions, and regarding statistics, the number of performances and of works performed is 10 percent above that of last season, the number of performing groups having risen by about 5 percent.

[1] From "In the Balance, U.S. Opera Survey, 1971-72," article by Maria F. Rich, executive secretary of the Central Opera Service. *Opera News.* 37:26-9. D. 16, '72. Reprinted by permission.

In spite of what many have predicted, opera is a healthy child of our time.

	1971-72	1970-71
NUMBER OF ORGANIZATIONS:		
Companies	321	309
Colleges	394	376
Total	715	685
NUMBER OF WORKS PERFORMED:		
Standard repertory	192	158
Contemporary repertory	172	166
Total	364	324
NUMBER OF PERFORMANCES:		
Standard repertory*	3,875	3,332
Contemporary repertory	1,848	1,914
Total	5,723	5,246

* Includes 516 Gilbert & Sullivan performances

Further proof of vitality lies in the continuing number of new works written for our stages: thirty-four world premieres in the United States last season. Of these the more important included two operas by the young American composer Thomas Pasatieri, *The Trial of Mary Lincoln* (NET Opera) and *Black Widow* (Seattle Opera), and Virgil Thomson's *Lord Byron* (Juilliard School). The premieres of Leonard Bernstein's *Mass* and Alberto Ginastera's *Beatrix Cenci* celebrated the inauguration of the Kennedy Center; John Eaton's *Heracles* opened the Musical Arts Center at Indiana University and Neil Slater's *Again D.J.* the University of Bridgeport Arts Center. *Flower and Hawk,* commissioned from Carlisle Floyd, honored Jacksonville's sesquicentennial. In Denver, New Year's Eve was rung in with a first performance of Dominick Argento's *Colonel Jonathan and the Saint,* while the same composer's *Postcard from Morocco* was introduced by Center Opera of Minnesota in November 1971 and enjoyed a total of nineteen performances during the season.

The multimedia field was led by *The Artist* (Composers Showcase at New York's Whitney Museum), a collaboration between composer Paul Reif and artist Larry Rivers and poet Kenneth Koch, while rock oratorio was represented not only with *Mass* but *Joseph and His Technicolor Dreamcoat* (Overture to Opera, Detroit), by the *Superstar* team of Webber and Rice. Seven new operas were written especially for children, another twelve new works being introduced by college and university opera workshops. Among these last, three were based on famous plays: *Cyrano de Bergerac* by Jack Jarrett, *Earnest in Love* (after Wilde) by Croswell and Pochriss, and *The Lib: 393 B.C.* (after *Lysistrata*) by Theron Kirk.

A one-year tally of the most successful contemporary American opera composers shows their significance as part of today's culture: Gian Carlo Menotti with nine operas, 689 performances (*Amahl* dropped from a high of 446 performances to 242); Douglas Moore with five operas, 84 performances; Carlisle Floyd with five operas, 68 performances; Dominick Argento with five operas, 39 performances; Thomas Pasatieri with four operas, 19 performances; and Virgil Thomson with three operas, 10 performances. (Two productions of *Four Saints in Three Acts* were offered in celebration of Thomson's seventy-fifth birthday.) We have not done equally well by foreign contemporary composers, the exception being Benjamin Britten, who literally flooded the American market last season with eight operas in 214 performances—90 of his *Noye's Fludde* alone. There were only nine American premieres of foreign operas, and of these there was only one by a living foreign composer, Aribert Reimann's *Melusine* in Santa Fe. But musicologists must have been hard at work digging up all the little-known older treasures. From the seventeenth and early eighteenth centuries we enjoyed the first American hearings of Cavalli's *Calisto,* inaugurating the Patricia Corbett Pavilion in Cincinnati; Cesti's *Orontea,* at the University of California at Los Angeles; and Rameau's *Naissance d'Osiris,* at the Uni-

versity of California at Berkeley. Later works introduced
here last season include Massenet's *Thérèse,* played on a
double bill with Malipiero's *Sette Canzoni* (Peabody Conservatory [Baltimore]), Nielsen's *Maskarade* (St. Paul
Opera), Delius' *Village Romeo and Juliet* (Opera Society
of Washington [D.C.]) and the first staging of Ezra Pound's
composition *Testament de Villon* (Western Opera Theater).

In addition to their premieres, opera workshops at uni-
versities, colleges and conservatories offered a great number
of unusual, interesting and sometimes demanding works:
Smetana's *Kiss,* Henze's *Boulevard Solitude* and Kodály's
Háry János—all at New York's Manhattan School, d'Albert's
Tiefland at Kansas State Teachers College (Emporia),
Dvorak's *Rusalka* at Stanford University, Rossini's *Comte
Ory* at USC [the University of Southern California], Schenk's
Dorfbarbier at St. Petersburg [Florida] Jr. College, Tchai-
kovsky's *Eugene Onegin* at John Brown University (Siloam
Springs, Arkansas), Britten's *Peter Grimes* at Baylor Uni-
versity (Waco, Texas), Kurka's *Good Soldier Schweik* at
Texas A & I University in Kingsville and at Florida State
in Tallahassee, where Blacher's *Abstrakte Oper No. 1* was
also performed. Monteverdi's *Ballo delle Ingrate* was heard
at the University of Arizona in Tucson, *Das Rheingold* and
Ariadne auf Naxos at Yale, with additional productions of
the Strauss opera at Catholic University in Washington,
D.C., at Oklahoma City University and at Northwestern in
Illinois. Verdi's *Falstaff* reached Indiana University, San
Fernando Valley [California] State College, Southern Illinois
University and the Eastman School [Rochester, New York]
last season; four performances of *Otello* and twelve of Wagner at college or university workshops are further proof of
ambitious programing.

Workshops have been undergoing a gradual but significant transformation. Five surveys ago we welcomed the
first signs of change: "No fewer than seventy-six workshops
at universities, colleges and conservatories have changed
their name to Opera Theater . . . aiming at professional

standards for the student performers." But the tables have turned to such an extent that we are now faced with Opera Theaters concerned more with accomplished productions of demanding works than with offering students stage experience in roles they can master. While only a few years ago Bob Jones University (Greenville, South Carolina) seemed unique in turning to professional singers for leading roles, this has become an accepted practice today. In the past an occasional faculty member may have filled an overly taxing part; nowadays, professional alumni and faculty members carry a heavy performing schedule in order to facilitate the production of difficult works. The creation of new facilities, of expensive arts centers with large auditoriums, may in part be responsible for this condition. In any case, the following comment contained in replies to the Central Opera Service [COS]/ *Opera News* questionnaires attests to the view held by some music department heads: "The new facilities will make it possible to invite guest artists from major opera companies to star in our productions next to some talented students"; . . . another says, "Regrettably, we will no longer be able to offer our students the benefit of participating in the variety of opera scene productions but will be limited to one major opera with professional singers and relegate the students to minor parts."

In some instances the situation has developed to its logical conclusion—a professional company spinning off from a workshop. Such has been the case at the University of Rochester in Oakland, Michigan (Detroit's Overture to Opera), at USC (the Opera Theater) and at Memphis [Tennessee] State University, whose opera department merged with the Memphis Opera Theatre.

Meanwhile, the regular professional and semiprofessional companies have continued their own accelerando. Due to higher costs and expanded programs, seven companies increased their budget to over $100,000 last season, thus becoming eligible to apply for Federal grants; they join the

112 The Reference Shelf

forty such companies reported in last year's survey. The increase in overall performances during the past season, almost 500, must be credited largely to greater productivity by professional companies rather than by workshops.

While the majority of these companies added performances to their main or home season last year, the significant expansion has taken place in tours and out-of-town performances, educational and sociological programs. This growth can be attributed to the need for longer employment of artists, for development of new audiences, for introduction of the arts into depressed areas and for education of the young. Federal and state agencies, though modestly funded, support just such endeavors, and foundations and corporations find these projects equally interesting. Unions too have been helpful, as in Jacksonville (Florida) and Hawaii, where grants from the Music Performance Trust Fund/Recording Industries of the AF of M [American Federation of Musicians] facilitated student performances with orchestra.

We find companies large and small embarked on tours, from the Metropolitan Opera to the Greater Utica (New York) Opera Guild to women's clubs and fraternities. Last season the New York City Opera spent three weeks at the Dorothy Chandler Pavilion in Los Angeles and two weeks at Kennedy Center; the Seattle Opera took some of its productions to cities in Washington, Arizona, Montana and Oregon; Center Opera of Minnesota visited Chicago, Culver City (Indiana), Houston and Glens Falls (New York); and the Kansas City Lyric Theater (Missouri) offered performances in Kansas, Oklahoma and South Dakota, sponsored by the Great Plains Federation of Arts Councils. An all-time high of nearly fifty companies gave out-of-town performances in one or more cities within their state (only twenty-two were recorded at the 1968 count). Finally there are the companies devoted exclusively to touring, though only those operating with a relatively modest budget seem to survive; these include the Goldovsky Opera Theater [Brookline, Massachusetts], the National Opera Company—celebrating its twenty-fifth anniversary this year, the Western Opera Theater, the Turnau Opera Players [Woodstock, New York], the New England Regional Opera and almost a dozen more. Some of them travel with chamber orchestra, others perform with piano and still others join forces with the local symphony. One thing is certain: more professional performances than ever are being brought to communities never before exposed to opera.

By the same token, artists and administrators alike have realized that their most effective educational programs are those allowing a more intimate contact between performer and young listener. Although professional companies still offer student matinees and reduced-price student tickets, a growing number are adding special projects for in-school presentation, not to be confused with pre-performance lectures in schools. Through the educational departments of Lincoln Center and the Metropolitan Opera Guild, nearly two hundred performances of various programs were offered in elementary and secondary schools by the New York City Opera Ensemble and the Metropolitan Opera Studio. Around the country, schools booked presentations prepared by such companies as San Diego Opera (75 performances of *The Old Maid and the Thief*), Houston Grand Opera (60 performances of *Bastien and Bastienne*), Seattle Opera (24 performances of the specially commissioned *Magical Marriage*), Opera de Camera in New York (50 performances of *La Serva Padrona* and 12 of *The Medium*), Chattanooga [Tennessee] Opera (10 performances of *The Telephone* and "Opera Caravan") and Overture to Opera in Detroit (24 performances of *Rumpelstiltskin*). Several companies specialize in children's operas at libraries and museums. And many opera departments at universities, colleges and conservatories have developed their own touring programs for schools, including special adaptations of full-length operas —*The Tale of Papageno* (Cleveland Institute) and *The Abduction* (Hartt College [Hartford, Connecticut]).

The most recent and perhaps most significant expansion of opera seasons comes in the area of community involvement, attesting to new social consciousness about the arts. In 1971-72 we find the Harrisburg (Pennsylvania) Civic Opera performing *The Old Maid and the Thief* at the governor's mansion under the Late Start Program; in addition there were Seattle Opera performances sponsored by the Washington State Cultural Enrichment Program; Palm Springs Opera presentations at retarded children's centers and at a crippled children's hospital; New York City Center Performances for Senior Citizens and Lincoln Center's Festival of Street Theater Productions. One performance of *Noye's Fludde* on New York's Times Square involved some one thousand local schoolchildren, while other scheduled and/or improvised street theater presentations were offered throughout the city on movable stages, several times in connection with block parties. Often these performances were sponsored by the Inner City Programs, part of the National Endowment for the Arts's funded Expansion Arts Program. . . .

Free opera concerts in city parks have mushroomed within the last two summers, sponsored mostly by state or county arts councils, parks and recreation departments, sometimes by major corporations. Besides the Metropolitan Opera in New York, the Houston [Texas] Grand Opera has initiated a season of such concerts, as has the Southern Regional Opera in Atlanta and in other cities in Georgia and Arkansas. Programs of somewhat older vintage include Grant Park in Chicago, Ithaca Opera (New York), Opera Under the Stars in Rochester (New York) and performances sponsored by the Department of Recreation in Richmond.

No COS/*Opera News* survey would be complete without a list of the ten most performed operas of the standard repertory. Since its predictability is notorious, let's look first at the losers, those operas expected to be up there among the top ten but missing once the returns were in. Here we do find two surprises: *La Traviata* and *Fledermaus,* favorites for so many years, do not appear on the list, both having had performances cut by 50 percent against the previous year. *La Traviata* slipped from 161 to 74 performances, *Fledermaus* from 121 to 64. *La Bohème* takes first place with 188 performances, the ever popular *Nozze di Figaro* is in second place with 147, followed by *Il Barbiere di Siviglia* with 143 and *Madama Butterfly* with 142. Pergolesi's *Serva Padrona,* always quite a favorite, never has shone to such advantage: thanks to a school tour last season, the one-act comedy was heard in 140 performances. Thereafter we record *Hansel and Gretel* (131, up from 70 in 1970-71), *Carmen* (116), *Gianni Schicchi* (111), *Rigoletto* (94) and *Tosca* (88).

In general, last season brought a healthy balance of rarely performed operas from the baroque period to the present. In addition to the Cavalli and Cesti premieres and performances of no fewer than eight Handel *opere serie,* revivals of more than usual interest included Vecchi's *Amfiparnasso,* appropriately staged at the Cloisters in New York, and Monteverdi's *Orfeo,* appropriately accompanied by original old instruments—at the Spring Opera in San Francisco. Moving forward in time, we find Mozart's *Oca del Cairo* given by the New England Chamber Opera, Bellini's *Capuletti ed i Montecchi* by New York's Bel Canto Opera and his *Puritani* by the Philadelphia Lyric. *Norma* received an unusually high number of performances, with productions by eight opera companies. Rossini's *Semiramide* featured Sutherland and Horne in Chicago; Donizetti's *Favorita* proved a favorite in Dallas and in New York (Bel Canto); and Verdi's first comic opera, *Un Giorno di Regno,* was performed by New York's Cosmopolitan Orchestra. New York's Little Orchestra Society gave a semistaged performance of Schumann's *Manfred,* a dramatic work known only for its overture, and Philadelphia's Rittenhouse Opera staged Leoncavallo's *Zingari.* Special interest centered around Berlioz' *Troyens* by the Opera Company of Boston, which gave two complete performances of the five-hour opera, presenting it in two sections—once on consecutive evenings, another time as matinee and evening performances on the same day. The same month, the Pro Arte Chorus and Orchestra [Hofstra University, Hempstead, New York] presented the work in concert form on one marathon evening at Carnegie Hall.

Summing up, it was a good year, busy and productive as the figures and performances prove. One can also see a new road ahead: the thrust for opera, the challenge, now seems to lie in community-oriented programs. Under professional guidance, projects are developing which will open new frontiers, hopefully sparking the imagination and enthusiasm of a new and young audience.

BACKSTAGE AT THE OPERA [2]

When the Metropolitan Opera opened its season in New York this fall with a new production of Bizet's *Carmen*, the audience rose from its $100 box seats and lesser perches to shout bravo through twenty minutes of curtain calls. At one point in the tumult, no fewer than 180 performers were taking their bows from the stage, 68 musicians were smiling up from the orchestra pit, and—suspended in between—conductor Leonard Bernstein beamed out from his hydraulically operated podium. Yet this was only the visible evidence of what is, behind the scenes, probably the world's most advanced factory of fantasy.

In the vast bulk of the Metropolitan Opera House in Lincoln Center, nearly one thousand employees work the year around in a maze of rehearsal halls, scenery lofts, wardrobe rooms, lighting booths, and workshops. Seamstresses, carpenters, designers, directors, lighting men, and other essential workers produce everything that the Met needs, down to its own wigs and mustaches. Photographer Burt Glinn spent three months backstage at the Met to record the creation of this new production of an old opera.

[2] From article by Walter McQuade, staff editor. *Fortune.* 86:118-27. N. '72. Reprinted by permission.

The Met first performed *Carmen* nearly ninety years ago, and the basic story has changed less in the interim than the Catholic Mass. But it is the Met's continued striving for perfection—its quest for a nuance of costume, setting, illumination—that brings new life to the old farm year after year.

If the new *Carmen* had been a Broadway musical, the producer would have read the glowing reviews and then gleefully settled in for a long run and a profit in the millions. But not opera, not at the Met. Partly because opera stars, like baseball pitchers, cannot perform day after day, the Met scatters its performances of various operas throughout the season; *Carmen* will play only eleven times this season. Seven times a week the enormous stage of the Met is built up and torn down. Out *Carmen*, in *La Traviata;* come *Lucia di Lammermoor,* go *Roméo et Juliette.*

The expense of this repertory system is staggering. The Met spends as much as all other opera companies in the United States combined—$425,000 a week. Wages account for about 80 percent of the budget, including fees for stars that run as high as $4,000 per performance. Launching a new production like *Carmen* can add several hundred thousand dollars for designing and building new sets and conducting extra rehearsals. Even at that, when the Met takes *Carmen* on tour it will have to build another set of scenery, because the stages out of town—some of them converted movie palaces—are so much smaller than its own. On the road the Met receives $50,000 per performance from a local sponsor, but the opera's managers figure that it costs far more than that to transport, house, and pay the wages for the big show.

There is nothing cheap about attending the opera. Tickets for most performances are $20 in the parterre boxes and $17.50 in the orchestra; on opening nights they are much higher. Nevertheless, every time that golden curtain goes up, the Metropolitan Opera Association, Inc., loses an average of $25,000.

In addition to the deficit from the sale of tickets, the Met has encountered other fiscal pressures in recent years. In 1966 the opera marched into its grand new quarters in Lincoln Center to the tune of a record $7 million deficit, which was finally covered by donations. In 1969 the orchestra, soloists, chorus, and ballet went on strike and the house fell dark for almost half the season, creating another deficit of nearly $6 million. After the strike the Met raised the price of tickets to the current level. In a recession year, that was too much even for opera addicts. Season subscriptions fell and attendance dropped to 87 percent of capacity from 96 percent; each percentage point of the decline cost the Met $100,000 a year.

Opera has a long history of patronage by royalty and the tradition has survived in Europe. The British government subsidizes more than 40 percent of the costs of Covent Garden in London. Government funds pay as much as 68 percent of the opera's budget in Munich, 90 percent in Stockholm, 45 percent in Vienna, and 72 percent in Hamburg.

By contrast, the Met received only about 2 percent of last year's $22 million budget from governmental sources—funds from Federal and New York State arts programs and a grant from New York City for three weeks of free public performances in the parks. All three subsidies were for specific undertakings, some of which cost more than the funds received. The performances in New York City's parks, for example, cost the Met about $500,000, against $190,000 allocated by the city. The stars cannot be engaged at benefit rates for civic purposes.

The patronage that permits opera to survive in the United States is private. The Met's sources include income from a relatively small endowment, $7 million, most of it willed by the late Mrs. John D. Rockefeller, Jr. There are also contributions of at least $1,000 each from a thousand Met patrons, and additional sums from affiliated organizations like the Metropolitan Opera Guild, whose members contributed $425,000 . . . [in 1971]. The National Council of the Met . . . contributed $100,000. A drive by all the Lincoln Center cultural institutions raised $1.2 million, of which a third went to the opera. Still, after all these and other large individual donations, the Met had to carry over an $840,000 deficit from the 1971-72 season.

It is up to the Met's unpaid board of directors to find ways to bridge the gap. The chairman of the board is lawyer Lowell Wadmond, and the president is George S. Moore, retired head of First National City Corporation, an agile banker and an ebullient opera lover. Moore hopes to build a secure future for the Met by increasing the endowment dramatically, by making recordings, and by developing ways to reach a broader audience through pay TV.

The day when we can produce the best opera in the world for 3,800 people in Lincoln Center is coming to an end [he says]. The Met buys a quarter of the time of the top twenty-five voices in the world. Why should only 3,800 people have this?

Moore is certain that the audience is out there waiting. For thirty-two years Texaco has broadcast Saturday performances of the Met to an estimated weekly audience of ten million people, and of these faithful, fewer than 1 percent have ever seen a Met performance, even on tour. But while Moore ponders ways to bring those lonely opera lovers into the act, the Met is determined to continue, in perpetual emotion, its tenacious quest for perfection: tonight, *Carmen*; tomorrow, *Don Giovanni*.

UP IN THE ADIRONDACKS [3]

Ten years ago, above the scenic waters of New York State's Lake George, vacationers and local enthusiasts crowded into a drafty, antiquated, barnlike place to witness something not usually associated with the Adirondack vacationland—opera. There was no soft red cushioning below or crystal above, and on more than one occasion the soprano

[3] From article by Denis Gray, an Associated Press writer in Schenectady. *Opera News*. 37:18-19. Ag. '72. Reprinted by permission.

and her accompanist had to compete with the patter of rain on the metal-roofed building. Going to the greenroom during intermission meant a stroll on the green grass outside, and one night a few patrons had to donate their cars' headlights to beef up some circuits in and around "festival hall."

That was ten years ago. . . . [In 1972 on] July 13 the Lake George Opera Festival Company—housed in a well-accoutered auditorium in Queensbury-Glens Falls, attracting some of the nation's first singers, directors and operatic craftsmen, the lone pianist replaced by a thirty-five-piece orchestra— began a six-week season that will undoubtedly enhance its reputation as one of the outstanding regional repertory companies. On its bill of fare are two East Coast premieres of recent American works, plus *The Threepenny Opera*, Britten's *Rape of Lucretia, Tosca* and, in keeping with the original festival mood, three sunset "champagne cruises" on the lake featuring the lighter side of the literature. The American works: Thomas Pasatieri's multimedia *Black Widow*, first seen last winter in Seattle, and *Postcard from Morocco* by Dominick Argento, a production by the visiting Center Opera of Minnesota.

Putting it all together is David Lloyd, with Lake George from the beginning and its artistic director since the death of the festival's founder, Fred Patrick, in 1965. Lloyd, who off-season chairs the opera division of the University of Illinois, began his strenuous annual cycle with the last curtain call of 1971 at Lake George. Through the fall and spring the energetic fifty-two-year-old director auditioned over three hundred young singers around the country for Lake George's apprentice positions and selected the fifteen principal performers, the conductors and directors needed to realize the 1972 productions.

In late June it all started to fall into place as everyone involved in *The Threepenny Opera* converged on the region from a dozen points across the country to begin the first of seventeen consecutive days of rehearsal. In a bare stageside room the first day, with props reduced to red tape on the floor, Patrick Bakman of the New York City Opera put the young, exuberant cast through a short slice of the earthy Brecht-Weill piece. "Both of you preen—preen like Venuses," he coached sopranos Carol Wilcox and Maria DiGiglio, engaged in a catty duel over faithless Mack the Knife. "You're in a tough spot," Bakman prompted Miss Wilcox two hours later, going over the same scene. "You should be trying to find an escape hatch. Don't worry—just think about it, and it will all fall into place." A furtive flutter of eyes from the pretty Metropolitan Opera soprano and the two women threw themselves again into their bitchy dialogue. From the piano, conductor George Posell suggested a rhythmic change, which the singers tried with good comic effect.

"We know what we can do," Lloyd had explained a few weeks before rehearsals. "Putting on *Aida* would not go very well with our resources, so we select intimate operas, sometimes modern ones, those that demand fine acting." In the company's five-hundred-seat home, with the farthest spectator only seventy feet from the footlights, nuances make a difference: an inert or inappropriate facial expression strikes a false note, a flick of a finger or eyelid conveys an inner mood. Intensifying this impact are the performers' words, heard by all in English. In such a setting, a singer stepping in and relying on generalized formula would threaten the performance. Lloyd rules out such substitutions: "Here we get away from all the things that gave opera a bad name, such as ignoring the person one is supposed to be making love to, staring at the conductor, walking backwards onstage." Lloyd, a tenor with Tanglewood's opera group under Boris Goldovsky in the late 1940s and subsequently with the New York City Opera, learned his lessons well.

Performers at Lake George have consequently been chosen for more than vocal opulence. They are generally young, attractive, American and on the way up. Typical of the breed is lyric tenor Harry Danner of the Metropolitan Opera Studio, featured in *The Rape of Lucretia*. Associated with the company since being "overwhelmed" by its 1969

Albert Herring, and dissuaded by Lloyd from knocking on the doors of European opera houses, Danner is looking for involvement. Summers with Lake George have made their mark: his voice does not fight the words or mood of the music, and few standby gestures creep into his performance.

This perspective on opera, blended with the teamwork atmosphere, generous rehearsal time and a chance to do new repertory, attracts more than up-and-coming talents. Many who elsewhere draw a far larger weekly paycheck than Lake George's $200 or $250 have also been on the scene—Frances Bible, Patricia Brooks, Frank Guarrera, Gimi Beni, Frances Yeend, Nancy Williams and others.

Directing . . . [the 1972] summer's singers are Adelaide Bishop (*Lucretia*), H. Wesley Balk (*Postcard from Morocco*), Bakman (*Tosca* as well as *Threepenny Opera*) and Pasatieri, making his directorial debut with his own opera. In years past, audiences have shared the insights of such directors as Corsaro, Anthony Besch, Henry Butler and Theodore Mann. All of them, says Lloyd, "can dig below the surface meaning in such a way that almost involuntarily the singers' voices take on richer tones, coloration and meaningful nuances." None are willing to compromise their concept with the dictates of a star.

Complementing this emphasis on stage values has been an innovative spirit, evident in new approaches to standard operas (the Bailey-Corsaro *Bohème* of 1970), experimentation with novel forms (rock 'n' roll and mixed media in 1970's nightmarish *Elephant Steps* by Stanley Silverman, "music theater collage" in . . . [1971's] *Faust Counter Faust* from Minnesota), plus freshness of repertory choice (the first English mounting of Rossini's *Otello*) and repertory structuring (the 1968 all-Shakespeare season). Most striking has been the exploration of modern works. At least one opera by an American composer has appeared in each season to date.

"Opera can become an American thing," Lloyd insists, "but only if we encourage American composers and singers and investigate. Such encouragement would attract artists who are now staying away from the medium." What about the public? Lloyd points to Lake George's box office records. In 1967, attendance at *The Crucible* equaled *La Traviata*. David Amram's *Twelfth Night*, given its world premiere in 1968, was seen by as many as *Rigoletto*. "Nobody here seems particularly prejudiced against modern opera. It's how a thing is put together that sells tickets," he says. The company's *Bohème* did not sell out for its first few performances, but once word got around about how unique the production was, a run on the box office began.

Whether for Puccini or for Virgil Thomson (Minnesota's *Mother of Us All*), Lake George receives the finest kind of support an opera company can ask for: attendance by the local community. Of the 12,000 who saw the 1971 season, two thirds came from the immediate vicinity or the nearby Albany-Schenectady-Troy area. To many each year Lake George offers their first live exposure to opera, and a sizable number become subscribers or donors. Despite this avid support, ingenious ways must be devised to cut costs and make the most of resources. Karen Johnsen, one of the company's four year-round paid staffers, has a number of "beg, borrow or steal" vignettes to relate—costumes from *The Marriage of Figaro* being altered to fit the *Italian Girl in Algiers*, sets being stored in a local farmer's barn. "It hasn't been easy here," she says, "but enthusiasm has often made up for a lot of missing money."

Ten years have brought a great deal of change at Lake George—the physical scale has magnified, artistic ambition and realization have expanded, recognition has come—but not at the expense of those elements that have energized the group since its first season.

DIRECTIONS OF THE DANCE [4]

To people who have watched the growth and ferment in American dance activity in the performing arts during

[4] From report by Yorick Blumenfeld, staff writer. *Editorial Research Reports.* v 2, no 24:961-6+. D 25, '70. Reprinted by permission.

the past two decades, it could hardly come as a surprise that
ballerina Natalia Makarova decided to leave her native Russia for these shores. The thirty-year-old dancer was one of
the leading stars of the Kirov ballet in Leningrad until her
defection to the West. Like the departure of Rudolf Nureyev
in 1961, Miss Makarova's decision in September 1970 was
based largely on artistic considerations. American ballet, she
said in London upon being granted asylum, moves "constantly ahead, progressing to other things."

That she chose to sign a year's contract with the American Ballet Theater is in one sense an indication of the
coming of age of dance in America. There is added significance in that the dance company's new home will be in
Washington, rather than in New York, upon completion of
the Kennedy Center for the Performing Arts on the banks
of the Potomac in October 1971. Although New York remains the ballet capital of the United States, balletomanes
are no longer confined to its environs. After Miss Makarova's
debut with the Ballet Theater in New York's City Center
during Christmas week, she and the company will perform
in Houston, Denver, Los Angeles, San Francisco, Chicago
and other cities before expected capacity crowds.

Interest in the dance across the United States embraces
everything from classical to African ballet and from modern
dance to Japanese Kabuki. What used to be a pleasant but
trivial entertainment has become an art form comparable
to music, painting or drama in its expressiveness and ability
to move audiences. Nor is the dance removed from international politics. Soviet officials on December 11 cancelled
plans for the Bolshoi Opera and Ballet Theater to tour the
United States on grounds that "Zionist extremists" had harassed other cultural groups from Russia on tour in America.

Soviet authorities long have taken great pride in Russian
ballet and consider it a major element in their cultural exchange programs with the United States. For years, these
exchange programs have flourished with any thaw in the
Cold War and withered with any new chill in Washington-

Moscow relations. Culturally, as well as politically, Russia and the United States stand poles apart. In ballet, Russia is almost the sole remaining repository of classical nineteenth century ballet. Innovation is discouraged under the Communist party line—the main reason Miss Makarova gave for her defection. But Soviet ballet achieves a technical excellence rarely achieved in the West and draws popular support at home unrivaled by any foreign ballet company in its own country.

In America, dance has been liberated to the point where Ann Halprin of the Dancer's Workshop in San Francisco simply defines it as the "rhythmic phenomenon of the human being reacting to his environment." This liberation, in fact, permits dancers to do everything from disrobing to yelling like jungle beasts. Such forms of self-expressive dance began as a rejection of what was regarded as the formalism and sterility of classical ballet, with its highly disciplined and stylized art based on a centuries-old tradition of movement skills. But ballet, at least in America, has been reveling in artistic innovation.

Widening of Deficits Despite Enlarged Audiences

American ballet has grown since the end of World War II from a small enterprise addressed primarily to the cultural elite in New York into an art form frequently viewed by millions over television. During the past decade, in particular, ballet and modern dance have received support from foundations and government for productions, professional training, and for reaching large new audiences. A million-dollar-program to send twenty-two dance companies touring thirty-four states, announced on October 16, 1970, by Nancy Hanks, chairman of the National Endowment for the Arts, was indicative of this trend.

There is a dearth of comprehensive statistics on dance audiences, total number of groups, or professional presentations, but it can be calculated that in New York City alone about a thousand ballets are performed a year. It was estimated in 1964 that 750,000 people attended live, professional performances of ballet or modern dance. These audiences were much younger than those attending opera or the theater, and the box-office take was lower.

Statistics on the fiscal side of ballet are seldom declared publicly, but the expenses of ballet production are so heavy that very few persons directly connected with the ballet receive an adequate reward. The economic restrictions on modern dance, for example, were such that for a long time Martha Graham and the company she formed could perform only for a few weeks at a time. Although her troupe is now able to stage prolonged stands, thanks to foundation support, ballet companies are straddling a widening gap between expenses and income.

Inflation has added to the rising costs of ballet presentation. The rent alone at the new Metropolitan Opera in New York's Lincoln Center is $45,000 a week. And a lavishly produced *Nutcracker Suite* at the Lincoln Center cost more than $280,000 to produce in 1964 and well over $500,000 in 1970. Nevertheless, tickets for ballet and modern dance in New York are cheaper than tickets for opera, concerts, or Broadway plays. The Ford Foundation reported in 1968 that ballet, "for every artistic step forward," takes "two steps back financially."

The Joffrey Ballet, whose members once toured America in a station wagon and danced to the music of a tape recorder, now has a budget of $1.5 million a year. Despite substantial grants from the Ford Foundation, the company keeps on running in the red. The American Ballet Theater also admits to many problems in trying to attain its specific aims of helping to discover and develop creative talents and of offering the public an opportunity to enjoy and appreciate dance. Almost since its founding in 1940 by Lucia Chase, it has been running a deficit. It is estimated that Miss Chase invested $17.5 million in the ballet company. When her money stopped in 1969 the company came close to disbanding.

One of the trustees, Sherwin Goldman, was elected president of the American Ballet Theater Foundation, and he began putting the company on a sounder financial and institutional basis. Private contributions have increased to $500,000 a year, the price has been raised for choice seats, and a system of cost accounting has been introduced. Even so, box-office receipts can cover only three quarters of the cost and this means a deficit of about $1.7 million for 1970, the London *Economist* has reported. Prolonged tours of short engagements were discontinued as economically and artistically unprofitable.

American Ballet Theater has established a network of "resident" companies. Those in Los Angeles, San Francisco and Chicago have been highly successful, Goldman contends. But local support has been slow in coming elsewhere. All this may change when the parent company moves to its permanent home at the Kennedy Center in 1971. Nevertheless, Washington can guarantee only a limited number of performances each year and the company still has no fixed base in New York.

Foundation Support for American Dance Groups

Principal dancers in the American Ballet Theater earn less than $8,000 a year, soloists average about $5,500 and regular dancers in the *corps de ballet* below $5,000 according to John J. O'Connor of the *Wall Street Journal*. Many of them cannot support their families without outside income. Goldman said that substantial pay increases were "required by conscience." "We cannot allow the principal subsidy to American dance to continue to be paid by American dancers."

With ballet costs rising inexorably, companies have become increasingly dependent on foundation grants. The Rebekah Harkness Foundation established the Harkness Ballet Company with a million-dollar grant in 1964. Smaller gifts have been made by the Rockefeller Foundation, the Avalon Foundation, and the Mellon Educational and Chari-

table Trust. It was a single grant of $7.7 million by the Ford
Foundation in 1963 that changed the entire economic position of several ballet companies.

That sum was being allocated, over a ten-year period, to
the New York City Ballet Company, the San Francisco Ballet,
the National Ballet in Washington, the Pennsylvania Ballet
in Philadelphia, the Utah Ballet in Salt Lake City, the
Houston Ballet [in Texas], and the Boston Ballet. And yet,
W. McNeil Lowry, vice president of the Humanities and
Arts Program for the Ford Foundation, soon discovered that
it was not enough. Unprecedented financial strains led to a
further grant of $2.3 million to City Center Joffrey Ballet
[in New York] and the School of Pennsylvania Ballet
Company.

Ford also granted about half a million dollars to enable
three large theaters to accommodate a total of twenty-five
weeks of performances a year by modern dance groups. Unlike established ballet companies, most modern dance ensembles exist as companies only while performing. While
the Ford Foundation could not regularly underwrite such
groups, it did try to meet a need for concentrated programs
in large theaters. The foundation was moved to declare in
its 1968 annual report that some $11.5 million it had given
to ballet in five years had "done more for the field's artistic
and training progress than its financial stability."

The Federal Government has also been a major bene-
factor of dance in recent years. Since its creation by Congress
in 1965, the National Endowment for the Arts—a division
of the National Foundation on the Arts and the Humanities
—has made grants totaling $3,785,742 to individuals, schools
and troupes to encourage and sustain dance, including ballet, as a performing art.

Growth of Ballet Schools and Training Programs

Four major regional ballet associations and almost one
hundred small civic or regional ballet companies exist in the
United States. The term "regional ballet" indicates a non-

professional company, usually based on a dance school or even a group of schools, which regularly appears before paying audiences. It serves to keep interest in ballet alive and sometimes provides students with useful experience leading to a professional career.

The goals of the regional ballet companies vary, however. The Ballet Impromptu ensemble in Richmond, Virginia, lists six reasons for its existence: (1) to present ballet programs of the highest quality for adults and children; (2) to elevate the art of regional performances to the highest degree possible; (3) to provide a medium of expression for regional choreographers, designers, musicians and dancers; (4) to stimulate interest and support of ballet and ballet schools; (5) to solicit and raise funds to further these purposes; and (6) to establish a regional ballet company which will partake in festival competition.

Some form of dance instruction is being provided today at every stage of the educational process. However, it was not until the 1920s that creative dancing was first taught in this country. Margaret H'Doubler at the University of Wisconsin had a vision of dance education as a liberating force. That university was the first to give dance full recognition with a degree program. Dance departments of note developed at Bennington and Mills [California] and today over three hundred colleges offer courses ranging from introductory steps in basic movement to advanced seminars in choreography. Colleges have also established summer dance workshops such as the Perry-Mansfield School of Theater and Dance at Steamboat Springs, Colorado, and the Jacob's Pillow School of Dance at Lee, Massachusetts. As an outgrowth of academic interest in the dance, the National Council of the Arts established CORD (Committee on Research in Dance) in 1965 to help guide the development of dance education.

Dance schools have also proliferated. Often they are directed by well-known performing artists. Many of the leading modern dancers, such as Martha Graham, have established their own schools of dance in which they teach their personal techniques. However, few of the close to two hundred ballet and modern dance schools or studios listed in *Dance Magazine* are competently staffed for professional development. . . .

Diversity of New Choreographic Trends

Ballet's image today is that of the spectacular, opulent fairy tale, such as *Nutcracker* or *Sleeping Beauty,* told in dance. The image of modern dance, on the other hand, is of controlled physical contortions or nervous, awkward movements performed to music. The United States was the first nation in which traditional ballet and modern dance developed side by side. A school of choreographers consciously set out to create a form of dance expression that partook of elements of both.

New ballet choreographers such as Eliot Feld of the American Ballet Theater and Gerald Arpino of the City Center Joffrey Ballet have been drawn to the creative energy of modern dance. And they have borrowed heavily from it to extend the expressive range of ballet. The new choreographers have, for example, brought the dance closer to the floor with the result that the freedom of movement gained by the lower center of gravity has, in many ways, liberated the ballet from two centuries of upward movement.

The career of Jerome Robbins (born 1918), which is so tied to the rising tide of the ballet's popularity in America, has shown that it is possible to appeal to wide audiences in a variety of dance media. His first ballet, *Fancy Free,* formed the basis of the broadway musical *On the Town* (1944), while later *West Side Story* (1957), on which he collaborated with Leonard Bernstein and Oliver Smith, enjoyed immense success both on stage and as a film. There were times when it seemed that he had succeeded in reconciling ballet with jazz dancing.

In 1958, after having worked both with the American Ballet Theater and the New York City Ballet, Robbins started his own company, Ballets: USA. However, after several tours abroad and a final performance at the White House in 1962, the company ceased to exist. Two of the principal ballets Robbins created for his company, *Opus Jazz* and *Events,* had symphonic jazz scores by Robert Prince. Robbins skillfully conveyed the coolness and detachment as well as the energy of American life. The impact of these works on European ballet companies was enormous.

After a lapse of four years, in which Robbins cut himself off from ballet to concentrate on plays and musicals at his American Lyric Theater Laboratory, he was persuaded to renew his connection with the New York City Ballet and created *Dances at a Gathering.* When danced by the Royal Ballet in London in the fall of 1970, it received the most praise of any ballet performed there in a decade. *Dances at a Gathering* is a plotless, hour-long work set to Chopin's music, mostly mazurkas. It evokes the ideas of a lost European past by combining dance steps with classical movements. A dozen dances of joy and elegance that are performed by a series of young couples are an ode to the choreographer's ability to continue inventing new dance games.

Boldness of New Generation of Ballet Directors

Robert Joffrey at the City Center in New York has done much to change the image of the ballet in America and give it a native flavor. The Joffrey Ballet dancers are noted for their strength, precision and spontaneity. There is the excitement of the western hoedown and the Virginia reel in much of their dancing. And the vitality and vigor of the troupe is due, in no small part, to the number of male dancers who have been recruited from the ranks of baseball, basketball and football teams across the United States.

About half of the City Center's repertory has been created by Gerald Arpino, the chief choreographer. Arpino's subjects have ranged in diversity from black magic to international athletics. Sometimes Arpino shows his virtuosity by mixing ballet techniques. The ballet *Shadow* requires the balancing skills expected of a gymnast. Arpino staged a ballet, *Trinity,* in the fall of 1970 for a regular orchestra and a rock group. The resulting beat and drive are particularly appropriate for the speed and exuberance of the dance troupe.

Eliot Feld, the choreographer and director of the American Ballet Players at the Brooklyn Academy, gets his ideas from listening to music. [Feld has since rejoined American Ballet Theater as a dancer and choreographer.] "My dances are about me, really; about my own fantasies and imaginations. . . . I know as soon as I play a piece if I can relate to it" [he said in 1970]. His dances may be set to the lieder of Richard Strauss or to the music of Prokofiev. What draws the attention of both the critics and the audience is Feld's daring. While daring is perhaps common to the new generation of choreographers, it is exhibited to an extreme in his work.

Just as [Isadora] Duncan rebelled against the classic ballet, so today there are avant-garde dancers who rebel against stylizations of modern dance. The collaboration between the choreographer Merce Cunningham and the composer John Cage, who developed "chance music," was an early reflection of this contemporary trend. In one work, *Variations V,* Cage's music was controlled in performance by the movement of dancers haphazardly activating photo-electric cells arranged around the stage.

Yvonne Rainer's choreography is rooted in a reaction against the narcissism she finds rampant in the dance world. To avoid exhibitionism, Rainer frequently works with such ordinary movements as walking, running and jumping. One of her newer works, *Continuous Project Altered Daily,* attempts to bring the spirit of rehearsals into the actual performance—with Miss Rainer criticizing the dancers or making them repeat their movements in front of the full audience.

Avant-Garde Choreography Without Plots or Music

Twyla Tharp is a choreographer whose ballets have no plot, no reference to character or emotion, no scenery or props, costumes only very rarely and, above all, no music. "I don't think Mozart needs my help," Miss Tharp has said. Asked what she is trying to do, Miss Tharp answers succinctly, "I do everything I know how in a dance." Her dancers' movements are generally free-flung, wildly energetic, deceptively haphazard, complex, very mental, and usually odd and cool, critic Tobi Tobias has observed.

At the 1969 American Dance Festival in New London, Connecticut, Miss Tharp produced a dance called *Medley,* which took place on a parade ground the size of two football fields, with the audience seated on a slope at one end. Six girls in Miss Tharp's company were at the other end of the field, looking small and remote. Gradually they moved closer, but never close enough for the public to see the intricate detail of the choreography. The climax of the performance came when thirty students joined the group and commenced one long sequence in which each person moved at the slowest possible speed, giving the effect of a field full of statues in a continuous but imperceptible state of change.

While Paul Taylor cannot be placed in the company of Tharp or Rainer, his approach, which was regarded as revolutionary fifteen years ago, is today thought of as modern dance classicism. In his early works Taylor was intrigued with "nondance" or "antidance." In one work he stood motionless for several minutes, and frequently his dances seemed more like happenings. Gradually, however, this ex-pupil of Martha Graham won the affection of his audience with humorous ballets like *Piece Period,* a parody on various affectations in style.

Another ballet, *Three Epitaphs,* was set to the music of a brass band and the dancers were dressed in ghoulishly black costumes. Eventually, with other dances such as *Party Mix, Scudorama* and *Orbs,* a dance flow began to enter his compositions. Now Taylor uses more classical music than anyone else in modern dance. Taylor says that his present development is a search for clarity. "I became interested in making things very clear, even if they were corny."

Nudity in Ballet; Quest for Novelty and Newness

Clive Barnes, dance critic of the New York *Times,* wonders whether the American public does not expect its ballet companies to be over-productive, to stage too many new works. Though ballets in Europe are being produced at a slightly more leisurely pace, the frenetic tempo is catching on there too. Various dance groups in England, the Netherlands, Belgium, France, Germany and Australia illustrate that without an active, prolific choreographer of quality, a company stagnates or falls into triviality. Ballet companies that have not developed out of a national style or have not succumbed to the spell of a first-rate choreographer often tend to look old-fashioned. The result is that in their desperate attempts to catch the international eye, they frequently revert to sensationalism.

Maurice Béjart, a forty-three-year-old French choreographer, whose *Orphée* in 1958 was an early example of the mixture of dance, electronic music, speech and myth, has shown enormous daring and enterprise. When he took over as director of the ballet company of the Royal Theater in Brussels in 1959, he renamed it Twentieth Century Ballet and set out to stage ballets in sports arenas, where he has drawn crowds of twenty thousand with programs specifically designed to appeal to "the masses." His themes are stunning, his decors extravagant, but the dancing itself is sometimes conventional and even banal.

Choreographic nudity is standard in the works of Hans van Manen of the Netherlands Dance Theater. The company opened the 1970 London ballet season November 2 with a van Manen work which concluded in an eight-minute dance sequence for four men and a young woman totally unclad. The reaction of the audience and critics was mixed. John Percival of the *Times* wrote that the nude scene was "moving, beautiful and innocent." James Kennedy of the *Guardian* dismissed the nudity as a gimmick. For the performers, all was not bliss; they complained of the cold theater and one performance was interrupted when some culprit threw itch powder on stage.

However, Londoners had been forewarned because the Netherlands Dance Theater, since its founding in 1959, has been the home of radical notions in ballet. Based in The Hague and subsidized by the Dutch government, it mounts no classics but each year produces ten new ballets written by young, contemporary composers. The Dutch government's tolerance for nudity in ballet has not yet crossed the Atlantic. The Smithsonian Institution in Washington refused to let a male soloist from the Yvonne Rainer dance group perform in the Smithsonian's Museum of History and Technology with only an American flag tied around his neck. The dance would have been performed in front of a national relic, the Francis Scott Key flag.

James Morris, director of the division of performing arts at the Smithsonian, said nudity in the performing arts would have been inappropriate in a national institution supported by taxes. Miss Rainer rejoined that since nudity is displayed in painting and sculpture at Smithsonian museums, why not in the performing arts. Jean Battey Lewis, dance critic of the Washington *Post,* found "an astonishing amount of naiveté on both sides."

Yet, stage nudity is already several seasons old, both on and off Broadway, and movies have gone beyond mere nudity —sexual acts are graphically depicted. In ballet, Rudi van Dantzig, another of the young Dutch radicals, has made his ballet *Monument for a Dead Boy* a case study of the development of a homosexual. The story is the classic Freudian tale of rejection by both parents and school friends and the inability to relate to the opposite sex. His inability to mix with normal society leads to his eventual death—which the program note suggests may be symbolic, merely celebrating his acceptance of his own nature and the death of his previous, self-tortured self.

Aided by the weird bubbles and gasps of Jan Boerman's electronic music, van Dantzig succeeded in creating a mysterious, nightmarish world of repression and sexual guilt. That this ballet has been so widely accepted and performed in Europe and the United States is an indication that ballet is keeping up, if not leading, the general sexual revolution in the arts.

Throughout history, it would seem, ballet has tended to reflect the social mores of both the choreographers and the dancers. And while in the past ballet may have lagged behind the other arts in delivering a revolutionary message, today it would seem to be gradually moving to the forefront as a powerful, symbolic means of expressing man's nonverbal, subconscious feelings and emotions.

SEEING BALLET SIDEWAYS: BACKSTAGE WITH THE CITY CENTER JOFFREY BALLET [5]

All dark. Black velvet side curtains, shakily braced on crude wooden stretchers, form the wings, those black nowheres into which the painted, soaring dancers will disappear to the audience. This is where we stand, one person to write, one person to take pictures, in the wings, in the dark. Heavy linoleum, black worn grey with endless abrasions of rosin, water, sweat, and footwork, stretches before us, laying a dull cover over the floor of the stage. Above, innumerable black light housings, lined up in rows, angle their secret faces center stage. These fat metal cylinders are like the leads of stained glass windows, enclosing their shining gels. Even the air in this space shimmers a soft glittering grey, with dust that filters down, illuminated in the beams of light, from the direction of the high catwalk. At the sides are poles of theater lights—the pros call them booms or tormentors—

[5] From article by Tobi Tobias, contributing editor. *Dance Magazine*. 46:44-50. O. '72. Reprinted by permission from *Dance Magazine*, October 1972 Edition.

standing like immovable sentinels, one to each wing. Massive black bruisers, they shoot paths of glare across the darkened stage. One by one, in this fake night, the dancers appear, and begin to warm up.

They come to the wings like refugees, clutching their bundles of supplies: extra shoes; plastic sweat pants or woolen leg warmers; a faded towel; a shapeless, favorite sweater; a small arsenal of makeup, hairspray, combs and Kleenex; a can of diet soda; and other odds and ends of the sporting life. One girl arrives with three pairs of new pointe shoes, drops them in a heap on the floor. The soft, plump curves of gleaming, pink satin lie nestled like newborn piglets against the dark folds of the side curtain.

In each wing now, there are one or two or three dancers, quietly, intently putting themselves through their barre, holding on to the wooden braces of the side curtains for shaky support. Pliés, tendus, frappés, ronds de jambe, punctuated by tentative balances and starry-eyed ports de bras. Sweat breaks out on their foreheads and necks; backs begin to glisten with effort. They work with terrific, searing, physical and mental concentration; a powerful line of energy seems to run down the center of each body, like a lightning rod. Their intense focus is turned inward, each one of them sounding out the absolute, necessary knowledge of his own body, his crazy, wonderful, idiosyncratic instrument.

Close to, the dancers look terribly vulnerable, all their small faults showing. An ankle that wobbles, struggling to support a high extension; the spine giving in to the fling of a grand battement; a flourish of beats that finishes in blurred uncertainty. At the same time you see flashes of their astonishing capability, of their unearthly graces and feats. They twist their exquisite bodies into phenomenal shapes, making the superhuman seem casual, like breathing.

They're a breed of exotics, these kids. They've got the gratuitous freshness of the young, a touching combination of great strength and great fragility. And they're marked, unmistakably, by their own peculiar kind of beauty, not birth-given, but self-made, created out of hours, days, years of work and dedication to their compelling trade.

Beside them, the stage crew is absurdly pedestrian. Hefty-set, coarse-mouthed stagehands, strictly union men, in baggy slacks and loose shirts, sleeves rolled up on burly arms, tough or friendly as they feel like it, looking possibly a little more busy than they really are, ignoring the dancers as they weave in and out among them, moving ladders around, adjusting lights, manipulating a backdrop into place. "On number thirty-six." "Coming in." "Little bit more now." "Hold it—too far." "Take it up about an inch." "That's it."

Brainier, slicker, stage-management types, in disheveled business suits, briskly talk technical details, practical, un-ruffled, knowing, totally capable. Over at the light board, with its complex tangle of switches and wires, one of them checks his watch, picks up the stage mike, and announces, "Half-hour please, ladies and gentlemen, half-hour." These are the people who make the invisible part of the performance happen. Next to the butterflies, they seem to walk heavy.

Beneath the Tulle, Leg-Warmers

The performers wear their costumes for the opening ballet, layered over with parts of their practice clothes, for warmth. The lead girl looks spun-sugar pretty, her tutu appropriately pink and flowered. Beneath the delicate tulle skirt, though, her legs are sausaged into filthy, baggy-kneed leg warmers, that are just ready to fall down. The effect is incongruous and endearing. Like a little girl, she yanks her woolies up, as she stands talking briefly with her partner, a strange Brummel, Mozartean-ruffled shirt and elegant tights obscured by an ancient plaid bathrobe.

Their makeup is fantastic. Each one is different. The boys are maybe a little less super. Some of the men keep to the minimal. No matte or gleam can compete with one huge black guy's magnificent bone structure; he knows it, doesn't bother much with the rouge and the liner and the shadow.

Some is tentative, amateurish. Some is flauntingly applied, a badge. With the girls, though, it's all party, a wild enhancement of lovely. The weird-dream exaggerated-*Vogue* heads are nuns' compared to these ballet birds'.

Here's one with a line of eyelashes deftly, defiantly painted on the ridge of her cheekbone. Another one has stenciled a curve of beauty-spot black dots just below the eyebrow. Eyes are outlined in swinging arcs, shadowed blue-brown-purple, eyelashed double, triple thick. Lips are made with luscious bright berry colors; cheeks blushed impossibly radiant pink. Planes and hollows are created at whim. And it's all been done with an unerring panache that makes this outrageous, gorgeous paint seem like second nature. You think of the faces they'll have when they leave the theater. Skin scrubbed down to reality, the girls always look so pale and sallow and tired as they say their quiet good nights. These brilliant stage faces they've made up are the ones that really seem to belong to them.

In pairs and trios the dancers exchange a little desultory banter, but not much, and their hearts aren't really in it. There's a careful holding back. It's as if these performers don't fully exist in this suspended, pre-curtain time, but are reserving themselves for what they will be when the curtain goes up, and they project their true, whole identities out to the audience—their fourth dimension. Now the curtain is down. It cuts, heavily weighted, like some symbolic statement, between the performers and the spectators, between the doers and the watchers. Here, on the dancers' side, only a center fold of glory-red velvet with its gold fringes can be seen; the rest is drab beige muslin.

"Fifteen minutes please, fifteen minutes."

They move their practice out to the center of the stage. The boys do soft, multiple turns; the girls, sharp, clipped pirouettes. Invariably, they spot to where the audience will be. They try out balances, some dubiously, some confidently. There's always an element of luck in these things, according to the night and the stars. Smiling, daringly or tremulously, they slash into pitched arabesques.

A long, lithe girl drops an oilgold chunk of rosin in a corner, kills it smash/flat to a white powder, then slicks her shoes through it, soles and pointes, and bourrées dit-dit-dit-dit into action. Another one tests her pointe, bouncing up to relevé, springing down again, with the inevitable pace of a child skipping rope. Suddenly both of them turn their heads, like animals alerted to awareness.

Their gaze picks out the director of the company, who has just appeared on-stage. A small, finely built man in very elegant, Italianate street clothes, he steps deftly into the midst of the action, scrutinizing every detail, then gives pointed, lucid instructions. As everyone knows, he's a man with a genius for ballet, in all its varied aspects, from administration to making dances and dancers. So when he tells someone how to point his foot, even if it *is* ten minutes before curtain time, that someone listens good and points it like the man says.

Matter-of-factly, he follows the shifting path of a soft, muscular nymphet who bourrées backward as she absorbs his last-minute admonitions. Brisk and calm, he delivers himself of a chain of specific advice. He questions, corrects, improves—a turn of the head, the thrust of an arm, the way a preparation is to be taken, the timing and execution of a beat. Everything he says is designed to make placement, action, and mood precision-honed. The girlchild soaks it up, raptly.

He stands back to watch another girl execute, badly, a rapid circle of turns, immediately knows what's wrong, and calls out to her, "Plié." She doesn't, can't, and sure enough she stumbles. He nods, deft guess confirmed. Turning aside, he corrects a boy's arms and realigns, beautifully, some entwined arabesques in a pas de deux, then catches sight of the turning girl again and calls, once more, urgently, "Plié! Use that plié!" This time she does, and the turns come right. He nods again, approving.

And Then, the Dark

All at once, without warning, the stage goes completely dark. In the pitch black, the dancers keep leaping, running, jumping, turning, without the slightest hesitation. You can see absolutely nothing, but you can hear the heavy rhythms of their feet and their breathing. Still the director stands there, next to us, and, incredibly, seems to watch intently as the dancers continue jumping and turning, jumping and turning, in total oblivion.

The stage lights flash on again—a quick, blinding blaze —then very slowly dim. "Places please, places," the stage manager announces, snapping his fingers. Everyone scurries. Like good little furtive mice. In the darkness, the beginners take their opening pose on stage. The rest of them disappear into the wings. Lots of giggles as they hide in a group in the dark. "House lights are going to half." A long, silent, breath-held pause. "House lights are out. Dancers stand by." The curtain goes up with a muffled roar, an ocean far away. The sound is very faint, but it has the ominous vibes of expectation. Now you can hear and feel the audience. Those hundreds of hungry eyes. You can just see the conductor, face rapt, bathed in a golden glow, baton arm uplifted, ready to take the opening cue from the stage, then, shadowed, bending over the music. The dancers begin to move.

Feet attack the floor, strong, supple, and sure. Arms curve and reach. Legs beat, push, whip. Bodies are bending, turning, meeting, soaring. It's too late for technique now, way past classroom and rehearsal time, past thought, consideration, calculation. This is living, happening performance. The dancers are daring their bodies and daring each other. They know their steps and changes, know the music, the choreography, and the timing as well as they know the shape of their own limbs and the beat of their hearts. This is the moment in which they must take everything they know and transform it into a magic action. This is the moment when, if ever, they realize why they've chosen their outrageously cruel profession.

Here's a boy, in a wildly strenuous solo, doing everything he possibly can: jumping, beating, spinning, leaping. Every fiber of muscle is straining, air and blood pushing through his body at a crazy pace. He's extended to the very end of his physical abilities. At the last moment he gathers himself together, with a ferocious concentration of energy and will, to thrust out a fierce surge of turns as he hurtles offstage.

Another solo: bravura, whiplash first variation done, the girl in pink exits on a flying leap, reaches the dark shelter of the wings. There, hunched over, she clutches her chest, panting and gasping for breath. A few seconds, timed by the music, go by. Then she straightens up, deftly adjusts the knotted ribbons of her shoes, tightens an already taut waistband, smoothes her sleek hair, crosses herself twice, firmly, and goes out and does it, double gargouillades and all. Onstage, in the blaze of light, music, and motion, she's all gaiety, all flirtatious theatrical allure, all dancing and forthright enjoyment. She finishes with total aplomb, bows to the wave of applause, exits, looking ecstatic, and is once again hunched over in the wings, chest pumping in and out, struggling to get a decent amount of air into her lungs. Her friends shoot past her to fill the stage with arcs of movement.

There is a glareshine of lights—yellow, purple—off the sweat on the dancers' bodies. The heat of the lights seems to bounce off their wet flesh. There's a terrific sense of community among the performers now. It's as if they all know the same secret and they're batting it back and forth to each other. They're communicating their own exalted physicality, and sending it out, like a comet's message, to the silent watchers in the dark.

The lights dim and brighten. The acrobatic antics splay in and out through the wings and over the stage. Offstage and on is a hot continuum of motion. Each dancer comes hustling off, panting, moves swiftly and surely to the spot set for his next entrance. A girl in yellow shoots into the wings, breathless from her own brilliant solo, sees the photographer focused on a boy onstage, executing a series of airborne jumps and leaps. "Yeah, get that," she carols, clutching the photographer's arm, and times him, urgently, out loud. "Now. Now." She's right. At the very peak of each soar the Pentax clicks and grabs the perfect moment. Then, suddenly, she takes off from the wings—a flash of pink tights, yellow net, and unleashed power—into stagespace.

Beyond Human Efforts

Now the ballet is at its height. The dancers are bathed in sweat, spraying sheets of sweat. Pounding turns. Wide-armed, wide-legged flights. Yellow girl pants her heart out in the wings while the pink girl, onstage, does fouettés, and the music goes on playing, and the audience claps with mindless joy. Pink girl finishes with a flourish, exits, yellow girl runs on, audience is yelling "Brava," piercing the air with whistles. Sweat pours down, flies off in heavy droplets as the dancers turn. Smiles get fixed, and a kind of physical ecstasy takes over as each one of them makes the largest effort he can, and then soars beyond his own, human, limits.

They're approaching the finish. Remorseless stop turns stamped out on the pulse of the music. Then a blind running for places, partners' hands reach, connect, a quick shifting, a fish dive flung out on hope, and the lights black out. The audience reassures them with warm blankets of applause, first loud, then abruptly muffled by the descending curtain. Sweat running down their backs, they walk away from the footlights, turn, join hands, smile brilliantly as the curtain rises, and bow, radiant, graceful, trembling with exhaustion.

The moment the calls are over, the choreographer is onstage—a slim, smart, live wire of a guy with all those shining Platonic images of balletic perfection running around in his head—showing them how they should have danced his piece. Our girl in pink gets the worst of it, an intense tongue-lashing illustrated with vivid, explicit gestures. As he demonstrates her faults, her face goes pale and stricken. Her eyes fill. In the eerie half-light, she looks desolate. You can't tell if it's tears or sweat drenching her cheeks.

The choreographer is ruthless. He takes her through it and through it again. He looks snaky mean, eyes narrowed on his prey, crouched over, coiled for another sharp swipe of words or motion. Anyone can tell it's time to stop, to let the victim go, but he continues, compulsively, insisting that his dancer make his choreography happen the way it should. Right now. It's as if he has to get at the clay while it's still wet.

Most of the company has moved a discreet distance away from the scene, or at least turned polite backs. A stagehand, however, placidly wetmops the stage right around them. Whatever it is, it sure isn't his problem. It'll blow over, anyway, same as it always does.

"Look at yourself," the choreographer says, grotesquely exaggerating a flaw he spotted in her performance. His version of her rond de jambe en l'air looks like it was being done by the hunchbacked stepsister in *Cinderella*. "But I didn't—" she protests, wincing. "You did. You did," he insists. "Look, here's what you have to do . . . ," and with miraculous deftness, his body breaks the step down into its essential elements, revealing it simple and pure. Her face lights up. "Oh."

Because She's Worth the Trouble

Now she gets some of her spirit back, pulls herself together, starts taking in his corrections, and gives him—by executing each step even better than she (or he) knew she could—as good as she's getting. Realizing she's made a breakthrough, she smiles, expectantly. He's still not smiling back. What he wants is that rond de jambe the way it is in his head. But she's into the secret now; she knows he's picking on her because, of all of them, she's the one who's really worth the trouble.

Finally he releases her with a word of grudging praise. She goes off looking humble but happy, crossing paths with the cast of the second ballet who chat together in a shadowed corner upstage.

This next one is a dramatic piece. A virgin-victim, her earnest-but-tormented young lover, and three effectively evil-looking badguys gossip, tense but amicable, as they wait for their opening cue. The girl is the image of sensual vulnerability, with her loose, full-blown, curling red hair. She wears a flimsy white dress; her legs are bare, luminously pale, fantastically muscled. As she talks, she's deftly pasting pink stickytape over her wedding ring.

Suddenly the young hero breaks away from their huddle and approaches the photographer. "Take some nice pictures of me in this," challenging, but begging. Photographer looks up from loading his camera, mildly astonished. Boy, melodramatic, "It's my last performance." Photographer stares back, bewildered. sensing the tone of real asking underneath the banter. Boy, cocky, pleading, persuasive, "I'll cry for you, o.k.?"

The music moans, the curtain goes up, the young couple dance out their lyric love, the monsters menace and lunge. The boy gives the photographer everything he could ask.

While he executes his heart-rending solo, the girl, who has been carried offstage, ostensibly to be raped by the savage gang, sits down quietly, cross-legged, in the wing farthest upstage. With yogilike serenity she makes the changes in her appearance that are supposed to indicate the unviewable violence. With slow, methodical calm she tangles her hair; using a small, shiny scissors, she cuts through the ribbons that hold her pointe shoes on. Then, barefoot, she stands up and gently removes most of the remaining pieces of her costume, leaving herself in a tan bodystocking hung with a few shreds of thin white nylon. Throughout the process her face is remote, totally self-contained. Yet a minute later, as she makes her entrance, she appears completely shattered, moving broken and benumbed, as if some terrible brutality has taken place.

At the end, the audience shouts with pleasure while the curtain is rung up and down by a stocky, bored, and angry stagehand. He seems to consider all of this theatrical nonsense outrageously foolish child's play. The hero, heading out for his solo calls, shakes his head, saying in the flat accents of his home town, "Damn, that's a hard ballet, man." The heroine waits her turn, musing over a lapse in the big duet with a friendly stage manager. "You know, we got a couple of bars behind the music and I guessed we'd have to leave something out. I thought we'd leave out the spiral turn, or maybe the . . . ," vaguely, she gestures a dispensable phrase. "Well," the technician points out, "you took a long time coming out of the arabesque, and when you went into the arm thing you took four counts, and then—" "Yeah, we were way behind, but we caught up," wonderingly, "I don't know how," she remarks with a kind of remote, abstract interest, as if the whole event were mystic, beyond her control, and glides out into the bright glow of the footlights.

The curtain closes, cutting off the light and applause. Behind it, the girl and her partner come face to face, nearly colliding, smile delightedly, and hug each other. "Thank you, honey." "Thank you, dear," they exchange, mocking (but enjoying) the *politesses* of their trade. "Hey, gimme a flower," he says, pointing to the bouquet of past-their-prime red carnations that was thrust into her arms on the bows. "At least I should get a flower," he urges. There's something teasing and gallant about him. She breaks one off short and offers it apologetically. They laugh, and walk arm-in-arm.

The photographer, who has shot fifty-six views of the hero's eloquent face, says, astonished, "You know, he was really very good."

The dancers for the closing ballets are already underfoot. Girls in delicate, wispy chiffon costumes walk glossily around in their new pointe shoes. They're a flurry of exotic beauties, painted, hair sleek and coiled, pasted with flowers and brilliants. They all wear perfume.

One of them, lightly holding on to the side curtain, grasps her ankle and effortlessly brings her leg up to the side of her head. In five minutes this exquisite, perfectly tuned body will launch into space to perform uncanny feats with lovely, courageous ease. Meanwhile, from her casual contortion, she gazes into the wings, eyes my clipboard enviously. "Do you write?" she asks shyly. "Yes." "Oh, wow," she says.

The lead boy arrives, carrying a lurid pink towel and an ostentatiously held cup of water. He stashes them in the wings, walks cautiously out onto the stage lino, like a skater testing the ice, tries a split, grimaces, . . . then looks up with a gratuitous, endearing smile, and a pained expression in his eyes. He chooses a spot downstage, takes a deep preparation, and swacks out spate after spate of pirouettes as if demonically possessed. One of the prettygirls teases him, "Will you please stop sweating all over our stage?" He gives her a mocking grin.

"Five minutes, ladies and gentlemen, five minutes."

The dancers let loose and fill the center stage, swirling like liberated butterflies, going through snatches of the ballet. It's a new one, and their pre-curtain practice is even more ardent, fast, and furious than ever. Buoyant excitement is in the air, a lot of unsure nerves, a gay, shaky bravado. In the shimmering halflight, swooping lifts are quickly rehearsed. Arms and legs are swung through tricky fragments of the choreography. Leaps are hastily flung into space, as if not so much to test the leap or the leaper, but to try out the air.

"Elegant." The director is here, instructing the stage at large. His tone is, self-protectively, half teasing. Who's willing to lay himself so wide open here in casual-hip 1972 as to ask anyone to be anything so square as elegant? But every single cast member present knows he means it. And knows he'd damn well better deliver just that. "Elegant," the director warns/pleads again, looking at them lovingly, "classic." "Oooh," moans a chiffoned child, who happens to be the ballerina of this piece, "I wish he wouldn't say that." "House lights to half," comes the remote, disembodied warning, and the kids line up nervously in the wings, clutching each other's hands, fingers interlaced, for their entwined entrance.

The chiffoned pretty can't keep her mouth shut now; fright's made her voluble. "Conductor, get out there, please. My legs are freezing, and I've got to get going." A second girl challenges the group, "Hey, listen, I may not make that second entrance because I'm changing my shoes in the middle." A boy who seems to know she'll have only half a minute offstage at that point echoes, incredulously, "You're changing your shoes?" "Yeah, yeah," another guy yells down the line, "she can do it. She's always doing some crazy thing like that." "I've got nerves!" a third gal squeals.

A Piece of Everest Ahead

They are really scared now, and not without cause. If you've seen this new ballet of what's-his-name's, you know the kids honestly have a piece of Everest ahead of them. But at the same time they're enjoying their own fright, taking to excitement and panic with a delighted, communal glee. Their eyes sparkle. They're like a bunch of ten-year-olds on Saturday afternoon in 1944, sharing a bag of salty, buttered popcorn at a double-feature horror movie.

"What are you scared of?" a lanky boy asks Girl Three, flatly. "You know, that part in my solo where I do . . . ," she lets go to wave her hands intricately in the air. "Well, don't get nervous until then," Lanky tells her firmly. "I've got to dance with you before that." A younger boy glances critically at this bit of callousness. "When she gets nervous, she throws elbows," the partner-presumptive explains, "and I've only got two eyes."

"House lights are out," the mike announces, like the voice of doom. "Is everyone's wool off?" a girl calls hurriedly from deep in the fifth wing. No answer. But they all take a quick look down. Leg and foot warmers of all descriptions are usually left on until the last minute, and several unfortunate instances of forgetfulness have left the dancers with a haunting fear. Dirty woolen socks under chiffon are *not* elegant.

Suddenly the orchestra waltzes into the introduction. One of the stage managers passes by and touches the baby ballerina on the shoulder. . . . "Thank you," she whispers, teeth chattering a little. She looks trustingly down the line of dancers holding hands in the almost dark. . . . The curtain goes up, and they're on. They swing out onto the lit-up stage. Where they're absolutely marvelous.

When the curtain comes down tonight, as always, there are two or three dancers (invariably the really good ones) who remain in the middle of the stage, doggedly, tenaciously repeating a few of the steps and combinations they've just performed, figuring out what went wrong what went right, and how it can be better next time. Here's one with the fresh coloring and the warm, cheeky, low-class charm of an Irish shopgirl, being devastated by the intricacies and pitfalls of her art. She's going over and over a pique arabesque turn. With each shot at it, now that the curtain's down, she floats suspended, twice round. But she's upset nearly to tears because she knows her performance of it, when it counted, wasn't any good. Flushed and unhappy, she tries it again and again. She can't figure out why it didn't connect before. Finally, shaking her head, she gives up, collects her sweat pants and leg warmers, her towel, her extra shoes, her can of Tab, and stalks off in the direction of the dressing room, wailing over the turns she gave the audience, "You should have seen them. You should have *seen* them."

Halfway into the wings she bumps into the director, drops her load of rags and bones, and pulls him onstage to look at her problem. As he watches her execute the turn, she falters visibly. "I'm off," she says. He nods, but clearly feels this is no time for sharp criticism. "I must be tired," she offers. "You are," says the director, sympathetically, willing to dismiss her. She's obviously one of the favorites of his flock. She doesn't give up so easily. Grittily, she attempts the turn again.

The director knows desperate determination when he sees it and helps her with it a few times, making apt suggestions about timing and balance. She tries it, taking his advice, and he comments, "That's better. Much better." He's very happy with her, but she's not hearing it. Looking frantic she stabs into the spin again. "Now less force," he says gently. "Don't look down. Freeze. Then just swing, lock, and go." He makes it sound so simple. She swings, locks, and goes, teeters, stops, exchanges a naked glance with the director, wordlessly walks into the wings, stoops to pick up her motley bundle, and continues out into the bleak corridor, almost crying, but not quite.

The stagehands are having trouble with the curtain. They warn everybody back, making a big deal of it. But the dancers are not interested in these mechanical problems. Their job done, for now, they head quickly to the dressing rooms to grab showers, street clothes. For the next ten hours or so they can be lured by the glitter of everyday pleasures—friends, food, sleep—before their strange, magic ritual starts again. The photographer packs cameras, film cartridges into his army sack; I stash notes, cheap ballpoints into mine. We sigh, like children after a party. Suddenly the curtain goes up to reveal the empty auditorium, warm in the glow of the house lights, row upon row of worn red velvet seats curving toward the stage in an expectant embrace. The director joins us and we look out, silently, on this horizon. A single worklight on a pole is placed downstage center. From the second balcony a matronly usher calls down her warning, "I'm closing up now." The director walks us across the deserted stage. "It's not easy at all," he explains. "This is one of the worst theaters for dance in the city. For one thing, the wings are so shallow and—" he stops abruptly, then says, "They do a beautiful job, don't they?" We smile yes, with no words, gather up our sacks of supplies, and file through the wings, across the dingy cement corridor with its red bulb glowing "exit," into the soft, dirty New York night. . . . Outside, where thronging mobs of autograph seekers are supposed to be waiting, there is no one.

IV. MUSIC: POPULAR AND CLASSICAL

EDITOR'S INTRODUCTION

The making of music can range from the efforts of young people in the high school band to the performance of the first violin with the Cincinnati Symphony, to the electronically hyped voice bouncing off the upper balcony of a sold-out rock concert. To survey the scene fully in a section is impossible; the variety is too great. The variety itself indicates the ferment that is the essence of the contemporary music scene.

This section moves from discussion of the more popular forms of music—rock, jazz—to the consideration of the problems faced by "serious" music organizations. First, in the realm of popular music, a *Time* essay explores the phenomenon of one of the superstars of the rock world, Mick Jagger of the Rolling Stones. Next, there is a look at rock festivals, which in the summer of 1972 regained some of their tarnished popularity. There is never any one type of music that captures all tastes at all times. Jazz, which all but disappeared commercially in the early heyday of hard rock, is capturing new audiences, regaining old ones. The revival is seen in a report on the transplanted Newport Jazz Festival, now happily taking root in New York City to the acclaim of every critic who attended its multiple events.

The next article turns to more serious music. Critic Alan Rich explores the question, "Who are the so-called youth audience?" Finally, two articles probe the problems of symphony orchestras. "The Silent Spring of Our Symphonies," forecasts the closing of some orchestras unless Government help is forthcoming. Amyas Ames should know whereof he speaks: he is chairman of a group called Presidents of Symphony Orchestras.

152

A witty piece by Harold Schonberg, a long-time observer of the music scene follows. Mr. Schonberg discusses the "Kashouk Syndrome," wherein those responsible for filling concert halls are forever crying doom, yet generally manage to stay in business. He concludes that serious music has never been a very popular art form but has always managed to draw enough enthusiasts to keep going.

THE STONES AND THE TRIUMPH OF MARSYAS [1]

In theory, the lyrics the white boy is singing ought to enrage the audience with their racism and sexism. In theory. . . .

But twenty, even ten rows back, the words can scarcely be heard. They exist not as nouns and verbs, but as a physical mass, a hot, indistinct slur like sausage meat: ground out of the famous lips, eaten by the mike, driven into banks of amplifiers and rammed out through two immense blocks of speakers high on either side of the stage. The vowels mix stickily with the air of the auditorium, already saturated by the fume of tens of thousands of packed bodies, the smoke of fifty thousand cigarettes and a few pounds of weed, forming an acrid blue vault overhead.

The Rolling Stones are on the road again, and the drums, electric guitars and vast sneering voice ride into another, undifferentiated wave of sound coming at the stage from the hall—the noise of thousands of kids. . . . Where these two walls of energy meet, above the stage and its blindly waving fringe of teeny-bopper arms, they precipitate a form. It is Mick Jagger, Jumpin' Jack Flash in person, laced into a white rhinestone-studded jumpsuit and painted like a Babylonian hooker, back-lighted by amber spots and frontlighted by a Mylar mirror the size of a movie screen slung from the roof trusses, belting into the chorus. . . .

When the Stones open at Madison Square Garden in New York on July 24 [1972], it will be the climax of their

[1] From *Time* essay by Robert Hughes, a staff editor. *Time.* 100:44-7. Jl. 17, '72. Reprinted by permission from *Time,* The Weekly Newsmagazine; Copyright Time Inc.

seventh US tour, which has been, in purely show-biz terms, a vast success. Every concert they have given has been packed solid, the tickets all sold weeks in advance; in San Francisco, the barter price for a $5.00 ticket was an ounce of grass and seven grams of hash, or, from scalpers, $50 cash; by Chicago, the price for a $6.50 ticket had risen to $70—accompanied by the rumor that someone had printed and sold a quarter of a million dollars' worth of fake tickets, which, mercifully, did not turn up at the gate; and in New York, it may well be around $100. The chance of getting a ticket over the counter has irrevocably gone. To frustrate scalpers, the tour managers set up a kind of electronic lottery in which suppliants sent postcards six weeks in advance, and the cards were selected at random. The news of this selection process appeared in smallish print at the bottom of the full-page ads in the New York *Times,* with the result that thousands of Stones fans who did not read it were still pestering the helpless box offices in early July.

The Stones' new album, *Exile on Main St.,* went to the top of the sales charts soon after the start of the tour and has stuck there since. Even the usual rock-concert freebies—to critics, columnists and the like—have been cut to a minimum. At this point of their career, the Stones need publicity about as much as the Second World War did, and the logistics of moving them around America have something in common with that military operation. There are the transport arrangements, involving the precise arrival of trucks, the private jets on stand-by at closed airfields, the split-second timing of those black, secretive limousines that proclaim and conceal the Superstar; the overkill technology of the staging, with its portable hydraulic lifts, remote-control mirrors and waving arcs; even the official correspondents, Truman Capote for *Rolling Stone* and Terry Southern for *Saturday Review.* And behind it all, invisible, the accumulated thrust of one of the most prodigious image-building industries the world has ever seen.

The Rolling Stones are the last of the sixties. The Beatles have split up; Dylan will probably never give another national tour. That leaves the Stones, survivors all, in complete possession of that territory where the superstar music of what was once the "counterculture" shades imperceptibly into the booming glitter of Las Vegas stardom. The Stones are not the world's most inventive band; far from it. Their music is almost—but not yet—an anachronism: straight, blasting, raunchy 4/4 time rock 'n' roll, coiling around the hall and virtually shaking the fillings out of the listeners' teeth. The Stones are the white musicians who make black music, and their work openly derives from black rock and black blues—from Chuck Berry and Slim Harpo, from Muddy Waters, Lightnin' Hopkins, Robert Johnson. Quite apart from Keith Richard's arrangements, Mick Jagger's lyrics are based on the taut, painful, elliptical images of "classical" blues. . . .

With the coming of the seventies some of the ground has begun to shift beneath the Stones. Perhaps rock will not become, as some pessimists think, the bubble-gum music of tomorrow; but the Stones' predominantly white, middle-class audience gets younger and younger (Jagger is no longer a twenty-year-old playing to other twenty-year-olds, but a twenty-eight-year-old playing to kids of fifteen) and, in any case, fewer and fewer musicians nowadays are interested in playing straight gut rock. The trend among musicians seems to be toward a more complex, melodic style that incorporates jazz fusions and extends the vocal phrases instead of locking them solidly into the beat. There are also signs that the mass concert may not be the Grail of musical ambition that it once was, that it may go the way of the three-day rock festival —into oblivion. It took the pop audience a few years to learn that giant concerts tend not to be events of ecstatic mass communion but uncomfortable affairs, jammed and hot, the music distorted, the vibes edgy. It takes a lot of dedication to stand like a parboiled wading bird on a rickety wooden seat through an hour of sound that you have already heard twenty times on your stereo at home, while straining to watch, a quarter of a mile away through the gaps in the jiggling mops of hair, a tiny gyrating mannikin whose face you cannot see but whom you know to be Jagger.

But the fans' allegiance is not to rock as music; it is to the Stones as a sociosexual event. The current tour is the Ascot of the hip, an event that cranks out the latent dandyism of every town the Stones play in and calls into action an elaborate pecking order of the In who possess tickets (to the Royal Enclosure, as it were) and the Out who do not. The point of the concert is not the sound but the presence of Mick Jagger, who is still arguably the supreme sexual object in modern Western culture.

Myth tells us that the god Apollo, whose instrument was the lyre, was challenged to a musical contest by a coarse satyr named Marsyas, who had learned to play the flute. Marsyas lost, and Apollo skinned him alive. In our day, this draconian triumph of reason over instinct has been reversed: Marsyas, the unrepressed goat-man, has won; the Rolling Stones are one of his incarnations. Unlike the Beatles—the very prototype of nice English working-class lads accepted everywhere, winning M.B.E.s [Member of the Order of the British Empire] from the Queen—the Stones from the start based their appeal partly on their reputation as delinquents. They were always too shaggy, too street smart; instead of creating the illusion of working within English social conventions, as the Beatles did, they simply ignored the rules. Long before [Stanley] Kubrick made *A Clockwork Orange* into a film, the Stones were acting out the fantasy of being Alex and his droogs. When, around 1965, England's subculture of Purple Hearts and winklepickers began to mutate into hashish and Moroccan caftans, it was the Stones who bore the full weight of Albion's reprobation. Three of them were busted, haled into court and subjected to a campaign of vilification from the English right-wing press. The Stones became the scapegoats of England's drug problem, and their legal vicissitudes provided London with the juiciest gossip since the Profumo scandal.

Yet it is a fact of the Stones' detachment that they have been as inaccessible to the left as to the right. One of the cherished fantasies of the sixties was the prospect of a generation sacking the Pentagon to the boom of electric guitars; but the Stones' only overt comment on this was "Street Fighting Man." ...

It was hardly a call to arms, and Jagger was much assailed for his "indecision"; indeed, an audience in Berkeley booed him for flashing both the peace sign *and* the clenched-fist power salute. But now that political pop is dead, the harsh, narcissistic irony of the Stones has lasted better than the maunderings of cult heroes like Abbie Hoffman or Jerry Rubin. In a sense, the Stones have lasted well because they never believed that a millennium was just around the corner....

Causes are forgotten, but effects, like DDT, accumulate in the social system: Jagger's Luciferian image is now absolute, fixed. He is even credited, in some quarters, with having "destroyed" the rock festival as a form through the Stones' famous appearance at Altamont in 1969, when a Hell's Angel knifed a man in the audience. It is an illusion that rock culture died or went sour *because* of Altamont. That event was merely a peg for a death announcement, just as Woodstock served to announce a birth that had actually happened long before. Yet the myth of Jagger's perversity is such that his music was believed to have turned the Hell's Angels into degenerate thugs—which, of course, they already were. There are some brutes whom not even Orpheus can charm, much less Marsyas. An essential aspect of the Orphic myth is that the sweet singer could attract the maenads to pursue him, but could not stop them from tearing him to gobbets; art, a magic key to the irrational, cannot always control the emotions it unlocks. Hence the idiocy of the comparisons that get drawn between Stones concerts and

Nazi rallies. Hitler was in command of his audience; Jagger not.

An essential part of Jagger's act is his vulnerability. He is a butterfly for sexual lepidopterists, strutting and jack-knifing across the stage in a cloud of scarf and glitter, pinned by the spotlights. Nonresponsibility is written into his whole relationship with the audience, over which he has less control than any comparable idol in rock history; Elvis Presley, who can still tune the fans up and down like a technician twisting a dial, is the opposite. Jagger's act is to put himself out like bait and flick away just as the jaws are about to close and the audience comes breaking ravenously over the stage. No other singer alive has transformed arrogance into such a sexual turn-on: it is the essence of performance, of mask wearing and play, and the spectacle has a curiously private appearance, as though the secret history of a polymorphic, unrepressed child were being enacted by an adult. (His narcissism is such that Jagger married himself, or a close facsimile: Bianca Jagger could be his twin.)

What still confounds the audience is Jagger's ripe compound of menace and energy; he seems an ultraviolent wraith from Fetish Alley. As king bitch of rock, Jagger has no equals and no visible successors.

NEWPORT IN NEW YORK—A REBIRTH OF JAZZ [2]

In the summer of 1960, there were those in the jazz world who felt that the worst enemy jazz had ever known was Boston impresario and sometime pianist George Wein. In the summer of 1972, some of those same people were saying that George Wein was its best friend.

Wein has been staging the Newport Jazz Festival since its inception nineteen years ago in Newport, Rhode Island. By the late 1950s, Wein had begun booking into the festival blatantly commercial acts—acts having little if anything to

[2] From "Newport in New York," article by Gene Lees, a contributing editor. *High Fidelity.* 22:26. O. '72. Reprinted by permission.

do with jazz—to bolster box-office receipts. Jazz admirers objected, feeling that these acts diluted the interest and value of the festival. Equally important, these performers began attracting to the festival a scruffy element of young people who came not to hear jazz (they didn't know what it was and didn't care) but to swill beer and chase chicks. . . . Various musicians and writers predicted that their presence would some day result in a riot.

On the Fourth of July weekend of 1960, the prediction came true. The riot was so bad that musicians had to leave the festival in convoys of cars for safety. As things deteriorated further, the state police and elements of the Rhode Island National Guard had to be called in to quell the disorders. As night turned into dawn, agitated musicians and press people at the Viking Hotel heard what sounded like tanks in the street. But it wasn't quite that bad: the noise was coming from street-cleaning equipment as rotary brushes swept up the mounds of beer cans.

Newspapers had a field day with the story, and jazz received the worst publicity black eye in its history—from people who weren't even jazz fans.

Jazz went into decline in the 1960s, both commercially and aesthetically. Record companies were pushing rock and building the myth of its profundity. Brilliant jazz musicians were hard pressed to make a living, much less create anything fresh and vital. Many, like drummer Arthur Taylor, trumpeter Arthur Farmer, composer George Russell, and tenor saxophonist Johnny Griffin, simply abandoned the United States for Europe, where jazz had always been treated with the respect it deserves. Some, like trumpeter and composer Johnny Carisi—one of the important innovators—took menial jobs in Broadway pit orchestras. By a bitter irony, Carisi ended up in the orchestra of *Hair,* performing music infinitely inferior to his own.

By 1971 Wein was interpolating rock groups into the festival. Their followers (now flying on grass instead of beer) gave him the Second Newport Riot. The disgusted city fathers of Newport let him know that as far as they were concerned the festival was finished.

They were wrong. Wein simply moved it to New York City. This year [1972] there was not a single rock act in the event—it was all jazz. And 100,000 people turned up to attend the many concerts (some of them held simultaneously) in Philharmonic Hall, Carnegie Hall, Radio City Music Hall, and even on the Staten Island Ferry. The festival, now expanded to a week in length, left musicians, fans, and critics alike in virtual euphoria, remembering the well-behaved crowds of young (and old) people, some superb music, the excitement, and a great deal of just plain fun. And some of Wein's most severe critics in 1960, including me, had nothing for him now but praise. The New York-Newport Jazz Festival was a stunning success.

Said pianist Bill Evans, one of the performers, "This is probably the greatest thing that's happened to jazz. I think the festival this year will put jazz back up there where it belongs. And George Wein did it."

The festival spread out, as it were, beyond its legitimate confines. Nightclubs around town booked jazz acts for the fans to hear after the regular concerts. For the first time in years they were able to hear the great guitarist Jimmy Raney, in a little club just north of Greenwich Village called Bradley's. In the jazz depression of the sixties, Raney had, as he put it, "developed a bit of a drinking problem" and went home to his native Louisville to vegetate. Now he was back, off the sauce, and picking up the pieces of his career and his life, and people who had not forgotten turned up at Bradley's to hear his subtle, thoughtful, modern music. Said singer Sylvia Syms, listening, "It's as if something light and airy touched your cheek, but you're not quite sure."

The return of Jimmy Raney, fit and healthy and productive, seemed to symbolize something that's happening to jazz itself. And that mood was all through the city. Raney off liquor, another great musician I know off heroin, and the brilliant Stan Getz off both.

Interestingly, some of the youngest festival-goers were deeply interested in some of the oldest music. When the Papa French Original Tuxedo Band performed in three successive trips on a ferry boat, three crowds of about two thousand each went along for the ride, the music, the dancing, the joy. Seventy or eighty per cent of them were under twenty.

At the other end of the musical spectrum, the avant-gardist Ornette Coleman impressed many people with a new composition for jazz quartet and orchestra called *The Skies of America*.

Duke Ellington got half the second front page of the New York *Times*. The Stan Kenton and Woody Herman bands appeared in concert together. Count Basie's powerful and still utterly fresh orchestra played the festival, then went into a two-week engagement in the elegant dining room of the St. Regis Hotel. For his opening there, a virtual Who's Who of show biz turned out to cheer him.

As the week wore on, the festival accelerated. Newspapers gave extensive coverage to the event, and as word went out on the wire services that this was the kind of jazz festival people wanted—no trash acts in it—fans began to pour into New York, some by plane from as far away as Texas, to get in on the fun.

It is impossible to list all of the artists who performed in New York that week; it was in fact impossible to hear them all. But Dizzy Gillespie, Freddie Hubbard, Eubie Blake, Herbie Hancock, Eddie Condon, Teddy Wilson, Kenny Burrell were there, along with a lot of little-known people who deserved (and for once got) the chance to be heard.

The fans, as a *Times* writer noted, were as intense as a chamber music audience. And the feeling of good fellowship among them was almost palpable.

As awareness of his success pressed in on George Wein, he said, "This festival will be in New York forever. New

York is the jazz capital of the world, and it should be the permanent home of the festival. . . . I feel as though I've been reborn."

So he has. So has the Newport Jazz Festival. So has jazz.

THE YOUTH AUDIENCE—WHO IT IS
AND WHO IT ISN'T [3]

There may be hope for us yet. My evidence for this revolutionary idea is a letter I got recently from a seventeen-year-old reader in Bucks County [Pennsylvania]. He writes of having heard a performance of Schubert's C major Quintet on the radio ("one of my favorite works," he writes, thereby establishing his credentials) in the RCA recording with Jascha Heifetz.

At once [he goes on], I was struck by the detached lack of warmth. . . . Mr. Heifetz and his colleagues played perfectly in tune, and at an impressively swift pace. But the beat seemed metronomical; there was no coloring, no warmth. . . . Yet, Jascha Heifetz and other musicians with his approach are extremely popular with the public. It upsets me to see such widespread lack of musical sensitivity. I have a Turnabout recording of this piece [with] Pablo Casals. Sometimes the musicians are not together and they are not always perfectly in tune. But the performance is *musical* . . . whereas the Heifetz performance was merely a shallow display of virtuosity.

Now, one sensitive, wise, seventeen-year-old music-lover cannot speak for all musical consumership in this country, but I still regard this letter as important and encouraging. I talk to a great many people, and read statements from others, who are concerned in one way or another with what is called the Youth Audience. Their concern is understandable; young people are becoming alienated from the musical establishment for a number of reasons (ticket prices, among them); they don't show up at the big halls in sufficient numbers to assure the future of musical audiences in this

[3] Article by Alan Rich, "Lively Arts" editor. *New York.* 5:50-1. Ag. 21, '72. Copyright © 1972 by the NYM Corp. Reprinted with the permission of *New York* Magazine.

city, and they also aren't buying serious music on records the way they used to.

Yet, I worry some at certain attempts to make serious music—or serious artistic products in any field—palatable to the youth market. One of the things that was wrong-headed, if not actually phony, about Lenny's *Mass,* for example, was that it projected a view of young people that was commercialized and, ultimately, patronizing. It created a stereotyped Young Person not at all different from the stereotyped blacks of thirties movies or the stereotyped Jews of vaudeville. Any intelligent kid should be insulted by such treatment, as he should be by such other acts of patronization as Virgil Fox's "Heavy Organ" acts, record-company ads that attempt to sell Bach and Beethoven as the hippies of their day, or Arthur Fiedler conducting the "Pops" in a Beatle wig. The sound of "groovy" on the lips of the aged falls sadly on the ears.

What my young correspondent proposes is that the best way to attract the attention of young audiences today is simply through *musical* communication. I happen to agree with his general estimate of the Heifetz brand of music-making, and in particular with his reaction to the Schubert record, which is ugly beyond belief. It is difficult to make any valid generalizations about the stylistic outlook of that era. Yet, it seems to me that a certain vague estimate *can* be made today of the kind of music-making most likely to appeal to today's younger music-lovers.

One of the things that impresses me these days is the readiness of young people to look beyond the old boundaries that separate "serious" and "popular" music. I imagine that most of the kids at Mostly Mozart these nights also listen to the Rolling Stones. The power of rock music lies in its very immediacy. Even without the bone-crushing impact of the sound level at most live rock concerts, this music (both its text and its tunes) is the most overtly emotional popular music in existence. When I listen to old Glenn Miller records, the stuff that my generation "grooved" to, I cannot believe how tepid, contrived and conventional it all sounds in contrast to even the simplest teeny-rock band of today. The rock generation has learned to differentiate between Stravinsky and the Stones, but it has discovered how to react to both. It has made a particular kind of musician its hero, the one who knows how to reach—not with overpowering levels of sound, necessarily, but at least with a musical line that expresses something beyond its own mathematical design.

It is impossible to generalize about these heroes. They include such elder statesmen as Stokowski and Segovia, middle-aged people like Rampal and Fischer-Dieskau, and a few authentic youth figures like Peter Serkin. You wouldn't expect as basically serious and uncharismatic a man as Pierre Boulez to figure in the list, but he does because of his Establishment-be-damned championship of difficult music. Bernstein at one time had a definite appeal for young people, but he lost a great deal of it when he became conscious of it and overworked the image. The same applies to Zubin Mehta, whom people simply laugh at because he works so hard at being a swinger. Ozawa runs that risk, too, but is redeemed by his musicianship.

That, in the long run, is what is really going to bridge the gap between old music and new listeners. Today's young audiences simply know too much about music, from constant exposure and from their schooling, to accept the kind of performances that put men like Heifetz on the map, when the emphasis was less on the music than on how its technical problems could be solved. The rock age has destroyed much of the technique-worship that used to be an important part of the musical experience. When you come right down to it, Ringo Starr was a rotten drummer; Mick Jagger has a voice that sounds like the mating call of a rusty file. Nobody is going to make it, with young audiences or any others, by playing serious music without the proper technique to realize the notes, but nobody—in the immediate future, at any rate, is going to get very far on finger work alone.

The future audience for serious music is, at the present time, wise and suspicious. Since they have discovered other and better values than those of audiences who live on memories of having heard Heifetz, they don't accept the necessity of dressing up like those audiences. They want music, and they want it for what they have learned it can be—a communication of a spiritual state that existed in the composer, expounded by a performer who is capable of dealing with that spirit. Nobody is going to reach this audience until he understands that basic fact and learns to respect its immense knowledgeability. When I heard Peter Serkin play the *Goldberg Variations* at Mostly Mozart the other night, casually dressed, absolutely involved for an uninterrupted hour in expounding to a large, attentive, enthralled crowd largely of his contemporaries on one of the great creative miracles in the annals of composition, I had the marvelous feeling of being privileged to sit in on an act of reassurance that our cultural life will go on. I have felt the same way when the small, still sound of Jean-Pierre Rampal's flute held a huge young crowd in an act of communion, or when Pierre Boulez told young people about Alban Berg at one of the Philharmonic's informal musical encounters. They didn't use words like "groovy" to make their points. The music took care of that.

THE SILENT SPRING OF OUR SYMPHONIES [4]

There is more than one way to kill. A lake or a river can be killed by the outpouring of our wastes; birds—the singing of the oriole—can be stilled by our enthusiastic use of DDT; we can kill music by starving our orchestras, leaving our cities dreary places indeed. We can surround our cities with great traffic interchanges that cost $25 million to $50 million apiece and not realize until it is too late that, for

[4] From article by Amyas Ames, chairman of the New York Philharmonic, chairman of Lincoln Center, and chairman of the Committee-of-the-Whole: Presidents of Symphony Orchestras. *Saturday Review*. 53:81-3. F. 28, '70. Copyright © 1970 by Saturday Review, Inc. First appeared in *Saturday Review*, February 28, 1970. Used with permission.

a fraction of the cost of a small one of these, we are depriving our people, committing them to lives without music. The silent spring came inadvertently. In the same way, music and dance can be stilled without intent.

That the nation's symphony orchestras are in serious trouble was dramatically demonstrated a few months ago when the presidents of the ninety principal orchestras of this country were invited to Philharmonic Hall in New York to discuss their plight. Almost to a man, these busy, public-spirited men from as far away as Hawaii, California, Texas, Florida, Maine, and Alaska dropped whatever they were doing and gathered. After two days of discussion, they formed a "Committee-of-the-Whole" and became united for the first time as a result of desperate crisis. They prepared testimony to present to Congress; an appeal for support to the National Endowment for the Arts; a request that, as a people, we support the performing arts of this country so that they may endure. Here briefly is what they are saying:

When we speak of the nation's symphony orchestras we are talking about some 1,400 different organizations, located in every state, in practically every city of more than fifty thousand people.

We are speaking of a total audience of at least twenty million men, women, and children who attend more than eleven thousand concerts a year.

We are speaking of aggregate expenditures totaling near-ly $100 million a year and a veritable army of musicians and supporters—contributors and civic-minded men and women who serve the symphony. Nearly every member of our Congress has a symphony orchestra of larger or smaller activity "back home."

Our symphony orchestras serve their communities in many ways. They are the center of the musical world in their home communities. The musicians of these orchestras teach in the schools, colleges, and music institutes. The truly talented young of the area come to them to learn. The orchestra musicians organize chamber music ensembles that play throughout their communities. In some areas, orchestras serve as the sponsoring and financing body for the local opera society (as in San Antonio) or as the parent organization for the local community chorus (as in Cleveland and Chicago, and many smaller cities). Symphony orchestras sponsor and give financial help to the local youth orchestra in their city. They search out and give awards, scholarships, and performing opportunities to young soloists and composers in the area.

Many of the orchestras' women's auxiliaries finance youth concerts. In Charlotte, North Carolina, the women actually have driven school buses in order to enable children to get to concerts. In Huntsville, Alabama, the symphony women go into the classrooms to help hard-pressed teachers acquaint the children with the music they are about to hear.

Some of our orchestras have taken their concerts to Indian reservations. They have played in hospitals, in ghettos, even in prisons; they have performed noon-day concerts in industrial plants and morning concerts in shopping centers to make it easier for young mothers with small children to attend. Other orchestras have organized jazz groups in order to serve varied tastes and interests. One orchestra presents a series of sacred music concerts each year. Another piles onto buses, traveling to small, isolated mountain communities, and plays concerts in any kind of building large enough to accommodate the musicians and an audience.

A generation ago, the subscription concert was the main activity of our orchestras. Now 70 per cent of the orchestras' activities are public service in nature. . . . [In 1969] they gave 3,500 concerts for children and students, and another 4,000 concerts for the general public, in parks and on tours. Many were educational or special in nature. They sponsor and present hundreds of small ensembles from the orchestra personnel giving performances in public schools—often in individual classrooms.

So, the orchestras of this country have greatly expanded their public service and educational work, their playing for people, but they have received little help. Who pays for this new generation of concerts—for the young, in parks, on tours? The loyal supporters have done so in the past and will continue to bear more than their share, because they love music and want it for themselves and for their children. But the public service concerts cost money, and inflating costs increase the burden of support beyond what the local loyal supporters can bear. Without help from Government, music —and the performing arts in this country—will wither.

The ninety orchestra presidents analyzed their operating problems, and presented figures to the congressional committee. The significance of these figures can best be understood by scanning the following table.

90 Principal American Symphony Orchestras

	Total Expenses	Cash Loss
1963	$28,820,500	$ 169,800
1969	66,794,500	5,215,800
1972 (est.)	87,090,000	13,222,000

Looking ahead to the year 1972, when the Ford Foundation grants that have so helped the orchestras will terminate, these figures show that:

Total expenses will be up 30 per cent (to $87.09 million). The greater part of the expense of orchestras is the salaries of the musicians. There is every reason why the musician should have his compensation comparable to wages of other sectors of our society, and rising as those wages rise.

Income will be up 20 per cent (to $40.045million). This figure includes income from tours, recording and broadcasting fees, etc., as well as ticket sales. Ticket prices cannot be raised much, for to do so would mean excluding large segments of the public—higher prices result in lost listeners; the number of seats cannot be increased; the competition from foreign orchestras limits income from record sales. Most important, the orchestras are undertaking many additional public-service programs that produce little income. So, income will cover only 46 per cent of operating expenses in 1972. Symphony orchestras are confronted by the same problem that schools and colleges have had to contend with—to raise tuition enough to cover good salaries for educators would close them. And so with symphony orchestras; without new support many orchestras will have to disband.

Contributions will be up only 20 per cent (to $33.463 million). There is clear evidence that the giving by individuals cannot keep up with inflating costs, and may even be sharply restricted by rising prices and changes in the tax laws. Contributions by Government are virtually microscopic when compared to either what other countries of the Western world do, or what we do for other interests of our people.

Cash loss will rise 150 per cent. The present loss of $8.5 million—a cash loss that threatens bankruptcy for some orchestras—is jeopardizing the existence of many orchestras across the country. The loss of an estimated $13.222 million in 1972 will begin to silence living orchestra music throughout the land.

The bitterness of the fruits of inflation is evident in these figures. Corporations can and do raise prices as wages rise; the Government increases taxes to pay the inflating costs for everything it buys. Orchestras cannot raise prices and find the very foundation of their support—the generous giving of individuals—undermined by the effect of rising taxes and prices. Looking ahead to 1972, each of our most famous orchestras will probably have to find some $500,000 of new money in that year alone. That is not their doing, but the act of our society. We can kill them with inflation.

The amount of Federal aid so urgently needed to maintain the orchestras' various activities is small indeed when compared to the practices long followed by other governments. Howard Taubman, the distinguished [former] critic-at-large for the New York *Times,* in his report on symphony orchestras abroad points out that the orchestras of Munich,

Berlin, Amsterdam, and The Hague are given annual government subsidies of approximately $1.2 million each—or more than 75 per cent of their total budgets. The four London orchestras and the Manchester orchestra are supported by government grants of about 20 to 30 per cent of their total budgets.

In Austria, a high government official told Mr. Taubman: "The arts are felt to be a great, perhaps the greatest, adornment of the nation's image—for itself and for the rest of the world."

And Taubman goes on: "It cannot be too strongly stressed that the main objectives of the subsidies are to keep the orchestras in existence and to insure that their quality will not be diminished. . . . One might speculate that there might be no orchestras at all in most countries without [them]—and certainly not distinguished ones."

The financial comparison between Europe and America is not exact, inasmuch as we operate under different circumstances—but the spirit is largely the same. It is clear that the American orchestras must have Government support. They have had remarkable success in finding the funds necessary to keep operating, but a whole new approach and development of a new set of priorities . . . are necessary. . . .

The request of orchestra presidents is not that our Federal Government assume responsibility for 75 per cent of the total operating costs of symphony orchestras as is customary in Europe, nor even for 20 per cent of the costs as is done in England. But rather that our Federal Government assist the orchestras in an amount less than 10 per cent of the current gross costs of our orchestras' operations—$8.5 million, an amount barely equivalent to the costs of one third of a modern traffic circle.

Furthermore, the orchestra presidents recommend that Federal funds should be used to support only those orchestras that (1) maintain a high level of earnings and local voluntary contributions for annual operations; (2) meet reasonable qualifying standards of operations and management; (3) maintain broad-based programs of cultural and musical services for the general public.

In light of the financial crisis, the orchestra presidents are asking for Government support through the National Endowment for the Arts, and are backing President Nixon's request for $20 million for the National Endowment for the Arts, even though that request is extremely modest when compared to the critical needs of our arts institutions. It will permit the Arts Endowment to provide only $3.5 million of the $8.5 million currently needed by the orchestras, because the Endowment is charged with responsibility to other arts fields of which the orchestras are but one segment.

Nevertheless, approval of President Nixon's request would achieve two goals. It would increase the actual dollar support available to the nation's arts efforts, and, secondly, challenge all other governmental entities (states, counties, and cities) as well as nongovernmental contributors, by the tested principle of fund matching. The orchestra presidents in their testimony before the congressional committee have asked for the flexibility that will permit them to come back for help if these matching funds cannot be realized.

Two hundred years ago, the people of this country fought for independence. Now we fight not only to save our rivers, our lakes, the very air we breathe, but also to save our music. This must be part of the drive of the people of this country to enrich the total life of its citizens and to work "toward a reflection of the goodness and grace of the human spirit." The arts, like nature, are more part of us than we think. Why else would people in twelve hundred cities, in every state of the union, organize and struggle to support symphony orchestras?

It is time to act—to stand up and be counted as a backer of the arts. What we ask is well within the power of our Government to give.

THE CONCERT BUSINESS . . . A BALANCED
APPRAISAL [5]

The concert business, one hears, is in bad shape. Audiences are down, expenses up. Young people are not supporting serious music. Inflation has forced ticket prices too high for most people. Artists are hard put to make a living.

All of which may or may not be true. Some of us have been hearing much the same stories for years. But are there any real statistics? One wonders how much of the lamentations is what Julius Bloom, who runs Carnegie Hall, refers to as the Kashouk Syndrome.

Michel Kashouk was a concert manager in the 1920s. He handled some important artists, and often sold out with them. But, to hear his cries and lamentations, he was always running a losing operation. No matter what he put on, he lost money, or so he claimed.

One day, after listening to Kashouk *kvetch* [whine] for a couple of hours, Sol Hurok, who was just beginning to make a name for himself as an impresario, put the question direct.

"Tell me, Kashouk," Hurok wanted to know. "If you always lose so much money, why do you stay in business?"

Kashouk looked at Hurok in astonishment.

"How else can I make a living?" he answered.

To Bloom, there always is a Kashouk around, and Bloom is skeptical of some alleged figures showing heavy losses. "The more complaining you do, the less people are apt to ask for money," he says. "Not everybody in the concert business is that way, but a lot are, and they get away with it. Who shows figures? Has anybody ever seen Hurok's books? Has anybody," says Bloom, in a spurt of honesty,

[5] From "Is Anybody Listening?" by Harold C. Schonberg, noted music critic and author. *Harper's Magazine*. 242:111-12. F. '71. Copyright © 1971, by Minneapolis Star and Tribune Co., Inc. Reprinted from the February, 1971 issue of *Harper's Magazine* by permission of the author.

"ever seen mine? Figures to me have always been very suspect."

Bloom, known as the philosopher of concert managers. concedes that there are areas where business is down. Those are counterbalanced in areas where business is up. Kurt Weinhold, the chief operative of the biggest concert agency in the business, Columbia Artists Management, agrees with Bloom. The concert business is spotty all over the United States, he says. In some cities, activity has increased, in others it has gone down, and he sees no discernible pattern. One thing is certain, and it is that there has been little change over the years following World War II (the Depression decades, of course, posed an entirely different set of problems): big-name artists and organizations continue to draw, as they always did.

The Chicago Lyric Opera reports its best season ever. "The people around here have a lust for opera," a spokesman says. Kurt Herbert Adler, who runs the San Francisco Opera, is happy. He too is having his best season, with almost 98 per cent of all houses sold out. The Seattle Opera reports its most ambitious, most highly supported season. At the New York City Opera the performances are almost all sold out. At the Metropolitan. where overall attendance is a little down, there have nevertheless been some weeks . . . [in 1971] where box-office takes have broken all records.

The irony is that all of these organizations operate in the red. Opera, symphony—these are expensive toys. The more sold-out houses, the greater the deficits, because every performance must necessarily operate at a loss. Running expenses are phenomenally high, and ticket prices are as high as they can be pegged without losing the audience. Government money will have to come into the picture, eventually, to save the performing arts in America. It cannot be said often enough that the United States is the only country in the world where a government ignores its artists. As a result, performing-arts organizations in this country are in des-

perate straits. But that is not for lack of public support.
More people are going to concerts than ever before.

Solo Recitals Are a Special Case

Where there has been a decided change in the concert
business involves the solo recital, especially in New York.
But even here the situation must be carefully examined. At
any time, there have been only a relatively few musicians
who had the mysterious magnetism that would fill concert
halls the world over. Some forty years ago, in a day of powerful and individual virtuosos, only a dozen at most could be
counted upon to sell out at every concert. Concert managers
would go crazy trying to fill halls for the other artists, some
of them great ones. In those days one could pick up student
tickets for such tremendous musicians as Mischa Levitzki or
Josef Lhevinne for 25 cents. Or one could get tickets where
only the admission tax had to be paid. Or, if one had any
contacts at all, there were countless free tickets to be had.
Managers would, and still do, "paper" a hall to get people
in. Anything to prevent an artist playing to a half-empty
house.

But a New York recital was mandatory. In a way it still
is, though its importance has diminished. The idea for a
New York concert, and especially for a debut recital, was to
get good or (hopefully) rave reviews, which seemed to impress the managers in the provinces. A sheaf of highly favorable reviews could sell an artist, even make his career for a
while (though in the long run, of course, an artist must
make his own career). In those days there were a dozen or
so New York newspapers, many of them with influential
critics. There also were the music magazines, especially *Musical Courier* and *Musical America*.

Now there are no magazines, and only one newspaper
that really counts around the country: the New York *Times*.
As a result, young artists are more and more reluctant to
give New York debut recitals. There is no longer even any
guarantee that the recital will be covered, as honest man-

agers are forced to tell their clients. "One newspaper," says Anne O'Donnell of New York Recital Associates, "is not enough for balanced reviews. A bad review in the *Times* is no longer offset by other opinions." The music critics on the *Times,* perfectly aware of the problem, can do nothing about it, and they curse the day when the *Herald Tribune* and the other newspapers went under.

Even artists of stature have in the past decade been avoiding the rigors of a New York recital. They get around it by other means. They may confine their appearances to dates with orchestra, in which case they get the publicity, the exposure, and a built-in audience. Or they may appear on one of the subscription series around town, such as the Hunter College Saturday night concerts, or the Great Performers at Philharmonic Hall, or on one of the Carnegie Hall-backed series, or at the Grace Rainey Rogers Auditorium [in the Metropolitan Museum of Art]. That way they get their normal fee and do not have to worry about taking a loss at an ill-attended concert. The subscription-series manager takes care of everything.

Antiseptic Artists Don't Fill Recital Halls

Younger artists have a harder time, as they always did. The geniuses on the order of a Heifetz, Horowitz, or Tauber never had much trouble; their unusual gifts were recognized from the beginning. Unfortunately, genius on that order is rare, and it seems to be even rarer today. Young instrumentalists today are invariably good, but they seem to lack the magic, the personality, the supreme confidence (call it arrogance, if you will) that so many of the older generation had. They are emotionally tight, and they tend to sound the same way. All over the world we are getting a class of pianists and violinists best described as competition types. They all have won competitions. To win competitions, you have to impress judges. To impress judges, often a pedantic lot, you have to play with careful and literal brilliance. Literalism means strict adherence to the printed note, something unknown to virtuosos of the Romantic period. A young artist, no matter how brilliant or imaginative, is not going to win competitions unless he plays in a pretty strict manner. That is supposed to show his "musicianship." (Historically this is all wrong, but that is another story.) And so we get these accomplished young people, all sounding alike, all accuracy and spit-and-polish (conductors, too), all failing in the central idea of being a great artist, and that is to impress one's own personality on the music without distorting the essential meaning.

Small wonder, then, that audiences have not taken this breed to their hearts. Antiseptic playing is great for the clinic but not for the concert hall. The young people come and go, but most of them under no circumstances can make a career, because they have so little of themselves to offer. That includes Van Cliburn, whose reputation among musicians is fading fast. Audiences should not be blamed for their failure, any more than audiences should be blamed for the failure of a composer. If hardly anybody likes a composer's music, the fault is not necessarily with the audience. It conceivably *could* be the composer's fault, you know.

Anyway, when one speaks of audiences, it should be remembered that there is no one audience. There are audiences. There are opera audiences, and even here there are subdivisions. Many will attend only Italian opera. Many others would not be caught dead near such an "inferior" kind of art as Italian opera, and will attend only Mozart or Wagner performances. There is a symphony audience. There is a singers' audience that would never attend a piano recital but will turn out en masse for Tebaldi, Sutherland, or Corelli. There are those who concentrate on piano recitals. Surprisingly few music lovers are responsive to all forms of music, though there are some, and they are the backbone of the industry. In metropolitan New York, an area taking in some twenty million people, the steady concert-going audience (managers say) is about thirty thousand. Managers presumably should know, though the figure does look small. Kashouk Syndrome?

There are, of course, certain factors operating today that were not in existence before the war. In big cities, people are increasingly loath to go out at night. With ticket prices at an unprecedented high, an evening at a concert or opera for a suburbanite (dinner, baby-sitter, parking and whatnot) can cost a small fortune. Television has made inroads. And, they say, young people are not supporting classical music, though that argument has something smelly about it. Did young people *ever* support serious music? Back in the 1930s, there were cries that they cared for nothing but Benny Goodman, Gene Krupa, and the other jazz heroes. All the experts went around saying that we had to bring young people into the concert halls or music would die. They are still saying it, and music is not dying. On the contrary, it is, despite the Kashouks, surprisingly healthy. Serious music, through history, has never been a very popular art form (and in the Anglo-Saxon nations it has been even less popular than in other countries), but it always has managed to siphon off enough enthusiasts to keep it going, and it will always continue to do so.

V. MOVIES—THE NOW ART

EDITOR'S INTRODUCTION

A very persuasive case can be made for the argument that movies are the most vital of the arts today. The medium has a devoted following among younger, under-forty audiences. It is studied seriously in colleges and universities around the country. Just as creative writing has always been offered as a course, so now film making is a legitimate field of study for creative young people.

Film flows effortlessly across international boundaries. The most hotly discussed films in any given year in the United States will include a half dozen from Europe or Japan. Similarly, audiences abroad are offered most American-made films.

The variety of films available is very large, although less commercial films often face distribution and booking problems. Because they are seen by an audience so much larger than will see even the most popular play, movies tend to be a common ground and conversational meeting place for a broad segment of the better educated younger portion of the population. Criticisms of movies are written today with a seriousness formerly devoted only to the printed word.

The first article in this section is a broad overview of the state of film today. Written by Richard Worsnop of *Editorial Research Reports*, the selection surveys the great popularity of film, the newsworthiness of film offerings, film rating codes, the effort to amass film archives before fragile old prints melt away, and the modifications the challenge of television has made on films and film making. The surprising popularity of old movies shown not on television but in theaters and museums is the subject of the next article, "Cashing In on Vintage Flicks."

An article from *U.S. News & World Report* follows, discussing the economics of Hollywood production today. Special emphasis is given to the impact television has had on film making. The last article in the section describes a new phenomenon in American-made films—movies made specifically for the newly discovered black audience. The first wave of these films has been exploitative, sex-and-violence, but Roger Ebert sees this phase as just the infancy of a new art form.

MOVIES AS ART [1]

Motion pictures have advanced, in three quarters of a century, from the nickelodeon to Lincoln Center [of the Performing Arts, in New York City]—from inexpensive entertainment for the masses to "the central art of our time." Most of the people who go to the movies are young, intelligent and, to an extent not fully appreciated, film-educated. A recent survey, commissioned by the Motion Picture Association of America, found that around 50 per cent of the contemporary film audience is under age twenty-four and that 75 per cent of the audience is under age forty. Today's average high school student spends 11,000 hours in the classroom before graduation. By contrast, the same student has watched television for 15,000 hours and has seen five hundred feature motion pictures by the time he is graduated. Around 75 per cent of the TV viewing time, moreover, has been taken up by filmed programs.

Small wonder, then, that young people consider film "their" medium. Courses on production and appreciation of motion pictures are proliferating in the country's colleges and even in high schools. The fourth National Student Film Festival was held recently at Lincoln Center in New York City. Some of the most sought-after directors now in Hollywood are relative newcomers to the motion picture industry —Mike Nichols (*Who's Afraid of Virginia Woolf?*, *The*

[1] From a report by Richard L. Worsnop, staff writer. *Editorial Research Reports.* v 1, no 21:413-19, 424-7. Je. 4, '69. Reprinted by permission.

Graduate) , Francis Ford Coppola (*You're a Big Boy Now,
Finian's Rainbow*), Noel Black (*Pretty Poison*), John Cassavetes (*Shadows, Faces*).

Youth-oriented movies have scored both critical and financial success. The most notable recent example is *The
Graduate,* a 1968 picture that in its first year of theater release became the fourth biggest box-office hit in the history
of the movies. Of the top ten films, ranked according to rentals received by American and Canadian distributors, no
fewer than seven were released in the past six years and four
of the seven had special appeal for young people.

Rising Stature of Movie Critics and Criticism

Because movies are taken more seriously than heretofore
by persons who regularly see them, film criticism has become more serious also. Movies were dismissed as trivial for
years, even by many of those who worked in them; the great
director David Wark Griffith initially was "ashamed at being
reduced to this low form of occupation." Accordingly, film
criticism tended to be hackwork. A conspicuous exception to
this general rule was the criticism of the late novelist James
Agee, who considered motion pictures an art form and treated them as such in his reviews for *Time* and *The Nation* in
the 1940s.

Today, some of the country's leading critics are engaged
in reviewing and analysis of films. They include, among
others, Pauline Kael (the *New Yorker*), Stanley Kauffmann
(the *New Republic*), and Judith Crist (*New York*). Charles
Champlin, principal film critic for the Los Angeles *Times,*
has written: "The revolution of rising interest in films and
film makers . . . sweeps along the film critic as well. He probably has more readers these days, and certainly more discerning readers. A plot synopsis and a 'Gee Whiz' won't suffice,
if they ever did."

More esoteric criticism may be found in the French journal *Cahiers du Cinéma* and the American quarterly *Film*

Culture. The guiding principle of the criticism published in both magazines is the *auteur* theory—the notion that every film has an "author," who almost always turns out to be the director. In other words, the collected films of a distinguished director can be expected to form a body of work with a distinctive, unifying vision. Opponents of the *auteur* school contend that it produces dogmatic criticism. A minor film by a highly esteemed *auteur* director like Alfred Hitchcock is apt to be overpraised, while a major picture by a lightly regarded director like John Huston is likely to be underrated.

Certain recent movies have become almost news events, as was the case with *The Birth of a Nation* and *Gone With the Wind* in earlier years. *Bonnie and Clyde,* a 1967 release that recounted the criminal careers of the bank robbers Bonnie Parker and Clyde Barrow in the 1930s, was dismissed initially as a routinely sensational film of the gangster genre. But soon several critics had second thoughts. *Bonnie and Clyde,* according to the emerging consensus, was a perceptive study of ambivalent American attitudes toward violence. In the end the film was nominated for several Academy of Motion Picture Arts and Sciences awards, and one of its stars, Estelle Parsons, won the 1968 best-supporting-actress award.

"The Public Has Been Underrated"

The Graduate, released a year after *Bonnie and Clyde,* was a critical and box-office hit from the beginning. Jacob Brackman, in a long article about it in the *New Yorker,* said:

[*The Graduate*] seems to have become something of a cultural phenomenon—a nearly mandatory movie experience, which can be discussed in gatherings that cross the boundaries of age and class. It also seems to be one of those propitious works of art which support the theory that we are no longer necessarily two publics—the undiscerning and the demanding—for whom separate kinds of entertainment must be provided. Its sensational profits suggest that Hollywood can have both its cake and its art. . . . *The Graduate* seems to be telling us that the public has been underrated.

Much of the appeal of *The Graduate* derives from its irreverent, even contemptuous attitude toward middle-class mores. Young people today often condemn America as a "plastic society." Thus, at a party scene occurring near the beginning of *The Graduate,* a middle-aged man draws aside the young hero of the film, Benjamin, and whispers to him the secret of success: "Plastics." Young people, it is said, readily identify themselves with the naive Benjamin, while middle-aged people are able to enjoy the film because they do *not* identify themselves with Benjamin's mother and father, Mrs. Robinson, and the other parents portrayed in *The Graduate*.

A number of recent pictures have made news because of their frank approach to sex. *I Am Curious (Yellow),* a Swedish film that includes several scenes of sexual intercourse, has been playing to capacity audiences wherever it has been shown. *The Killing of Sister George,* based on a play about lesbianism, contains a scene depicting a sexual act between two women. Director Edward Dmytryk said . . . [in January 1969] that he had been ordered to insert a homosexual rape scene in the forthcoming *Act of Anger*. Scenes of nudity have become commonplace in both American and European films.

Revision of Code Handling of Sex and Violence

These developments have led to demands that movies be censored. State police in Connecticut ordered theater managers to delete the sex scene in *Sister George,* and the managers complied. They did so despite the fact that the Supreme Court, in a series of rulings, has held prior censorship of motion pictures unconstitutional and has severely limited the powers of state and local censors. Freed from such outside restraints, the American motion picture industry has instituted a system of self-regulation which in effect delegates to parents the decision of whether their children should see a given movie.

The Motion Picture Code and Rating Program, drawn up by the Motion Picture Association of America and put into effect November 1, 1968, established a Code and Rating Administration which assigns to every film exhibited in the United States one of the following four ratings: G—suggested for general audiences; M—suggested for mature audiences (adults and mature young people); R—persons under sixteen years of age not admitted unless accompanied by parent or adult guardian; X—persons under sixteen not admitted. . . .

[Effective January 25, 1972, the ratings were changed to the following: G—All ages admitted. General audiences; PG—All ages admitted. Parental guidance suggested; R—Restricted. Under 17 requires accompanying parent or adult guardian; X—No one under 17 admitted. (Age limit may vary in certain areas.)—Ed.]

In determining what rating a picture should be given, the Code Administrator is expected to take into account the following standards laid down by the MPAA:

1. The basic dignity and value of human life shall be respected and upheld. Restraint shall be exercised in portraying the taking of life.

2. Evil, sin, crime and wrongdoing shall not be justified.

3. Special restraint shall be exercised in portraying criminal or anti-social activities in which minors participate or are involved.

4. Detailed and protracted acts of brutality, cruelty, physical violence, torture and abuse shall not be presented.

5. Indecent or undue exposure of the human body shall not be presented.

6. Illicit sex relationships shall not be justified. Intimate sex scenes violating common standards of decency shall not be portrayed.

7. Restraint and care shall be exercised in presentations dealing with sex aberrations.

8. Obscene speech, gestures or movements shall not be presented. Undue profanity shall not be permitted.

9. Religion shall not be demeaned.

10. Words or symbols contemptuous of racial, religious or national groups shall not be used so as to incite bigotry or hatred.

11. Excessive cruelty to animals shall not be portrayed and animals shall not be treated inhumanely.

The foregoing standards roughly parallel those contained in the old Motion Picture Production Code, which was drawn up in 1930 after widespread protest against licentiousness and crime on the screen. The old code, however, was considerably more detailed than the new one, and mar of its taboos seem quaint or incomprehensible today. Prohibited words and expressions included *fanny, tomcat, nerts* and *hold on to your hat.* Even after revision in 1956, the old code banned utterance of such words as *chippie, pansy,* and *S.O.B.*

Fate of Old Films; Effort to Build Up Archives

Such matters are of only passing interest to film scholars. Their primary concern at present is the preservation of motion pictures in film archives. Numerous films of the past, masterpieces as well as potboilers, may be irretrievably lost. The American Film Institute, after surveying the field, found that one half of all films ever made in the United States no longer were accessible.

Thousands were never copyrighted and could not be located. Thousands more, printed on fragile nitrate stock, had turned to dust and been discarded. Countless others were scattered in depositories and private collections all over the world.

Many American classics—films such as *Scarface,* with Paul Muni; Theda Bara's *Cleopatra; Stagecoach,* John Ford's great Western; *The Hunchback of Notre Dame* with Lon Chaney, Sr. —no longer could be found in complete 35mm safety prints. Of the approximately 200,000 motion pictures released in the United States since 1894, less than one tenth were stored in major film archives on safety stock.

The perishability of film stock complicates the task of preservation, even when negatives or prints are available.

Until 1952, motion pictures intended for theater release were photographed on film with a nitrocellulose base (nitrate film). The chief advantages of nitrate film were flexibility and wearability. But it has one fatal flaw: the nitrogen compounds of which it is composed are highly unstable. "Nitrate film begins to decompose from the moment its production is completed."

Disintegration of nitrate film usually is slow but always is irreversible. In the course of decomposition, the film releases noxious gases, shrinks, and becomes even more highly inflammable than it is ordinarily. The film emulsion—on which the photographic images are recorded—undergoes progressive discoloration and fading. Finally, the entire film congeals into a solid mass and then disintegrates into a brownish powder.

Fortunately, a more reliable kind of film stock is now available. Its raw material also is cellulose, but it is treated not with nitric acid but with acetic acid, so as to form acetyl cellulose. This acetate film is more stable and much less inflammable than nitrate film. In good storage conditions, it may be expected to have a life of two to three hundred years.

Film archivists are constantly searching for rare nitrate negatives and prints with the object of reproducing them on acetate stock before they are lost to decomposition. The resulting copies inevitably are of lower image quality than the films from which they were made; the latter, in turn, usually are several prints removed from the original camera negative.

One of the principal goals of the American Film Institute, a nonprofit corporation founded on June 5, 1967, is "to preserve, catalogue and provide for the increased accessibility of outstanding American films." On December 11, 1967, the A.F.I. board of trustees approved allocation of $1.2 million, nearly one fourth of the institute's initial budget, for the conservation of America's film heritage. The intended re-

pository of this heritage is the National Film Collection
housed in the Library of Congress, Washington, D.C.

Although the Library of Congress is America's largest
film archive, with around 25,000 titles, it had, until recently,
a serious gap. The gap resulted from the fact that only thirty
feature films were deposited as evidence of copyright between
1912 and 1942. To dramatize the situation, the A.F.I. and a
panel of film historians drew up an initial rescue list of 250
important American films believed to be lost or in danger
of being lost because good 35mm copies of them were not
known to exist in any archive. Seventy-five per cent of those
films now have been located.

Long-unavailable and presumably lost films sometimes
turn up in private collections or in foreign film archives. For
example, Gosfilmfond (State Film Archives of the Soviet
Union) recently donated to the Museum of Modern Art two
D. W. Griffith features released in 1919—*A Romance of
Happy Valley* and *Scarlet Days*—in return for some early
Russian newsreels. But discovery sometimes comes too late.
One of the classics of the silent screen was Erich von Stroheim's 1923 movie of the Frank Norris novel *McTeague*.
Meticulously faithful to the book, Stroheim's film ran to
fifty reels—more than eight hours—and was trimmed by him
to twenty-four reels. When the director refused to cut it
further, Irving Thalberg, the new production chief of
Metro-Goldwyn-Mayer, reduced it to ten reels and released
it under the title *Greed*.

Film historians have long wondered if an uncut version
of *Greed* existed. It transpired that, until about 1960, the
M-G-M vaults contained a print of the film about six reels
longer than that which was put into theater release. But the
longer version was filed under the working title of *McTeague*,
not *Greed*, and by the time it was discovered in the vaults,
the film had disintegrated. . . .

CASHING IN ON VINTAGE FLICKS [2]

Lanky, pickle-pussed Charlotte Greenwood takes a quick look at Carmen Miranda's hat, an inverted Dixie-cup affair wound with a braided rope, and says: "Oh, boy, I'll have to watch my lampshades and bellcords with her around." In the Murray Hill Theater in New York, where a 1943 movie called *The Gang's All Here* is playing, that line invariably brings down the house.

To laugh at such gags, and to grow misty-eyed while a youthful Alice Faye sings a World War II lament . . . , moviegoers . . . paid $14,000 at the Murray Hill box-office [in one week in December 1971]. Downtown, crowds jammed a tiny off-Broadway theater and paid $3,500 to $4,000 to see *The Wizard of Oz*, a film shown regularly on television. In Chicago, Denver, Boston, Houston, and elsewhere, theaters are finding that a revival of a distinguished picture from the past—or even an undistinguished one—often draws more customers than a new, big-budget production.

Though the "nostalgia boom" has fed the surging interest in oldies, a more pressing reason is the shortage of new films from depressed Hollywood. Several Broadway theaters in recent weeks have closed down temporarily while they waited for new pictures to come their way. Others fill empty weeks with live vaudeville and rock-music groups. Some are being forced to lower their standards by running "porno-flicks."

"There aren't too many good new movies coming out right now," explains Mark Mitchell, manager of Houston's Park III theater, which is showing *A Night at the Opera* with the Marx Brothers. "As a matter of fact, there aren't many new movies, period."

The film shortage has provided an opening for enterprising newcomers. Theatrical producer Arthur Whitelaw noted the lines . . . [in 1971] when the [New York] Museum

[2] From article in *Business Week*. p 25. D. 18, '71. Reprinted from the December 18, 1971 issue of *Business Week* by special permission. © 1973 by McGraw-Hill, Inc.

of Modern Art showed such antiques as Bob Hope in *Fifty Million Frenchmen* and Al Jolson in *The Singing Fool*. He approached Howard Otway, owner of the theater where his stage production of *You're a Good Man, Charlie Brown* played four years, about going after the same audiences with a series of old musicals. Since . . . [August 1971], the series has drawn such crowds that Otway and Whitelaw stopped giving away penny candy as an attraction.

Obtaining good old films is as difficult as getting new ones. Eric Spilker, a thirty-two-year-old former writer for *TV Guide* and *Variety*, liked *The Gang's All Here* when he saw it on television in black-and-white. He spent more than a year negotiating with Twentieth Century-Fox and others for the rights to re-release it in color. Some $3,500 needed for an option to get the picture and to prevent more TV showings was scraped together. Eventually, theater owner Don Rugoff, whose Murray Hill house was doing poorly, came through with $2,000 for a new color print of the 1943 musical. Rugoff and Spilker ran a major ad campaign, and they talked United Fruit Company into supplying huge plastic bananas and palm trees to make the lobby into a fruit-salad replica of a typical Carmen Miranda hat.

Spilker estimates that it cost $20,000 to $30,000 to open the film in one theater, but he figures to make a profit before Christmas. Rugoff now plans to exercise an option to distribute *The Gang's All Here* countrywide.

Denver's Ronald Hecht, manager of The Flick, notes that New York is not necessarily an accurate barometer of national tastes. His theater did well with a Humphrey Bogart festival, W. C. Fields, and *King Kong*, but "bombed" with Busby Berkeley. In Philadelphia, where the Bandbox Theater scheduled a summer-long festival of 1940s musicals, the result was disastrous.

"There's more to the business than simply showing old films," says Mrs. Ursula Lewis, owner of uptown Manhattan's Thalia Theater, which claims to have started the "repertory films" trend and has shown old pictures regularly since 1955. "You must schedule each picture properly, and make sure you get a good print," she says. On the one hand, obtaining prints that are not scratched or brittle is easier these days, since the interest in old films has led some producers to make new prints from their original negatives. But, Mrs. Lewis notes, the increased competition for old pictures is driving prices skyward. "We played *Citizen Kane* one hundred times over the years," she says, "and now we can't afford it."

Some theater owners are surprised at the audiences turning out to see Garbo and Mae West. "We expected an older, nostalgia-seeking crowd," says Howard Otway, "but we're getting families with young children, and college kids, as well."

The success of the backwards-looking entrepreneurs has stirred Paramount Pictures to dust off its 1927 silent feature, *Wings,* with Clara Bow and Buddy Rogers, and release it as a major 1971 picture. A sex-film distributor bought the rights from Warner Bros. to reissue a 1950 horror film, *The House of Wax,* and it grossed $32,000 in its first week at Grauman's Chinese Theater in Hollywood. When Twentieth Century-Fox found it was making money off *The Gang's All Here,* it tossed in free 1943 newsreels. Now audiences who go to see Carmen Miranda can also watch American planes drop bombs on Japanese-held islands and the Russian army march toward Berlin.

Innovations to Meet Radio and TV Competition

In their short history, motion pictures have proved remarkably adept at fending off challenges from competing mass media. The first such challenge came from radio in the late 1920s. Box-office receipts then were in decline, and introduction of vaudeville and novelty acts did not help. Then, in 1927, Warner Brothers persuaded the popular singer Al Jolson to make the first "talking" picture. *The Jazz Singer* actually was a silent film for the most part, but it contained three Jolson songs and a snatch of dialogue. The film was an instant success, and the "talkies," though still to be perfected, were on the way to reviving and revolutionizing the industry.

The next—and more serious—challenge did not come until two decades later, with the arrival of network television. The home screen offered free entertainment, as had radio, and movie attendance slumped. This time the movie industry mounted a many-pronged counterattack. Many more films than formerly were made in color, and wide-screen projection processes were developed. Three-dimensional movies, including use of special glasses, enjoyed a brief vogue in 1953-54.

The most important change, however, was that of subject matter. Television freed Hollywood "from its thrall to the twelve- or thirteen-year-old mentality for which, in the past, the [movie] moguls cheerfully admitted they aimed." At first, the strictures of the Motion Picture Production Code prevented anything more than gingerly treatment of a host of controversial subjects. Then, in 1956, the code was revised to remove the total ban on portrayal of drug addiction, drinking and miscegenation. A further revision in October 1961 sanctioned films containing "references . . . to . . . sex aberrations, provided any references are treated with care, discretion and restraint." The industry took full advantage of these new opportunities.

In the late 1940s and throughout the 1950s, the American film and television industries remained mutually hostile. Sylvester L. (Pat) Weaver Jr., president of the National Broadcasting Company, in 1953 extolled the presentation of live entertainment on television and condemned the use of "sterile kines [kinescopes]." For their part, Hollywood studios declined to sell to television even the old feature-films stored in their vaults.

A major breakthrough occurred in the autumn of 1961, when NBC began to show feature films in prime time on Saturday nights. The viewer response was so favorable that a prime-time movie was scheduled on one network or another seven nights a week in the 1968-69 season. Eight such programs are in the works for the 1969-70 season. Difficulties may arise, however, when some of the current crop of sexually outspoken films become available for television showing. The author of a letter printed in the Washington *Post*, April 16, 1969, complained that a censored version of *The Chapman Report* shown on a local channel had been "so distorted that at times it didn't even make sense," and that the censorship "caused the audience to assume that certain acts occurred which in fact did not occur in the original movie."

Additional changes in film technology are in the offing. Cinerama, employing a curved screen of 140 degrees, may be supplanted by Dimension 150, which would employ a 150-degree screen. The average person's range of vision is between 160 and 170 degrees. A 360-degree screen is feasible, and was demonstrated at Montreal's Expo 67, but it does not lend itself readily to story-telling.

Dr. Richard Vetter, a former University of California professor who helped to develop Dimension 150, believes that holography, a 3-D process not requiring glasses, eventually will be adapted for theater films.

It will be three-dimensional, but not as we've known the process. You will see a total image, but if you wish a total perspective you can walk behind it and see it from the other side. It will need neither a screen nor, after a while, the circular-style dome most theaters will eventually become. Anywhere will do. The method of projection will be a laser beam and the viewer can watch from any perspective at all, just so he doesn't obstruct the beam.

Vetter has no idea exactly how the process will work: "All we know is that it is possible and should become commercially feasible by the year 2000."

Takeover of Movie Companies by Conglomerates

The current good health of the movie industry in general has made film companies one of the favorite targets of expanding conglomerate corporations. In recent years, Paramount has been acquired by Gulf & Western Industries, Inc., whose basic business activities include metals, chemicals, and electronic products; United Artists has been merged with Transamerica Corporation, a concern which deals primarily in real estate and insurance; Warner Brothers has become part of Canada's Seven Arts Productions Ltd., a company engaged in leasing of theatrical films to television; Embassy Pictures has become a subsidiary of Avco Corporation; and Universal Pictures has been acquired by the Music Corporation of America.

Only four independent film studios remain: Metro-Goldwyn-Mayer, Columbia, Walt Disney Productions, and twentieth Century-Fox. Wall Street analysts believe Fox will be the next takeover target. The studio, anticipating this possibility, has recalled its convertible debentures in the hope of persuading shareholders to exchange them for common stock. Warner-7 Arts, already a merged company, was the object of a takeover bid by the National General Corporation. When the deal fell through . . . [in January 1969], Commonwealth United Corporation and Kinney National Service Inc. submitted rival bids to acquire the company. . . . [Warner Brothers is now a subsidiary of Kinney Services, Inc.—Ed.]

THE HOLLYWOOD COMEBACK [3]

Reprinted from *U.S. News & World Report*.

America's motion picture industry, after years in the doldrums, is enjoying a new lease on life—thanks in large part to an old adversary, television. All this summer [1972] film studios have been humming to turn out the weekly adventure, comedy and variety shows to be seen on network

[3] From "Big Success Story—The Hollywood Comeback." *U.S. News & World Report*. 73:38-40. Ag. 28, '72.

TV starting in September. At the same time, studios are shooting more and more full-length movies expressly for television.

This comeback of the movie industry still falls short of levels of activity in "the good old days." Many sponsors pulled back during the recent business slowdown and have not resumed big spending. Networks, using more reruns, included fewer episodes in their weekly series than they once did.

All the same, studio executives are talking more bullishly than they have in years—and for more reason. On top of soaring earnings from TV, attendance at theaters is showing a real pickup and substantially adding to studios' profits.

Says Richard Lederer, a vice president of Warner Bros., Inc.: "It's been a scary business, but it's an awfully healthy one for us right now. All signs run counter to what the doomsayers predicted for Hollywood just a few years ago."

In the first six months of this year [1972], Warner Bros. reports receiving about $70 million from its worldwide rentals of theater films. That is more than double the firm's receipts for the same period last year and an all-time company record. "There's been a marked upturn in box-office receipts since 1971," says Mr. Lederer. "We hope this means the industry has finally bottomed out."

To Pay the Rent—TV

Hollywood executives can point to a growing number of films that are returning record profits. *Summer of '42,* made by Warners for about $1.5 million, has already earned for Warners $18 million at theaters. *Airport* cost Universal Pictures some $10 million to make and has brought the producer more than $50 million. A new Alfred Hitchcock film, *Frenzy,* cost about $2 million to make and is expected to return more than $12 million to Universal in theater rentals alone.

For now, however, most studios are looking to television for their big growth. "Television has become the bread-and-butter operation today," says one studio official. "TV pays the rent." Some movie executives go even further. "Television has saved this town," one declares. "Without TV, no studio could exist." In . . . [the summer of 1972] the Hollywood *Reporter,* a trade paper, listed 152 television films in current production, compared with 124 in the works at the same time last year. No fewer than forty-two different producers are involved in today's output.

The Screen Actors Guild reports that television is now the biggest source of income for its performing members. . . . [In 1971] members of the union had total earnings of about $114.3 million. Of that total, some 30 per cent was paid by TV film makers and an additional 51 per cent by companies producing television commercials. Only 18 per cent of guild members' income was from making motion pictures for theaters.

High Unemployment

Despite all this, because so many feature films are made on location—that is, away from studios and often overseas—unemployment here in Hollywood continues to run high. Major West Coast studios, in a continuing battle against rising production costs, are getting more and more businesslike in the way they operate. Whipping a paper from his pocket, Lew R. Wasserman, president of MCA, Inc., says: "I can tell by noon each day if a production company is off schedule."

The average thirty-minute TV program now is filmed in just three days. A two-hour "special," with a budget of from $750,000 to $1 million, is expected to be completed in twenty days or less.

Studios have all but forgotten their traditional rivalries with one another—harsh and bitter ones in many cases—and are even working together to reduce fixed overhead. Last spring [1972], for example, Warner Bros. and Columbia Pictures pooled their equipment, sets and other major properties to form Burbank Studios. Columbia is disposing of its old Hollywood studios. From now on, both companies will rent everything from costumes to cameras from Burbank Studios, Warners' old property. The two companies have invested more than $3.5 million to modernize, an amount neither could afford alone. The facilities being installed include three special video-tape studios, which will be rented out to make, among other things, TV talk and game shows.

Some new and costly equipment at Burbank Studios will even do double duty. By day, producers will make the sound portion of movies using a new 16-track quadraphonic sound stage. At night, after film work is over, this million-dollar equipment will be used to cut high-fidelity phonograph records.

All twenty-seven of the Burbank sound stages are now in use, and schedules call for them to remain busy through year's end. Fifteen different TV programs are being filmed there this summer—all but three of which will be new to TV audiences.

Some 2,700 cameramen, actors and technicians jam the one-hundred-acre lot each day. Says Robert Hagel, general manager of Burbank Studios:

"There's not an empty stage on the lot. It's insane, but it's beautiful."

Already, a need for more office space has developed. More than $2 million was spent on a Columbia/Screen Gems administration building. MCA, Inc., parent company of Universal Studios, soon will begin the construction of a second office building in its 420-acre Universal City complex. About half of this five-story structure will be used by independent film companies shooting on the adjoining lot.

MCA also is building a second film-processing laboratory for Technicolor, Inc., to handle the increased work.

Universal, meanwhile, to accommodate the overflow of production people now at its studios making TV films for this [1972] autumn and winter, has taken over a nearby motel and converted its rooms into temporary offices. All thirty-four sound stages at sprawling Universal City are now in use. By late summer, officials expect more than six thousand actors, technicians and craftsmen to be working there on twenty different shows, all at the same time. "We've never been busier," says a company executive. The motion picture industry in Hollywood is looking for even more work next year.

Ahead: Fewer Reruns

Greater demand will come, it is hoped, when the networks increase the number of new episodes presented in each of their series during a season. "The public is tired of reruns," says one industry source. "It wants more fresh material." Hollywood producers and the unions are engaged in a concerted campaign to get TV networks to expand the number of new episodes in a series from the present twenty-two or twenty-six a year.

The industry, as part of this campaign, has formed a Film and Television Co-ordinating Committee. It hopes to collect one million signatures on a petition to the Federal Communications Commission. The Committee wants the FCC to prevent networks from using reruns for more than 25 per cent of the prime-time hours in any given year.

If networks cut back on their use of old programs over and over, the co-ordinating committee says, as much as $50 million in new production would result. The Screen Actors Guild, for its part, warns that unless networks reduce their reliance on reruns, the guild in its next contract will seek a 100 per cent payment every time an actor's work is repeated on TV.

Whatever happens in this "numbers game," says Sidney J. Sheinberg, who is an MCA vice president and president of Universal Television, "there's absolutely no question that television is entering a new period of quality growth." As examples, he plans more of what are called "limited editions" and "miniseries." These are shows which last only a fixed number of weeks instead of running through an entire season and returning year after year, if successful. Such a "limited edition" is being made in conjunction with the British Broadcasting Corporation in London. It will consist of twenty-six one-hour programs based on Winston Churchill's *History of the English-Speaking Peoples*.

Stars usually not associated with TV are becoming more attracted to the medium. Starting in September [1972], for example, Yul Brynner and Samantha Eggar will be featured in a new series, "Anna and the King," on CBS. The series is based on the motion picture, *The King and I*. Producing the new program will be Twentieth Century-Fox Television, Inc. Another movie, *M*A*S*H*, will also become a TV series. . . . William Self, president of Twentieth Century-Fox Television, says the two programs reflect a trend toward adapting successful motion pictures to television.

A sign of the new profit-potential in film making is the appearance of more outside investors in the field. Major corporations are backing new movies, and even entire production companies. As a result, some names that are household words for consumer products are behind movies soon to be seen on TV or in neighborhood theaters.

The Quaker Oats Company was among the first to take such a plunge. It financed a series of four one-hour TV shows and a $3 million musical. General Electric Company recently formed a subsidiary called Tomorrow Entertainment, which will engage in a variety of leisure-time activities. Mattel, Inc., until recently known mostly as a toymaker, has formed a joint-venture film company, Radnitz/Mattel Productions. . . . "Movie making is a natural extension of the company's interest in family entertainment," says Spencer Boise, a Mattel vice president, and its movies will be designed for family audiences.

The New York-based perfume company, Fabergé, Inc., also has formed Brut Productions, Inc., which plans to make five major feature films. The first will star Elizabeth Taylor.

"We're witnessing a new form of financing in the film business," says a veteran producer here. "Hollywood certainly welcomes the move."

There are also purely private backers behind some major films now in production. One is J. Cornelius Crean, founder and chairman of Fleetwood Enterprises, a company based in Riverside, California, that mainly makes trailers and mobile homes.

Mr. Crean points out that the nearly $3 million invested in one movie, *Hammersmith Is Out,* is his own money and not that of his corporation. . . . Mr. Crean startled Hollywood by deciding to rent theaters himself to show his movie, and thus cut out the distributor-middleman.

Another innovation by Mr. Crean was to get big-name stars to work for a percentage of the gross revenues realized, plus a generous but unspecified amount for expenses. Usually "superstars" command salaries in excess of $1 million per picture, plus an almost open-ended expense account.

As investors like Quaker Oats and Mr. Crean start to produce movies, at least one major studio is turning in another direction. Metro-Goldwyn-Mayer, Inc., now plans to go into other leisure-time businesses. At a cost of $54 million, it expects to build three cruise liners, which are designed to accommodate young, budget-minded vacationers.

This firm also has started to build in Las Vegas what it bills as "the world's biggest hotel," a $90 million resort complex. Kirk Kerkorian, a board member, says the two-thousand-room project marks the company's entry into a "significant and far-reaching diversification program."

Even so, movie making remains the No. 1 business for the studio giants, and TV ranks as their most important market. Says one executive:

"We used to be a studio that also made films for television. Now, it's turned completely around—we're a studio that produces mostly for TV, and also makes some feature movies for theater audiences."

BLACK BOX OFFICE IS BEAUTIFUL [4]

The first Hollywood film directed by a black man was Gordon Parks's *The Learning Tree,* released in 1969—or just seventy-three years after Edison unveiled his Kinetoscope. It was set in the rural Midwest during a hot summer of some forty years ago, and was based on Parks's own autobiographical memories. There was murder in it, but it was not a violent film. There was also hope, love, a measure of nostalgia, and a marvelous saloon with a whorehouse upstairs that might have been celebrated by Ben Hecht, had Hecht been black and born in Kansas.

The Learning Tree is generally mentioned as the first break in Hollywood's pattern of behind-the-camera racism, but it has gathered two other distinctions that in some ways are more interesting. It is the only black movie to date that is neither contemporary nor set in the old West, and it is the only black movie so far that does not depend on the exploitation of sex, violence or racism for its fundamental box-office appeal.

Depending on how you define a black film, there have been fifteen or twenty. About the same number are currently in production. Most of the black directors are former actors, for the obvious reason that the acting profession was open to blacks for years while the craft unions were closed. Compared with the thousands of features that have been filmed in America, black movies are still a tiny minority, but they represent a beginning and almost all of them have been financially successful. At a time when no traditional combination of genre or star seems able to guarantee a profit, black movies are just about the only sure thing at the box office.

And, increasingly, they are being made by blacks as well as starring them. *The Great White Hope,* which was written, produced, and directed by whites, was not widely ac-

[4] From article by Roger Ebert, film critic for the Chicago *Sun-Times. World.* 1:67-9. S. 12, '72. Copyright © 1972 by World Magazine. Reprinted by permission.

cepted in the black community and was, in fact, one of the few black-oriented movies with a mediocre gross. Jules Dassin's *Up Tight* was another. They may turn out to have been the last ambitious, major films about blacks by whites. Although the race of the director of a B-grade black action film is of little interest, black film makers are increasingly claiming the more important black subjects as their own. Plans to film *The Confessions of Nat Turner* were dropped after a national protest by black artists and intellectuals, and Anthony Quinn's current project to star as Henri Christophe, the legendary black king of Haiti, has come under attack from the same coalition.

The problem, however, is not whether major black movies will be controlled by blacks; it's whether an important critical and artistic success can be expected in the near future from a black director. There's an abundance of talent available, but hardly any opportunity to get financing for a serious film. Black film makers can usually find bankrolls only if they turn out what *Variety* has already termed "blackploitation" movies. There is a large black audience for sex and violence, of course, just as there is a large white audience. But the major sources of financing, having identified a dependable black audience for exploitative action pictures, are playing safe by investing *only* in films which are aimed at this particular audience.

The black directors and actors I've spoken with during the last few months do not like this situation, although many of them are living with it for the moment in hopes of financing their personal projects in a year or two. A few, like Ossie Davis, have given up waiting for the white movie establishment to come around and have developed support from the black community. Davis is in pre-production on *Black Girl,* from the off-Broadway play, and James Baldwin is also said to be working on a personal film.

Such pioneering films may bear fruit in a year or two, opening the way for others to follow. In the meantime, however, the black characters who find their way to the screen all seem to be cowboys, cops, detectives, and gangsters. Even Sidney Poitier, the first black superstar and one of the few with the clout to generate his own projects, has played policemen or outlaws in five of his last eight films. Black men in movies never seem to hold jobs that don't require carrying a weapon.

Part of the problem in finding financing for non-violent black films may be the track record of the few exceptions, like *The Learning Tree*. It was released while Warner Bros. was in the throes of its divorce from Seven Arts and marriage to Kinney, and the film received inadequate promotional and booking support. It was a moderate success all the same, but to this day studios are turning down projects for ambitious black movies with a sigh and a mention of *The Learning Tree*. For his second film, Gordon Parks made an almost coldblooded decision to shovel in elements of exploitation. The result was *Shaft,* an enormously successful caper movie involving a private eye.

Shaft was also the first black movie to include scenes in which whites were put down semiritualistically as incompetent in matters of intelligence, sexuality, and survival. This summer's big black hit, *Come Back Charleston Blue,* features a white policeman who is so comically inept, cowardly, and stupid that the racist movie characterizations of the 1930s and 1940s seem to have been reversed and even improved upon. Melvin Van Peebles' *Sweet Sweetback's Baadasssss Song* also had lots of antiwhite stereotypes, but it contained so many *black* stereotypes that it managed to offend almost everybody except the huge audiences that consumed it on a basic level of carnality and bloodshed. Judging from the many audience responses I've observed in big-city theaters playing black films, black audiences seem to enjoy the current racism much as white audiences enjoyed the racism of thirty years ago. There is probably a degree of justice somewhere in this, however sad.

Degrading Black Women

If whites are not often depicted favorably in black movies, there's another category of character that fares even worse: the black woman. She has been portrayed as an inoffensive middle-class housewife in some of the Poitier films, and Gloria Foster played a strong and dignified frontier woman in Bill Cosby's neglected *Man and Boy*. But for the most part black women are used as sex symbols viewed in classically chauvinist terms.

There is a typical scene that turns up time and again: the woman is making love with the superhero when a telephone call summons him back to headquarters. The woman lies on her side, nude and expressing chagrin, while he promises to be on the case in fifteen minutes. Sometimes she gets a line or two of dialogue. Occasionally a black actress is allowed to play a secondary character fitted awkwardly into the corner of a male-dominated plot.

Yaphet Kotto, who wrote, directed, and starred in this summer's *The Limit*, talks about the screen treatment of black women with some bitterness. After the Chicago opening of his film, he said, a woman in the lobby told him: "This is the first time in a movie I ever saw a black man take a black woman out on a regular old-fashioned date."

She was right [Kotto said]. Usually a black woman has a very definite role in a film. It's just slap her, rape her, beat her up, take her into the back room. The rest of the time she stands around in sexy clothes. Most of the scenes involving black women pander to violence and obscenity and say they're telling it like it is. I can't dig that. A movie like *Sweet Sweetback* degrades black women.

Gordon Parks, who followed *Shaft* with the even more successful *Shaft's Big Score*, is also disillusioned by the difficulty of creating a black movie that is not simply violent and sexist. "I'm not going to direct any more black action movies," he says. "I liked *The Learning Tree* better than both Shafts put together, and I don't want to get typed as an action director. I want to try my hand at all kinds of films."

If he succeeds, he may become the first black director of a white film—a bridge no black has yet crossed, although whites routinely make the opposite journey. In its exclusion of blacks from the ordinary range of film making, the movie industry has become the most reactionary of America's entertainment industries. In a way, the contemporary black exploitation film is an equivalent of the "race" or "rhythm and blues" categories by which record companies used to segregate black music.

If the range in subject matter is largely limited to episodes of violence and interludes of sex, the time settings of black movies are just as restricted. They are set either in the urban present or the Western past, and there is a great gap of nearly a century in between.

The first film since *The Learning Tree* to attempt to open up this unexplored territory is *The Book of Numbers*, currently shooting on location in Dallas [Texas]. Raymond St. Jacques, who has played his share of gunslingers (he was TV's first black cowboy on "Rawhide," and played the detective Coffin Ed Johnson in *Cotton Comes to Harlem* and *Charleston Blue*), is producing, directing, and starring. Like most black film makers with unusual subject matter, he found his financing in an unusual place: the new Brut Productions division of Fabergé, the cosmetics company.

The Book of Numbers is described by St. Jacques as the "first black nostalgia film." It is set in the ghetto of a small Arkansas city in 1933, and concerns a prosperous black criminal class that makes a fortune during the Depression from the numbers racket. The movie's hero, Blueboy Harris, spends his money on fast cars, flashy clothes, and high living, and goes into partnership with a fancy woman named Pigmeat Goins.

This is the kind of subject matter white Hollywood has studiously avoided since the disappearance of "Amos 'n Andy" and the rise of self-consciousness about racial stereotypes. But now several black movies have delineated the difference between offensive stereotypes on the one hand,

and colorful character performances on the other. Leading roles tend to remain uniformly cool and heroic (and Fred Williamson is so aloof in *The Legend of Nigger Charley* that he resembles a monument to himself), but in the background some eccentric and wacky characters are beginning to pop up: Moses Gunn's rackets boss in the Shaft pictures, D'Urville Martin's fainthearted sidekick in *Nigger Charley,* or the black Tarzan dressed as Santa Claus in *Charleston Blue.*

One of the first impressions I received on the Dallas location was a delight in the 1930s fashions and hair styles. Black heroes such as John Shaft have been routinely costumed as refugees from the Brooks Brothers catalog, but in Dallas there were diamond stickpins, picture hats, wide lapels with carnations, gold watch chains and two-tone shoes all over the place.

"This Is the Way We Dressed, Talked, and Felt"

Hope Clarke, the young actress who plays Pigmeat, said she thought *The Book of Numbers* was the first film to show black people joyfully as they really lived in the recent past. "This is the way we dressed, talked, and felt," she said. "The older people tell us we aren't really living these days. Despite the oppression black people lived under in the 1930s, they developed a life-style we can love and respect, if we understand it."

The company was filming in the searing ninety-five-degree heat of Hall Street, in the Dallas ghetto, and the location had been dressed with painstaking attention to detail. There were pool hustlers hanging around the front of the Congo Café, old Lucky Strike billboards, a WPA office, shoeshine parlors, a bus terminal, and 1933 automobiles advertising (in the state's own spelling) the "Arkansas Sentennial."

It's hard to direct the young black actors in a period film like this [St. Jacques said]. They instinctively reject some of the attitudes we need in the picture; they do their militant number. But what I'm after here is a re-creation of the whole ambiance of the period, of the richness of our people.

He had hoped to make *The Book of Numbers* an all-black production, he said, but that was impossible because of the behind-the-camera craft unions:

They're the most blatant holdouts. There's not one black union cinematographer in America. Recently, the first black was made a union camera operator. We opened up as many black production jobs as we could, but because of the . . . unions there's no way to open up some jobs. No way.

St. Jacques said he could understand why so many black movies, up to now, have dealt primarily with violence and exploitation, and have presented a severely limited view of black culture and history.

The question is, what do you mean by "up to now"? How many black movies have there been? Fifteen? Sixteen? We broke into Hollywood three or four years ago. We're just getting started. The industry doesn't give a goddamn about black power or white power; all it knows is green power. If our movies make money, we get to make more. If we make a lousy movie, at least we're getting the experience that racism denied us for many long years.

I've been in some pieces of crap: *Cool Breeze* was an example of absolutely cheap, shoddy, gross exploitation. But it's part of getting things moving. . . . People put down Steppin Fetchit. He paid his dues. Because of him, there could be Poitier. Because of Poitier, I'm here. It's a question of what you have to do to survive, and you had to bend a lot more in 1930 than you do now. That's what the movie is about, in a way.

If a movie like *The Book of Numbers* is a success in the terms St. Jacques hopes for, it may be one of the transitional films in the gradual development of a more three-dimensional black cinema. When it comes, it will have to involve two primary areas of advance: greater black control over pictures, especially in the area of finance, and more latitude and imagination in subject matter.

Some of the superhero pictures, despite their fierce blackness, seem at times to be made with a subterranean consciousness of white attitudes and prejudices. They feel like commercials for black heroes, instead of adventures. John Shaft is sometimes described as the black James Bond, but the character lacks the self-kidding humor of Bond. Shaft is too humorless, too blankly heroic, and so we look to the supporting characters for moments of relaxing humanity. The same is true of many of the black cowboy pictures. There are black John Waynes now, but where are the black Robert Mitchums with a bottle in their saddlebags?

The Book of Numbers project is interesting because it doesn't seem inhibited by fear of feeding white prejudices, and is cheerfully willing to portray blacks as less than perfect. The characters in it are positive not because they are superhuman. The movie is a crime comedy, but no doubt there will be movies soon that will explore the black experience at sea-level, so to speak, instead of underground with the gangsters or on the mountaintops with superspade.

The challenge of getting more blacks behind the cameras will be much more difficult. If it took a white cinematographer like Haskell Wexler twelve years to break into the cinematographers' union, the first black director may be retired before he gets his card. In terms of getting the black experience onto the screen and into the consciousness of the American movie audience, however, it's more important that the key creative people—the directors, writers, producers, actors—be black. These are the artists who create the vision of a film, no matter what color the crew is, and the black film makers now finally, firmly, hold the tools of their art.

VI. TELEVISION—THE MASS ART

EDITOR'S INTRODUCTION

On a normal Saturday night an estimated fifty million people in this country tune into one TV program—"All in the Family." The figure fairly jumps forward, inviting comparison with the numbers of people attending live theater in a year. An author elsewhere in this compilation notes that three million people attended the performances of all twenty-four "regional theaters" over the course of a full season.

If one considers a single work presented live and on TV, the results are even more startling. Friday, February 2, 1972, CBS telecast a heavily-advertised version of Shakespeare's *Much Ado About Nothing*. Joseph Papp, whose production it was, introduced the telecast by saying that more people would see the single showing on CBS than would have seen *Much Ado* in the 373 years since Shakespeare introduced it at the Globe. The telecast was a success, but the live theater performance closed as a result of this success.

Television is there—in the living room and maybe elsewhere as well. One does not have to pay for it, or dress up and go to town to see it. It is, without a real rival, the mass art form. The vast majority of American households—even the very poor ones—have television. And it is "on" a great deal of the time.

All of this is self-evident, perhaps, but important to remember in placing television in context with the other performing arts. Critics don't take TV very seriously—but it has the audience no other art form has.

Like the other performing arts, television is permitting language and themes that were forbidden just a decade ago.

It is still the most strait-laced of the arts, because it goes directly into homes, where it is watched by children and adults alike. But the trend is definitely toward more open discussion of society's problems.

This liberalized trend is the focus of this section's opening article, "Archie Bunker and New Trends in Television." That article, which is from *Time*, surveys the new programing. The following article discusses (with the pride of one who writes for them) the ever-popular daytime serials or soap operas.

Bill Marvel of *National Observer* describes the ways of television censors (or editors, as they prefer to be called). Their big job today is whittling away at movies to be shown on television to make them "suitable for home viewing." Standards may be easing, but there is no immediate likelihood that the new crop of sex and violence movies will come to the home screen soon.

The final articles discuss the "other" network, once called educational television but now operating under the title of Public Broadcasting. After enjoying a surge of creative programming ("Sesame Street," "Masterpiece Theater," "The Great American Dream Machine"), PBS faces drastic changes because of decisions by the Nixon Administration. The first of these articles, "Can Public Broadcasting Survive?" by James MacGregor, discusses financial problems. The concluding article discusses the impact of Nixon Administration decisions on the public network.

ARCHIE BUNKER AND NEW TRENDS IN TELEVISION [1]

The "Jack Paar Show," 1960: Paar walks off the show because NBC has censored some terrible words he uttered on the air. The words were not really words but initials: w.c., for water closet, the British equivalent of toilet.

[1] From "The Team Behind Archie Bunker & Co.," a *Time* cover story. 100:48-58. S. 25 '72. Reprinted by permission from *Time*, The Weekly Newsmagazine; Copyright Time Inc.

"Petula," 1968: the sponsors, Chrysler Motor Corporation, try unsuccessfully to quash a shocking sequence in this Petula Clark special. In the sequence, Petula's white hand rests momentarily on the black arm of guest star Harry Belafonte.

"The Smothers Brothers Comedy Hour," 1969: the brothers, already in jeopardy with CBS for their satirical barbs, lose their show after an allegedly blasphemous guest spot by David Steinberg. The vein in which Steinberg took the Lord's name was comic.

Incomplete

That was the way it was on network entertainment shows. Scripts were judged not only by what they said but by what they did not say. Blacks were visible but untouchable, and bathrooms simply did not exist. By and large, any subjects were fair game except those that bore on the reality of viewers' lives. The result was prime-time programming that was at once obvious and incomplete, like connect-the-dots pictures without the lines drawn in. Reduced to japes about mistaken identities and absent-minded fathers losing their car keys, even situation comedies had few situations with which to make comedy.

But no more. TV has embarked on a new era of candor, with all the lines emphatically drawn in. During the season that began . . . [in the fall of 1972] programmers will actually be competing with each other to trace the largest number of touchy—and heretofore forbidden—ethnic, sexual and psychological themes. Religious quirks, wife swapping, child abuse, lesbianism, venereal disease—all the old taboos will be toppling. Marcus Welby . . . [in August 1972] joined the abortion debate with a patient who had not one but two in a single year. An upcoming ABC "Movie of the Week" will feature Hal Holbrook explaining his homosexuality to his son. Just for laughs, Archie Bunker's daughter will be the victim of an attempted rape.

NBC's "The Bold Ones" will be getting bolder, mainly by knifing into such delicate surgical issues as embryo transplants and lobotomy. The lobotomy episode will also depict that rarity on TV medical shows: a crooked doctor. No new adventure hero, it seems, will be admitted to the schedule without an ethnic identity badge. ABC's "Kung Fu" is a sort of "Fugitive" foo yong—a Chinese priest permanently on the lam in the American West of the 1870s, nonviolent but ready to zap troublemakers with the self-defense art of *kung fu.* The title character of NBC's "Banacek" (one of three rotating shows in the NBC "Wednesday Mystery Movie") is not only a rugged insurance sleuth but also a walking lightning rod for Polish jokes.

Indeed, the twenty new series making their bow this fall add up to a veritable pride of prejudices. CBS's "Bridget Loves Bernie" concerns a well-heeled Catholic girl who falls for a poor Jewish cab driver. In . . . [the] first episode they got married and promptly gave birth to dozens of Jewish-Catholic in-law gags. "M*A*S*H," also on CBS, is a surprisingly faithful adaptation of the grim-zany 1970 movie about an army medical unit in the Korean War. It mixes sex, surgery and insubordination until they are almost indistinguishable. . . .

The culmination of the whole trend may lie in NBC's "The Little People," which is contrived to capitalize on nearly every current vogue. It deals with the adventures of a pediatrician (thus getting into the medical bag) who practices with his rebellious daughter (the generation gap) in Hawaii (ethnic tensions) on patients whose problems go beyond mumps to things like mental retardation (controversial topics).

Bolder is not necessarily better. It is just as possible for TV shows to be inane about sex as about fathers losing their car keys. After all, the daytime soap operas have been doing it for years. By the standards of today's movies or cocktail parties, bolder is not even much bolder. Nor are all of the season's shows cultivating a racier-than-thou attitude. . . . [Fall 1972] will offer a spate of conventional programming in every category.

But on TV, a medium that magnifies the importance of things even as it shrinks their size, small gains loom large. Even allowing for a wide margin of *shlock* in the new season, some of it will be the *shlock* of recognition. With a gibe at anti-Semitism here, a humorous insight into sexual hang-ups there, home screen entertainment is beginning to be a little less of a window on a void. It is becoming a little more of a mirror.

Who is behind this transformation on the tube? A new, iconoclastic generation of creative talents? An insurgent band of reformers from outside the wasteland's preserve? Hardly. If any individuals can be said to be the catalysts, they are a pair of tanned and creased Hollywood veterans named Alan ("Bud") Yorkin and Norman Lear.

Both are canny professionals who grew up with the medium. Lear served an apprenticeship as a comedy writer in the fifties and sixties with Martin and Lewis, George Gobel, Tennessee Ernie Ford and Andy Williams, among others. Yorkin staged such shows as Martin and Lewis's, Gobel's and Dinah Shore's, later directed specials for Jack Benny and Fred Astaire. Together, as partners in a venture called Tandem Productions, they revolutionized TV comedy by adapting a British TV hit into "All in the Family."

The night "Family" went on the air in January 1971, a nervous CBS posted extra operators on its switchboard to handle the calls of protest. An outvoted censor prepared to say "I told you so," and several programming executives felt premonitions of the guillotine tingling at the backs of their necks. The network did not know whether the show would be a scandal or a flop. It was neither, of course, but instead a piece of instant American folklore.

Archie Bunker burst on-screen snorting and bellowing about "spades" and "spics" and "*that* tribe." He decried miniskirts, "bleeding heart" churchmen, food he couldn't put ketchup on and sex during daytime hours. He bullied his "dingbat" wife Edith and bemoaned his "weepin' Nellie atheist" daughter Gloria. Above all, he clashed with his liberal, long-haired son-in-law Mike Stivic, a "Polack pinko meathead" living in the Bunker household while working his way through college.

No matter that Archie tripped up on his own testiness and lost most of his arguments. He mentioned what had previously been unmentionable on TV. As played by Carroll O'Connor, he was daringly, abrasively, yet somehow endearingly funny.

With his advent, a mass-media microcosm of Middle America took shape, and a new national hero—or was it villain?—was born. It was not long before more than fifty million people were tuning in to Archie's tirades each week, making "Family" the highest-rated series on TV.

Yorkin and Lear repackaged excerpts from "Family" as an LP album and a book of Bunkerisms. Archie Bunker T shirts and beer mugs appeared. Well before Archie received a vote for the vice presidency at . . . [the 1972] Democratic Convention, columnist William S. White revealed that Washington politicos were talking about a "Bunker vote," reflecting a lower-middle-class mood of anger and resentment at a tight economy and loose permissiveness. In the White House, Richard Nixon watched an episode in which Archie's attack on "airy fairies" was blunted by the discovery that one of Archie's pals, an ex-football star, was homosexual. "That was awful," said Nixon. "It made a fool out of a good man."

Fool? Good man? Yorkin and Lear soon learned what it might have felt like to be Cadmus, the legendary Greek who sowed dragon's teeth only to see them spring up from the ground as armed men fighting each other. From the dragon's teeth of Archie's vocabulary, the producers reaped a crop of ethnic spokesmen, psychologists and sociologists, all armed with studies and surveys and battling each other over whether "Family" lampooned bigotry or glorified it. The debate seemed rather top-heavy for such light humor, but that was precisely the issue: whether "Family" was not all the more dangerous because it made bigotry an occasion for cozy chuckles and portrayed Archie as an overgrown boy, naughty but ultimately harmless.

Laura Z. Hobson, who prodded the public conscience with her 1947 novel about anti-Semitism, *Gentlemen's Agreement,* complained that "you cannot be a bigot and be lovable." Lear replied that bigotry was most common and most insidious when it occurred in otherwise lovable people. Since then, Northwestern University sociologist Charles Moskos has supported both the Bunkers and the de-Bunkers by arguing that ... [the] humor cuts two ways: "It is a cheap way for tolerant upper-middle-class liberals to escape their own prejudices while the bigots get their views reinforced." Lear concedes that the humorous treatment of bigotry means "we don't have to think about it now." But he maintains that "we're swallowing just the littlest bit of truth about ourselves, and it sits there for the unconscious to toss about later."

Meanwhile, Yorkin and Lear's breakthrough with "Family" has prompted a host of imitators—led by Yorkin and Lear. The best of the shows to explore the comic territory they opened up is their "Sanford and Son" (also adapted from a British original), which made its debut on NBC last January [1972].

New Door

"Sanford" is built around the love-hate relationship of a black father and son who run a junk business in Los Angeles. But it is no "Family" in blackface. Its humor plays *with* prejudices rather than on them. "Were they colored?" the police asked the elder Sanford about a gang of thieves in an early episode. "Yeah," he replied. "White." The old man, played by Redd Foxx, has none of Archie's anger. He is simply an engaging con artist who will resort to any ruse to keep his son from quitting the business and leaving home.

The show's true novelty stems from its relatively realistic portrayal of poor blacks in a warm, natural relationship. "My friends in the black community told me they're gonna be at home watching, just like it's a Joe Louis fight," Foxx said when the show began. "Means a lot to them." It must have meant a lot to other people as well. In one of the fastest ascents in TV history, "Sanford" shot up into the top-ten-rated shows, close behind "Family."

"Those two shows, 'All in the Family' and 'Sanford and Son,' have opened a new door for television," says NBC's vice president in charge of programming, Lawrence White. "They have made it clear that we can do broad-based entertainment shows that deal in reality as a source for comedy."

Among the first through that new door for the ... [1972-1973] season were—once again—Yorkin and Lear. This time they have a spin-off from "Family" called "Maude," and already it ranks as one of the fall's top prospects. Maude is Edith Bunker's cousin who lives somewhere in upstate New York. As played by the formidable (5 feet 9 inches), husky-contraltoed Beatrice Arthur, she may do for liberal suburban matrons what Archie has done for urban hardhats.

"The flip side of Archie," is the way Lear describes Maude. "She is a Roosevelt liberal who has her feet firmly planted in the forties." Maude knows how to arrange all the right-thinking enlightened attitudes around herself, but when she is challenged they open up like gunwales on a galleon, and she blazes away with broadsides at feckless repairmen, greedy cab drivers and her priggish right-wing neighbor.

She first hove into view on a "Family" episode. ... The entire Bunker family fell ill and Maude took over the household—especially Archie ("You can either get up off that couch and eat your breakfast or lie there and feed off your own fat ... and if you choose the latter you can probably lie there for months"). The CBS brass was watching and, in Norman Lear's words, "saw a star." A second episode—in effect a pilot—was concocted, in which Archie and Edith visited Maude on the eve of her daughter's wedding to a Jew: it clinched the deal for a new series.

"Maude breaks every rule of television from the start," says Robert Wood, head of CBS-TV. "She's on her fourth husband, and she is living with a divorced daughter who has a son. It's not so long ago that you couldn't show a woman divorced from one husband, let alone three." In . . . [an] opening episode, Maude had fairly tame set-tos with a door-to-door salesman and a psychiatrist, but her future outings will include a look at legalizing marijuana and a fling at black-radical-chic party giving à la Leonard Bernstein. In one episode . . . , she even gets pregnant and decides to seek an abortion, while her shaken husband looks into the vasectomy market.

With "Family," "Sanford" and "Maude" going for them, Yorkin and Lear have emerged in a big way from the twilight of anonymity behind the scenes in TV. Johnny Carson was barely exaggerating when he introduced . . . [the 1972] Emmy Award ceremonies as "an evening with Norman Lear." After Lear had collected one of the seven Emmys won by "Family," Carson quipped: "I understand Norman has just sold his acceptance speech as a new series."

Of course it isn't just the recognition; it's the money. Yorkin and Lear's profits from their three shows . . . [for 1972-1973] could reach $5 million, not counting the take from books, records and other byproduct merchandising. With offers of further projects pouring in, their Tandem headquarters is the hottest TV production office in Hollywood. So busy are the partners nowadays that they rarely get a chance to be in the office. They run the business by remote control, communicating with each other by memo. Occasionally they rendezvous for a quick huddle in the parking lot of a studio where one or the other is coming from or going to work.

Lear, who spends most of his time at CBS as executive producer of "Family" and "Maude," is a dapper, droopy-mustached man of fifty with the comedy writer's congenital air of melancholy, like a sensitive spaniel; he tends to be the spokesman for the team. Yorkin, forty-six, who concentrates on being executive producer of "Sanford" at NBC, is a beefy, genial soul with a flushed face and a habit of punctuating his speech with a stabbing thumb that one senses could easily become a fist. Both men, in their divergent styles, bear down hard on their staffs to achieve the gloss and precision that have become characteristic of Yorkin and Lear productions.

Ruthless Rehash

Each of their shows is taped before a live audience. Yorkin or Lear then leads the cast and staff through a ruthless rehash session, and another performance is taped before a second audience. The show that eventually goes on the air combines the best of the two performances. This system provides a TV equivalent of the Broadway theater's "tryout experience," says "Family" Producer John Rich. "We're doing a play a week and we're trying to be entertaining every minute. We don't have a Hartford or a Boston for tryouts."

No shows on TV are more heavily rewritten than Yorkin and Lear's. Whether a script originates with their staff or is one of the 60 percent that come from freelancers, Yorkin and Lear usually see that it gets torn to pieces. The story line acquires new twists, the dialogue is recast, sometimes new characters are added.

"When a writer says, 'I'd like to see Edith Bunker in menopause,' I know we can peel back layers of Edith and Archie," says Lear. "When I hear an idea like that, I'm like a dog hanging on to a bone. I'll hang on forever until the show is right." One of this season's early "Family" episodes, about Archie's infatuation with the brassy wife of an old Air Force buddy, was conceived in June 1971. After eight major rewrites, it was scheduled for taping . . . [in February 1972]. Lear withdrew it at the last minute for more work when it was already in rehearsal. By the time it was finally taped . . . [in the] summer, everybody had had a crack at it, including the actors.

This is where Yorkin and Lear's flair for casting shows up—in picking seemingly unlikely performers who will grow into their roles and shape them with their own temperaments. Veteran Comic Foxx won his "Sanford" role partly on the strength of his only other dramatic appearance—as a junkman in the 1970 movie *Cotton Comes to Harlem*. He and co-star Demond Wilson now work with . . . producer and chief writer Aaron Ruben, who is white, to "translate the scripts into spook," as Foxx puts it. "The writers are beginning to learn that black is another language." (Meantime, Ruben is training black writers for the show.)

Lear thought of Carroll O'Connor for Archie because he recalled O'Connor's "outrageous but likable" general in the 1966 movie *What Did You Do in the War, Daddy?* O'Connor's participation in the development of Archie's character has become so passionate that it frequently causes tension on the "Family" staff. At times he flatly refuses to perform a script that does not conform to his conception of the role. An example was . . . [the] episode about Archie's being trapped in a stalled elevator with a middle-class black and a Puerto Rican girl about to give birth to a baby. It was used only after Lear overrode O'Connor's objections that it "wouldn't work." (Such difficulties with O'Connor made the renegotiation of his contract . . . "a bloodbath," according to one Tandem source.)

"When we see a helicopter land on the roof of the CBS building and a man in a dark suit from New York get out," jokes one of Lear's writers, "we know we're in censorship trouble." Network censors are rarely as melodramatic as that. Usually they are a task force of some two dozen men and women, each of whom oversees a portion of a network's total programming (including commercials); they review scripts and sit in on tapings and screenings, questioning anything that seems to conflict with Federal broadcasting law or their network's standards of taste.

But if the helicopter is more writer's fancy than fact, the censorship troubles of Yorkin and Lear are all too real. "Family," particularly, has at least one big crisis a season. . . . [In 1970] it was over the episode about homosexuality that President Nixon so disliked; last winter, a show on which son-in-law Mike's exam jitters made him sexually impotent. Smaller crises abound, as when CBS succeeded in knocking out the word *Mafia* from one script, the term *smart-ass* from another.

So far, Lear has staved off every major threat with a combination of logic, persuasion, threats to cancel a whole episode (or the whole series), and scathing contempt for the censors' "think-tank mentality," his term for the corporate and governmental attitude that underestimates "how wiseheart a great many Americans are."

Doing things over is one thing; overdoing them is another. Amid all their taking of pains, Yorkin and Lear rarely forget the importance of not being earnest. Their shows are, after all, only situation comedies. The scripts, however inventive, tend more toward formula than organic form. The characterizations are still exaggerated cutouts from the fabric of real life.

"Sure we want to get the social theme," says "Family" writer Alan Ross, "but the show is a half-hour comedy on commercial TV, and if it's not funny you might as well be on the lecture platform." As George S. Kaufman pointed out, speaking of Broadway, the savage moralizing of satire is what closes at the end of one week; sitcoms must go on week after week. Acknowledging this, Yorkin and Lear are entertainers who brandish the weapons of satire but use them sparingly. Their Bunkers and Sanfords are sheep in wolves' clothing—domesticated in every sense from a tougher breed of British precursors.

The BBC's arch-Archie is Alf Garnett, a spiteful, bitter dockside worker in "Till Death Us Do Part," the model for "Family." The fathers of Sanford and son are Steptoe and son, on the BBC series of the same name, a pair of cockney rag-and-bone men who batter themselves and each other relentlessly against a dead end of life. Both Yorkin and Lear adaptations follow the same recipe: take one BBC show, add the milk of human kindness and stir for thirty minutes. "One of our major concerns was not to make 'Sanford' look too grim," says Yorkin. "The 'Steptoe' set in England was dark and gloomy; we took pains to make ours poor but not depressing."

Yorkin and Lear grew up in such a milieu—poor but not depressing—and both reach back to early days for authentic touches to bring their shows home to viewers. Lear's salesman father, though a second-generation Russian Jew, was almost as much of a source for Archie as Alf Garnett was. He used to call Norman "the laziest white kid I ever saw" and order his wife to "stifle"—both expressions that were to become Archie's. The family shifted restlessly from New Haven, Connecticut, where Norman was born, to nearby Hartford, then to Boston and New York City, as the elder Lear pursued a variety of get-rich-quick schemes with a lot of gall but little success. Norman decided to become a press agent like his uncle Jack, "the only relative on either side of my family who could throw a nephew a quarter when he visited."

After a year at Boston's Emerson College and another three with the Fifteenth Air Force near Foggia, Italy (since enshrined as Archie's old unit), Lear was laid off his first job with a Manhattan publicity firm. Then he went bankrupt with his own novelty ashtray business. He took his wife and infant daughter to Los Angeles, where half of his luck improved. He at least survived as a door-to-door salesman of furniture and baby pictures.

Lear and a fellow hawker named Ed Simmons decided that the street they really wanted to work was comedy writing. It was 1949; the infant medium of television was ravenous for material; the new team needed just one break in order to kiss baby pictures goodbye—and Lear typically made it for them. Posing as a New York *Times* reporter, he got Danny Thomas' phone number from an agent. He called Thomas and offered him a piece of material for a benefit engagement that night at Ciro's in Hollywood. "How long will it run?" asked Thomas. "How long do you need?" replied Lear. "Seven minutes." Simmons and Lear wrote and delivered a routine in two hours, and Thomas liked it enough to use it. In the audience was David Susskind, then a New York agent, who was so impressed that he signed Lear and Simmons as writers for a TV show called "The Ford Star Review."

By the time Yorkin and Lear crossed paths on the Martin and Lewis show two years later, the Lear-Simmons partnership was doing so well that it had to farm out some of its work to the younger team of Neil Simon, the future Broadway playwright, and his brother Danny. "To me Norman was big-time," recalls Yorkin, who was then a lowly assistant director. "He lived at the Waldorf and moved in a different world from my own."

Yorkin was born and raised in the coal-mining town of Washington, Pennsylvania, where his father, a women's-wear merchant, was part of a tiny and somewhat beleaguered Jewish community. Anomalously armed with a degree in electrical engineering from Carnegie Tech, he went to New York in 1946 with the intention of becoming a theater director. A daytime job as a TV repairman supported his night classes in English literature at Columbia University. "My partner and I used to find excuses to fix sets in good restaurants so we could get free meals from the waiters," he says.

Eventually Yorkin's engineering background landed him a job as a cameraman at NBC. Zealously he sent executives a steady stream of critiques of the programs he transmitted. They were never answered. He moved up anyway, first to stage manager and then to the control booth, where producers and directors sit. There Lear spotted him and prevailed upon Martin and Lewis to make him their director.

Two Unicycles

Yorkin and Lear's flourishing careers over the next eight years defied geometry, being two parallel lines that finally intersected. In 1959, well after Lear had drifted apart from Simmons (now a script developer at Universal Studios), the new partnership of Tandem Productions was founded. The first joint venture was the movie *Come Blow Your Horn,* adapted from a play by former Lear assistant Neil Simon, which everybody agreed would be a perfect vehicle for Frank Sinatra.

Everybody, that is, except Sinatra. When Sinatra failed to respond to a barrage of calls and telegrams from Yorkin and Lear, they hired a plane to fly over his house and sky-write their phone number. After eight months of such stunts, Sinatra agreed to do the picture "just to get you guys off my back."

Their wives gave Yorkin and Lear a two-seater bicycle to mark the launching of Tandem. Two unicycles would have been more appropriate. After the initial box-office splash of *Horn,* their subsequent movies (*Never Too Late, Divorce American Style*) fared only so-so. They decided to become parallel again, maintaining a loose, collaborative relationship and splitting their pooled earnings.

Today they kibitz freely about each other's projects, but friction is minimized because each supplies a different emphasis to the partnership. "Lear can put words in your mouth like nobody else," says Dick Van Dyke, who has starred in Yorkin and Lear efforts for both TV and movies. "Yorkin, as a director, is the ideal interpreter of Lear's writing." Lear is more preoccupied with creative matters. Yorkin, with more business acumen, is by his own admission "the heavy in financial deals."

Lear has the sort of temperament that might be described by Archie Bunker as "hebe Hollywood egghead"—or, if Archie knew the word, compulsive. The only eye in the hurricane of activity that he whips up around him each day is the moment when he retires to the men's room for a thorough perusal of the New York *Times*. One of his two outside interests is writing letters to Presidents and other political leaders on such topics as Viet Nam, the ICBM debate and school desegregation. His voluminous correspondence with four Administrations is filed in a cabinet at his ten-room colonial house in Brentwood, where he lives with his second wife, ex-department-store-executive Frances Loeb, and their two daughters. His other interest is psychoanalysis. After some four years in it, he is such a believer that he has been known to present young writers with $25 gift vouchers for initial sessions with analysts.

Yorkin blends more readily into the gregarious California life-style. Usually calm and direct, he can be stern at work (after being directed by him in a special, Fred Astaire give him a bull whip), but he enjoys relaxing with a wide circle of friends. He and his wife—former actress Peggy Diem, by whom he has a son and a daughter—shuttle between a Spanish-style home in Beverly Hills and a rented beach house at Malibu, where Yorkin occasionally dons an Archie Bunker sweatshirt and barbecues hot dogs for neighbors like the Henry Mancinis. Although, like Lear, he describes himself as a putative liberal, he sometimes turns up for dinner with Henry Kissinger when the presidential adviser makes one of his forays into Hollywood salons.

"I've seen Norman cry and I've seen Bud kick a door because things weren't working," says one of their aides. "But they've never attacked each other." Why not? "We have no ego problem," says Yorkin. "We know that whatever either of us succeeds in doing is good for both, because it all goes in the same pot." The pot is growing bigger; what to do next is becoming a multimillion-dollar question. Indeed, what else is left for Yorkin and Lear now that they have given TV a new system of dating—B.B. and A.B. (Before Bunker and After Bunker)? How much longer can they compete with themselves for the top audience ratings?

Quite a while, no doubt. Already in the works is a one-hour special on Duke Ellington. Lear is preparing yet another sitcom series for a possible January [1973] debut on CBS, this one about a black family named Jones. " 'Sanford' isn't trying to reflect real ghetto life," Lear maintains. Compared with ghetto dwellers, those two men live very, very well. What I would like to do is a real black-ghetto family show."

Above all, though, Yorkin and Lear yearn to make it in the movies. The failure that each nurses most lovingly is a film. With Yorkin it is *Start the Revolution Without Me,* a 1970 farce about the French Revolution that he produced and directed. With Lear it is *Cold Turkey,* a 1971 satire in which he directed his own script about an Iowa town that collectively kicks the smoking habit. Erratic but lively and intriguing, both works were just slightly out of sync with the shifting rhythms of public taste that Yorkin and Lear's TV shows have always caught so uncannily.

But their timing is improving. Yorkin has directed, and Lear has partly written, a new movie due out early next year. It stars Ryan O'Neal as a burglar whose passion, as luck would have it, is chess. The original title was *The Thief Who Came to Dinner.* Now, their eyes aglow at the thought of the mania sweeping the country after the Fischer-Spassky match in Iceland, Yorkin and Lear are eagerly dreaming up a good chess title. [The movie was released early in 1973 with the original title.—Ed.]

IN DAYTIME TV, THE GOLDEN AGE IS NOW [2]

The term [*Golden Age*] must be defined, of course; its usage analyzed. Since the phrase is customarily employed to

[2] Article by Agnes Eckhardt Nixon, a script writer for several daytime serials. *Television Quarterly.* 10:49-53. Fall '72. Reprinted by permission.

designate the past, it would seem that a certain interval of time is required to give any era the full, connotative glow of those words.

Thus, one wonders if Aeschylus or Sophocles knew, while in the throes of creation, that *his* was a Golden Age? Indeed, did Paddy Chayefsky, Tad Mosel, or Horton Foote, as they struggled to fit their work to the dimensions of the small screen console themselves with the thought that they were making television history?

Or were they, rather, plagued by the medium's then inexorable limits of space, time and money? Did they anticipate the catastrophes which can befall a live show? Finally, were they upset by the sure knowledge that the result of their labors, no matter how brilliantly produced and acted, would—after that one performance—vanish forever into the ether?

To be sure the script remained, as did the director and the actors—save those who had been knocked unconscious by a boom mike, broken a leg by tripping over a cable, or suffered a nervous breakdown from those thirty-second costume changes. And so, pragmatically speaking, the show could be recreated. But the mystical coalescence of all that talent, the special moment of magic was irretrievably lost.

Still it *was* a Golden Age of creativity and credibility—as we all acknowledge now—perhaps *because* of the traumas as well as in spite of them.

Well, the trauma may have been forgotten, but it wasn't gone. . . . It simply moved to daytime, where the dramatic serials grapple with the same old perils and pitfalls five times a week, fifty-two weeks a year, with never a hiatus and nary a rerun.

In case you're interested, that's 260 original half-hour episodes per annum, each produced in a single day, either live or live-on-tape. And how we do it is a question we frequently ask ourselves, since all our nighttime neighbors are too busy—doing thirteen or maybe six originals a year—to inquire. We suffer all the illnesses, births, deaths, psychic traumas, accidents, and natural disasters known to man. Yet the show must—and always does—go on.

Now, I wouldn't want you to get the wrong impression; if the above sounds covetous it's only because we are. Not greedy, just envious. We envy evening hours their vaster amount of time and money, their lavish style of planning, casting and rehearsing. We covet the space and freedom for interior shooting as opposed to our daily ration of four small studio sets. Upon occasion, we even become paranoid over the fact that our efforts, once aired—no matter how good— are gone forever.

We'd also enjoy the residuals. Having heard that daytime TV provides more than 60 percent of the networks' profit, we may be forgiven for feeling unappreciated now and then.

Despite all these handicaps, the daytime drama with which I have been associated has held to a high standard of excellence. We're *professionals,* from stagehands to leading ladies. Still, our art has not been accorded the high respect it deserves, though it surely is rising in public esteem.

If we're unappreciated, you may ask, why do we work so hard in daytime TV? What drives us? That our jobs pay well is surely part of the answer. But it is not the basic one. Moreover, our salaries are meagre alongside the prevailing nighttime scale. No, some other factor must account for the amazing esprit of these companies. I believe it is the pride and stimulation that comes of performing well in the face of all our restrictions and handicaps.

Aside from ability, our work requires a stamina, a tenacity and self-discipline of which many people—even talented people—are incapable. Thus a sense of elitism, as intense as it is idiosyncratic, sustains us. (After all, if the Roman gladiators could have it, why not we?) Creative satisfaction also comes from presenting a type of dramatic fare—and often, in the process, performing a public service—which, by its very genre, is unique in television.

For a serial to be successful, it must tell a compelling story about interesting, believable characters. Characters with whom the audience can personally identify or emotionally empathize. The ingredients are the same for any good dramatic presentation, except for one basic difference: the continuing form allows a fuller development of characterization while permitting the viewers to become more and more involved with the story and its people.

In a nighttime series, though the leads are placed in different situations and challenges week after week, their characters are fairly set. They do not progress or undergo mutations, as the program continues. In the serial, however, some characters work toward maturity while others regress; they go through psychological cycles, run emotional gamuts from weakness to strength, from love to hate, from cowardice to bravery. Gone are the days of the cardboard cast, the super-saccharine Helen Trents, Young Dr. Malones and Mary Nobles. Protagonists with whom the viewers most identify today, the ones they champion most, often take the wrong step, make the wrong judgment and must suffer the consequences. They're human.

That suffering of the consequences is, this writer submits, key to a serial's popularity and longevity. For any dramatic entertainment to be a success in 1972 it must be relevant. And relevance repudiates the cliché of the sunset fadeout, of Nirvana on earth. In contemporary society, the mind viewing the small screen knows, if it knows anything at all, that life is not perfect, and that man has caused the imperfections. Has caused them and must "suffer the consequences"—from a family quarrel to a global war. Thus a certain kinship is established between the fictional characters with their problems and the viewer at home with his. The viewer naturally wishes to see how these TV neighbors cope with their misfortunes, day by day, week in, week out, year after year. Audiences are bound, not by the chains of hero worship, but by the easily recognized common bonds of human frailty and human valor.

Naturally, staying contemporary and topical means that our plots and our style are more sophisticated now than ten, or even five years ago. But *all* forms of entertainment are more sophisticated today. Soap opera is simply keeping pace with that trend. We must, however, always bear in mind the motley nature of our audience, and the responsibility which that wide spectrum of viewers—from preschoolers to octogenarians—imposes.

Still, observing all guidelines we have gone far. We have done the story of a young college couple living together without benefit of clergy. We had the first legal abortion on television. We have dealt dramatically with the subject of male infertility and, in the near future, we shall explore the problem of female frigidity.

Perhaps the most gratifying aspect of "relevance," is the way it has permitted us to incorporate into our "soaps" many socially significant issues, to educate viewers while we are entertaining them.

One is not suggesting for a moment, however, that this service has been performed solely by daytime shows. But implicit in the serial is the opportunity to give an important subject an in-depth treatment, over weeks and months, which is impossible on any nighttime series that must have a new theme, or message, in each episode.

Thus, a five-month campaign to inform women of the efficacy of the Pap smear test in detecting uterine cancer in its early stages brought a bonanza of mail from appreciative women across the country, many of whom, having followed our advice and discovered the condition in themselves, claimed we had saved their lives.

For almost two years we told the story of a young Negro woman of light pigmentation who passed as white. This sequence was done primarily because it furnished us with an intense, absorbing drama that attracted viewers. But the mail response substantiated our belief that it was absorbing *because* it was relevant and because it explained to the viewers the sociological motivations for such a denial of heritage and race, due to the rejections suffered by the young woman from both the black and white communities. The ultimate tragedy we were presenting was simply another instance of man's cruelty to man, instigated by ignorance and prejudice.

In a drug-abuse sequence, after taking six months to bring a teenage character—in whom the audience had great interest—to the point of serious drug involvement, we made a daring departure from our fictional format by introducing "Cathy" into the reality of the Odyssey House Drug Rehabilitation Center in New York City.

Once on location there, with eight real-life teenage ex-addicts, no thought was given to prepared scripts or rehearsal. We simply taped, hour after hour, over three consecutive days, marathon group therapy sessions. Here these intense, highly articulate kids related their own experiences and the messages they had for young Americans, and their elders, on the subject of drugs. . . . The tapes of the sessions were then edited into briefer, self-contained segments, and presented throughout the summer in twenty different episodes.

When seventeen-year-old Austin Warner calmly spoke of having slashed his wrists, not because he wanted to die but because he was a lost, confused youth seeking affection, his words had a devastating impact. An impact I challenge the best writer or actor extant even to approximate.

When Wendy Norins said, "Cathy, it's not a weakness to ask for help; if people hadn't cared about me eleven months ago when I first came into the program, I would probably be dead on a slab," young viewers knew, by the magic transmitted only through truth, that Wendy was not speaking solely to Cathy, but to each of them personally.

Our "pitch" to Dr. Judianne Denson-Gerber, executive director of the various Odyssey Houses in and around New York, had been that the medium of a soap opera—many of whose viewers, of all age groups, are not the sort who read periodicals or even their daily newspapers, and who would be apt to turn off a documentary program on drug addiction —could be the means of disseminating a vital message to the people most in need of receiving it. The huge number of letters, telegrams and phone calls—for which we were at first totally unprepared either in manpower or emotionally— showed us how right our thesis had been.

More recently, we have had an eight-month campaign to educate viewers—particularly the young ones—to the endemic proportions of venereal disease and all its ramifications. We followed this with an article on the subject—supposedly written by a young reporter on the program—which we offered free to any viewer who requested it. "Venereal Disease: A Fact We Must Face and Fight" also gave the address of the Venereal Disease Branch of the Public Health Service for Disease Control in Atlanta, Georgia, for anyone wishing to get further information on setting up some type of educational program in his (or her) own community.

Over ten thousand requests for the article were received by ABC and, according to William Schwartz, educational consultant for the Public Health Bureau, letters arrived at his desk from all over the country in a steady stream, all as a result of the story and the printed piece. To quote Mr. Schwartz, "We were never before able to reach, effectively, the teenagers who are most in need of this information but you have now shown us how it can be done."

Our next project, still in the planning stage, is the subject of child abuse which is rarely mentioned because it is so abhorrent even to consider. Yet it does exist, to a horrifying degree, and needs to be brought to light.

Other relevant topics we have dealt with include ecology, mental health—particularly the very common anxiety-depression syndrome—the danger of carbon monoxide poisoning in the home, a returned POW and a young soldier missing in Vietnam.

These are only some of the subjects treated on only a few of the soaps. There are many other fine serials, on all three networks, done by talented, dedicated writers, producers and actors, similarly motivated and equally effective. . . . It is surely superfluous to add that if they were not garnering an audience they would be taken off the air.

No form of entertainment receives more criticism, or ridicule, than soap opera. The term has become a cliché of literary denigration and we are the frequent butt of jokes and parodies within our own industry, even on the air. Certainly we should be the last to say that we have no faults. But occasionally we do wonder how nighttime's offerings would look, by comparison, if they had to meet our output and our production schedule? We ponder how much they might accomplish under the same circumstances.

It is what we manage to achieve in this regard, despite our failings, that fostered the temerity of my title. We *are* in a Golden Age and we are making the most of it.

THE (SNIP)SDAY NIGHT (BLEEP)IE [3]

Millions of viewers of the ABC "Sunday Night Movie" a few weeks ago, watched Jack Lemmon and Sandy Dennis as *The Out-of-Towners* who lose their battle with New York City and retreat in dignity. At the end of the film, as broadcast by ABC, the jet bearing the couple back to their small Ohio home town wings off into the blue.

Only it didn't happen that way. In the version seen by millions of moviegoers over the past year and a half, the couple have settled comfortably into their seats when a swarthy man waving a pistol announces that the plane is being hijacked to Cuba. So much for dignified retreats.

Many in ABC's audience never knew they had missed a typical Neil Simon fillip. Many who did undoubtedly

[3] Article by Bill Marvel, staff correspondent. *National Observer.* p 24. N. 25, '72. Reprinted with permission from *The National Observer,* copyright Dow Jones & Company, Inc. 1972.

shrugged it off as another example of network meddling. A few were angry enough to phone ABC the next morning.

You say that your favorite movie was on television recently too? And you waited and waited for your favorite scene? And suddenly the screen was blank and the movie was over? Blame the networks' broadcast standards and practices departments, television's censors.

"We Never Censor"

Correction. At the networks, nobody censors. "Censorship is a dirty word," says Tom Swafford, CBS vice president in charge of broadcast standards. "And in this department we hate dirty words." Censorship, to Swafford, implies some outside force, such as Government, controlling what goes on and gets taken off television.

"We never censor anything," avers Grace Johnsen, ABC's director of standards and practices and the person who cut the hijacking from *The Out-of-Towners.* "We do look at films for good taste, however." And over at NBC they do what Herminio Traviesas, vice president in charge of those same standards and practices, calls creative editing. The aim of creative editing is to help get a movie onto television, Traviesas explains, adding, "The question we try and answer is, 'How do we save the program?' "

NBC performed one notable salvage operation on *The Anderson Tapes,* which in its original screen version included erotic scenes, nudity, dirty words—just the sort of things that cause a censor's scissors hand to twitch nervously. "When I first sat down and looked at it," Traviesas recalls, "I said I really didn't see how we could ever show it on the air."

Nevertheless, NBC's management asked him to draw up a list of objections to the film. The distributor, Columbia Pictures, sent in two editors to work on the listed scenes.

The picture concerns a former convict plotting to pull off the big job while the police listen in to his plans by electronic surveillance. "Because the picture had a gimmick," Traviesas says, "we could always switch to a tape if there was something objectionable in a scene. For example, we got rid of one shot of a girl on top of a guy and put in one of two people listening to the same scene on tape." In other scenes the hanky-panky went on off-camera, suggested by on-camera dialog; removing the suggestive dialog rendered the scenes harmless enough, though Traviesas concedes a few viewers may have wondered what was going on.

Herminio Traviesas hardly resembles a hysterical blue-nose conducting search-and-destroy missions through some director's work of art. An urbane, chatty man with thirty-five years' experience in the broadcast business, mostly in advertising, he regards his job as the embodiment of NBC's collective attitude in matters of good taste. Mrs. Johnsen, who has held her job for twenty years, sees to it that complaints from viewers get passed around the office and answered promptly. Both are, in short, business people, because in an industry that depends upon a mass audience, censorship is good business—like it or not.

Nobody knows that better by now than Tom Swafford, who became head of CBS' program standards just in time to get caught in the outcry early this year after CBS aired *The Damned*. To date, *The Damned* is the only X-rated film to appear on television—and, Swafford adds, it may be the last for some time to come.

"We rather naively assumed," he says, "that anybody would understand that if we edited the thing properly there wouldn't be anything offensive." Some thirty-six minutes were cut out of the film, an editing job that makes NBC's surgery on *The Anderson Tapes* look like a manicure. Scenes involving child molesting, transvestism, and various other unwholesome activities were snipped, but still people were offended and the protests rolled in—seventeen thousand of them at the last count.

The Anderson Tapes and *The Damned* notwithstanding, the networks' biggest headache is not the wave of permissiveness in recent movies but the trend toward graphic violence. How violent is too violent? Herminio Traviesas recalls with chagrin the time he turned down a picture for excessive rough stuff only to have it turn up on a competing network. "ABC ran it and creamed us in the ratings," he sighs.

Is ABC more permissive than NBC? ABC's Grace Johnsen laughs. "In the industry we have the reputation of being the most cautious," she says. Cautious or not, almost everyone in the industry agrees that the ABC "Sunday Night Movie" is the strongest movie package on television. Among other blockbusters ABC has acquired all seven James Bond pictures (*Goldfinger* has already pulled astronomical ratings, but the other six won't be seen until 1974), *Love Story*, which may have been shown to the largest television movie audience in history, *The Odd Couple, True Grit, Patton*, with its seven Academy Awards, *Lawrence of Arabia, Dr. Dolittle*, and *Z*.

Before a penny of ABC's cash went out—for the James Bond pictures and *Love Story*, the cash reportedly flowed in record amounts—Grace Johnsen sat through the films under consideration, stopwatch in hand, notebook ready. This procedure, roughly the same from network to network, results in a report containing a short synopsis of each film and a list of deletions recommended by broadcast standards and practices. This report goes to the program department and, in Mrs. Johnsen's words "initiates the cutting process."

Often the report is just a list of words that must be expunged. In *Love Story*, ABC excised Jenny's scatological favorite expression. On the tube, love apparently means never having to say a certain eight-letter barnyard epithet. "Such a shame," says Mrs. Johnsen, meaning that it's a shame the word was there in the first place, not it's a shame that she had to take it out. "It's a beautiful story." The few other dirty words that found their way to the television screen during *Love Story* apparently passed unnoticed. The few telephoned complaints to ABC the next morning had to do with a scene in which the lovers appeared in bed together naked (at least from the shoulder blades up), and another scene in which they expressed antireligious sentiment.

George C. Scott's language in *Patton* is something else again. Movie generals are permitted to say things that Radcliffes are not, and so Mrs. Johnsen has allowed *Patton* one *sonofabitch* and a couple of *bastards,* including the famous lines: "No poor bastard ever won a war by dying for his country. He did it by making some other poor bastard die for his country." Most other dirty words have been taken out because ABC feels there are limits, after all, even for generals.

Film editors can do lip surgery so skilfully that an audience is seldom aware that the character on their television sets is not saying what he said on the silver screen. "With obscenity you normally have the word at either the beginning or the end of a sentence, so it's easy to take out," Mrs. Johnsen explains. "The great difficulty comes when it's in the middle of a sentence and the character is facing the camera."

When this happens, editors search the movie's sound track for another, unobjectionable word that fits the occasion—and the character's lip movements. Then the nice word is dubbed in. (The same technique has occasionally been used to edit speeches for politicians and other public figures.)

According to Ralph Charell, director of feature films for ABC, less than one minute has been cut from *Patton's* 167-minute length—and the longest single cut was made because of network sensitivity to cruelty to animals, not humans. The excised scene shows two donkeys blocking the road in front of General George Patton's convoy until they are simply blasted out of the way. After the public outcry over televised bullfights a few years ago, ABC decided that scene had to go.

Despite frequent allegations, mostly by politicians, that they are not responsive to public opinion, television networks are vulnerable to myriad public pressures. Nowhere is that vulnerability more evident than in the broadcast standards and practices departments.

"Two years ago," recalls Mrs. Johnsen, "we had to go back and rescreen all pictures because of violence and the public change in attitude in regard to it. We found some of the old Westerns had a lot of sadistic violence." Often such reviews lead the networks to drop a movie that has been shown once before.

Today's news can often torpedo yesterday's movie. *The Out-of-Towners,* with its jolly hijacking scene—made before air piracy and terrorism had become such prevalent problems—is a good example.

Films also can get in trouble by their treatment of formerly docile minority groups. "We have to be very careful how we portray Indians, blacks, and Mexican-Americans," says NBC's Herminio Traviesas. His review of NBC's film backlog turned up one that was no longer acceptable because of derogatory references to Mexican-Americans and another that could be shown only after extensive cutting.

At ABC, Marshal Rooster Cogburn's passing mention of a bandit named Mexican Bob was cut from *True Grit.*

Not surprisingly, the public still connects the job of censor with sex, and the network censors' offices inevitably spend a lot of their time reassuring nervous viewers that they are not about to air stag films on the Sunday- or Monday- or Tuesday-night movie. Trouble is, the movies being made these days make it harder to find a film that *is* suitable for television. Ralph Charell, who shops for ABC's movies, says the networks in effect have plowed through Hollywood's entire output—twice, since network movies are repeated once.

Movies in Two Versions

The supply of television films is diminishing so fast that ABC is now screening movies released in 1970 and 1971. NBC still has a large backlog, so its situation is not so critical. But NBC's Traviesas admits that "if I had to go out into the market tomorrow and buy films I would be faced with tremendous problems." Perhaps the solution, he suggests, is for directors to shoot two versions of a film: one for the violence-loving, sex-ridden movie buff, the other for the family television audience.

Extra footage not used in the original screen version, according to Tom Swafford, saved Richard Brooks' *The Professionals* for CBS. A scene in which a group of Mexican troops are executed, one by one, by revolutionaries—all in graphic close-up—was replaced by footage showing Lee Marvin and Burt Lancaster watching the executions from nearby hills.

Neither Traviesas nor Charell believes that the answer is widening the censorship gate to let randier movies reach the TV viewers. "The movie industry is pushing standards ahead," Charell says, "and by and large we must go in the directions standards are going at the time. But we inch forward."

While CBS permitted viewers of *The Professionals* a quick glimpse of an undraped female breast—silhouetted against a campfire—the network has flatly turned down a chance to air *Carnal Knowledge* and the once X-rated *Midnight Cowboy*. There was no way they could be edited, says Swafford.

X-rated movies on NBC? Never, says Traviesas. "I was at a meeting in Denver recently," he says, "and after my talk I asked if there were any questions. One man stood up and said: 'No questions. I just want to say one thing: Keep up the good work.' Sure, standards change—but we just can't forget this country is basically puritanical."

CAN PUBLIC BROADCASTING SURVIVE? [4]

Remember "The Great American Dream Machine"? No commercial TV station would have risked letting it alienate one or another segment of its audience. But public television is supposed to do what no one else will, so "Dream Machine" made the air and by turns stimulated, puzzled, charmed and infuriated a lot of people.

Did. Not does. Earlier this year, "The Great American Dream Machine" died. It died not because the audience had resoundingly tuned it out, nor because something better had been found. It died simply because no one had the money to keep it going any longer. Since "Dream Machine" cost about half the going rate for a commercial network evening program, its demise should tell you something about public television's current financial situation. In a word, it's precarious.

This is the season [fall 1972] when—its construction phase nearly ended—public television was to have begun exploring the vast potential its architects believed it possesses. Instead, this is a season of many cutbacks, postponements and cancellations across the nation. A few smaller stations have been forced to halt local program production, picking up only the national PBS [Public Broadcasting Service] schedule. In Washington, an official of the Corporation for Public Broadcasting [CPB] gloomily predicts "fewer hours on the air, fewer episodes of continuing series, fewer original productions and a general lowering of program quality" as the season progresses.

Against that backdrop, WNET/13 [the New York PBS station] looks fairly healthy. Its 1972-73 budget of $16 million to $16.5 million is the largest in public TV, but it's also some $5 million less than last year. Staff and programming have been trimmed already, and more cuts may come during the year. Completely missing from the budget are the pro-

[4] Article by James T. MacGregor, a free-lance writer who reports on broadcasting and advertising. *Image.* 10:12-13. N. '72. Reprinted by permission of *Image,* monthly magazine of Station WNET/13.

visions for long-range planning and for spontaneous special efforts, both hallmarks of the top-quality TV station.

WNET is important to public television. Its viewing area comprises a tenth of the nation's TV homes, and a fourth of the current public TV audience. Only Los Angeles even thinks of rivalling New York's reservoir of talent, and no one contests its access to all forms of wealth. If WNET cannot make it big, the reasoning goes, who can?

Understanding the financing of WNET/13 begins with its two somewhat overlapping identities. On one level Channel 13, like 223 other public TV stations, is a local broadcaster, receiving, buying or producing programs and broadcasting them over its transmitter. Like the 223 others, it also picks up the shows broadcast nationally by the Public Broadcasting Service. But WNET is also a national production house. Along with a half-dozen other big-city public TV stations, it is commissioned each year to produce program series like "Black Journal" or "Playhouse New York," which are delivered to PBS and distributed to all public TV stations as part of the national schedule.

Under the Public Broadcasting Act of 1967, the Federal Government gives funds to the Corporation for Public Broadcasting, which is supposed to split it up three ways— some to PBS, which operates the public TV distribution "network"; some to the "production houses," which provide the programs for that network, and some to the individual stations, to partially subsidize some of their operations.

The Public Broadcasting Act was based on the report of the Carnegie Commission on Educational Television, which figured the CPB appropriation would be $75 million to $100 million a year by now, on a long-term basis. Instead, CPB this year may, at best, receive a one-year, $45 million allocation, very late. President Nixon this summer [1972] vetoed a bill providing $65 million this year and $90 million next year.

The reason for the veto depends on whom you talk to. The White House cites excessive concentration of power in public TV, asserting that CPB, PBS and the biggest production centers are imposing their will on everyone else (most of that "everyone else" disagrees). But many public TV leaders say the Administration's real objection is to news and public affairs programming, especially political commentary. White House criticism has been aimed mostly at the new National Public Affairs Center for Television, forum for Sander Vanocur, Robert MacNeil, Elizabeth Drew, et al.; and at WNET, which is also a few paces to the left of the President.

Since WNET has another problem—it costs more to produce shows in New York than in, say, Milwaukee—it's not surprising that CPB, in trimming this year's national program budget, took the biggest slice out of WNET's piece. At the moment, the $7.8 million for WNET's national programs breaks down to $2.7 million from CPB, $4 million from the Ford Foundation, and $1.1 million from several corporations and foundations to underwrite specific shows.

You might think a cut in this national budget wouldn't have much effect on local operations, but it does. National program money helps pay the overhead—facilities, staff and the like. You can't lay off half a camera if its use is cut in half, so the other half-user has to pick up the whole cost. In effect, reducing national production at WNET makes local shows cost more.

Perhaps more important, national shows have more impact than local shows, because more people see them. WNET can't compete with commercial stations on a dollar basis, so the national show is a big lure in drawing top talent to the station. Fewer lures, less talent. Ditto when WNET talks to potential backers: past and present achievements count a lot with prospective donors.

The Ford Foundation is the largest single contributor to WNET's local operations, with some $2 million this year. Channel 13's subscribers will account for another $2 million,

while $1.8 million will come from the State of New York
and the station's School Television Service fees. A variety
of business and charitable organizations add another half-
million and a final $750,000 comes from specific under-
writings (for example, the Helena Rubinstein Foundation
supports "How Do Your Children Grow?"). Two of these
avenues of support have distinctly limited horizons. The
Ford Foundation has done as much as anyone to make public TV a reality in New York. But the foundations don't
usually bankroll anything indefinitely. They prefer to provide a few years of seed money to get projects off the ground.
"WNET is terrifically dependent on Ford now, but it is not
going to go on forever," says Ward Chamberlin, former
WNET executive vice president.

What's to take up the slack? Only a few corporations,
most notably Xerox, Mobil and Standard Oil of New Jersey,
have consistently supported public TV shows. But John Jay
Iselin, vice president and managing director of WNET/13,
is spreading a new gospel to ad agencies and the like: "We
have no clutter [piled-up commercials] and a very involved
audience. Maybe we have a cost-per-thousand-viewers that
agencies should look at." That's Madison Avenue jargon for
a good vehicle to present yourself or your message. Some
recruits: Nestlé, Kraft, the Bowery Savings Bank. The message to foundations is similar, that they can further their
charitable mandates through public TV.

No one could fault the corporation or foundation for
asking who is watching. That's where the $15 check that
brings you this magazine [Image] comes in. WNET will
never match Archie Bunker for mass appeal, but Archie's
fans don't send CBS $15 to help keep it afloat. The sub-
scriber is, by definition, involved. This year WNET hopes
to boost membership to 100,000 from the current 70,000.
The real potential ought to be far higher. Public stations in
Boston and San Francisco draw as members 7 per cent of
the TV homes regularly viewing the channel in their areas.

In New York, 7 per cent would mean 210,000 members and $3.5 million in support for WNET.

That sort of support would take WNET back to the $20 million annual budget Mr. Chamberlin thinks is minimum, with no increased help from Washington or the Ford Foundation. It would provide working capital so Channel 13 could launch spur-of-the-moment coverage of Knapp Commission hearings [on police corruption in New York City] or chess championships without going round town with hat in hand. And it would allow for long-range planning. Commercial TV plans two to three years ahead; in public TV, even at WNET, it's more like two to three weeks.

Public support would also do just what Government support is supposed to do, prevent WNET and public television in general from becoming merely a collection of operas, plays, lessons and sporting events. Corporate support for public TV comes out of the advertising budget. "Once you get past education and culture into the area of national problems," says Mr. Chamberlin, "you can't find anyone to underwrite those things. Mobil is wonderful about 'Masterpiece Theatre,' but who will support a '51st State'? Of course, we keep on trying."

WHAT FUTURE FOR PUBLIC TV? [5]

For most of its five-year history, public television has been caught up in controversy and confusion. On one side have been those—in control until now—who have wanted something like the BBC, a vigorous national alternative to the commercial networks. On the other have been those—mostly in the Nixon Administration—who have wanted to spread Federal money to strengthen local public stations as a "complement" rather than an alternative to commercial TV. With . . . [the October 1972] installation of Nixon stalwart Henry Loomis as president of the Corporation for Pub-

[5] From "A Novice for Public TV." *Time.* 100:94. O. 16, '72. Reprinted by permission from *Time,* The Weekly Newsmagazine; Copyright Time Inc.

lic Broadcasting [CPB], the localists appear to have won the battle—at least for the moment.

Though the ostensible issue is centralization versus decentralization, ideology is the major consideration. Conservatives in both the Administration and Congress have strenuously opposed what they consider the liberal tone of public broadcasting news shows, like one that features former NBC commentator Sander Vanocur. They have also protested segments of the "Great American Dream Machine," a hip magazine of the air, which they thought expressed radical viewpoints. "Despite its supposed educational purpose," complained Republican Congressman Clarence Brown [Ohio], "public TV is showing more and more strictly one-sided programs: anti-Establishment, antiwar, anti-Government, anti-this, and anti-that."

Fourth Network

Clay Whitehead, policy director of Nixon's Office of Telecommunications Policy, warned public broadcasters against trying to become a fourth network. To put bite in those words, the President . . . [in June 1972] vetoed a bill that would have raised Federal spending for public TV to $65 million this year and $90 million next year (compared with the current $35 million). There would have to be, Nixon declared, a much more careful look at the direction public TV was taking. Discouraged, former CPB president John W. Macy resigned. Through presidential appointments, Nixon's men gained a majority of the fifteen-member governing board of the corporation, an independent body that actually determines how Government funds will be spent.

The change in direction at CPB should be almost immediate, since Loomis seems to agree with Nixon on every major point. Like the President, he believes in decentralization of the public broadcasting system. "The ultimate program choices," he says, "must be made by the stations, and they should have a considerable voice in national programming." Last year only 13 per cent of CPB's funds went to local TV stations; Loomis would give them at least 30 per cent.

News broadcasts of national affairs, which seem to have been a particular irritant to the White House, will be minimized under Loomis' guidelines. In a near-perfect echo of Vice President Agnew, he is particularly opposed to a newsman's coming on after a televised speech to offer his commentary on what has just been said. "Frankly," he says, "I think 'instant analysis' is lousy because the commentator who is sitting there hasn't had a chance to think." He is not opposed, however, to local stations airing local controversies.

What, then, should public TV do? "We should be trying to meet the specialized needs of a specialized audience," Loomis says. He would emphasize educational cultural shows like "Sesame Street" and 'Masterpiece Theater," which this month began showing a British-made five-part serialization of *Vanity Fair*. Indeed, if funds become any tighter, many more shows will have an English accent since it is cheaper to import a show than produce it. "Public broadcasting," Loomis asserts, "is complementary to the basic system in this country—which is commercial." He has no intention of asking for long-range financing of public TV for a while, a move that would mean greater freedom from political control. He adds: "One thing I feel pretty confident about is that this activity is going to have to be accountable to the Congress and to the Administration, any Administration. These are public funds."

With nineteen years' experience in top-level civil service positions, including almost seven years as director of the "Voice of America," Loomis, fifty-three, is regarded as an excellent administrator. He admits to having had no previous knowledge of public TV. Until his appointment, he had never even watched Washington's public station, WETA. When he was approached to become president of the Corporation for Public Broadcasting, his answer was

simple: "What the hell is it?" Democratic Representative
Lionel Van Deerlin [California], a longtime advocate of
strong public TV, . . . greeted CPB's new boss with understandable sarcasm: "It seems about the same as selecting to
coach the Washington Redskins someone who detests football. Let us hope for some avid on-the-job training." Other
critics saw Loomis' appointment as a victory for the commercial stations, which presumably will now have less worry
about popular public broadcasting shows stealing their
Nielsen ratings—and their profits.

Both Loomis and the Administration must now make
good their own ideas for public TV, however. Although decentralization would give greater attention to local concerns
and local talents, it is far from certain that this attractive
concept can be made to work. Various experiments with local
programming in the early sixties were notably disappointing.
Viewers in Cedar Rapids, Iowa, are as accustomed as viewers
in Manhattan to glossy, big-budget shows from the networks.
They are not likely to tune in to less professional shows on
the public channel, even if they do come from their area.

BIBLIOGRAPHY

An asterisk (*) preceding a reference indicates that the article or a part of it has been reprinted in this book.

BOOKS AND PAMPHLETS

Associated Councils of the Arts. Directory of state arts councils 1970-71. The Councils. 1564 Broadway. New York 10036. '71.

Associated Councils of the Arts. Washington and the Arts: a guide and directory of Federal programs and dollars for the arts. The Councils. 1564 Broadway. New York 10036. '71.

Baumol, W. J. and Bowen, W. G. Performing arts: the economic dilemma. Twentieth Century Fund. '66; paper ed. MIT press. '68.

Bloomfield, A. J. The San Francisco Opera, 1923-61. Appleton. '61.

Burgard, Ralph. Arts in the city: organizing and programming community arts councils. Associated Councils of the Arts. 1564 Broadway. New York 10036. '68.

Cutler, Bruce, ed. The arts at the grass roots. University of Kansas Press. '68.

Eaton, Quaintance. Opera caravan; adventures of the Metropolitan on tour. Farrar. '57.

Graf, Herbert. Producing opera for America. Atlantis. '61.

Humphrey, Doris. The art of making dances. Grove. '62.

Kirstein, Lincoln. Movement and metaphor; four centuries of ballet. Praeger. '70.

Knight, Arthur. The liveliest art. Mentor. '57.

Kostelanetz, Richard. The theater of mixed means. Pitman. '70.

Martin, George. The opera companion, a guide for the casual operagoer. Dodd. '61.

Mayer, M. P. Bricks, mortar and the performing arts. Twentieth Century Fund. '70; paper ed. Kraus-Thompson. '70.

Read, Herbert, consulting ed. Encyclopedia of the arts. Meredith. '66.

Terry, Walter. The ballet companion, a popular guide for the ballet-goer. Dodd. '68.

PERIODICALS

American Record Guide. 38:438+. My. '72. Contemporary music: whence, and whither? Jack Ringo.

Art in America. 59:96-7. S. '71. Joplin and Hendrix: a note on the rhetoric of death. Mary Josephson.

Atlantic. 227:75-9. Ja. '71. Anatomy of pretentiousness.

Atlantic. 227:98-101+. F. '71. Jazz meets rock. Albert Goldman.

Atlantic. 228:144+. N. '71. Our misanthropic movies. David Denby.

Business Week. p 27. N. 21, '70. Networks to cut prime time gladly.

*Business Week. p 25. D. 18, '71. Cashing in on vintage flicks.

Christian Science Monitor. p 9. N. 3, '71. Lincoln Center saga. John Beaufort.

Christian Science Monitor. p 12. Mr. 10, '72. Blanche Thebom lifts opera appeal sights. Leslie Coram.

Commentary. 53:77-81. My. '72. Movie musical. W. S. Pechter.

Commonweal. 93:466-9. F. 12, '71. Rock and rebellion, from modern jazz to hard rock, a sociological view. I. L. Horowitz.

Commonweal. 95:155-8. N. 12, '71. Exile of pirates and princes; escapist films. T. S. Reck.

*Cultural Affairs. 10:43-4. Spring '70. Regional theater: filling the vacuum. Thomas Fichandler.

*Cultural Affairs. 15:12-18. My. '71. New spaces for new arts. Peter Blake and E. P. Berkeley.

Dance Magazine. 44:52-64. Mr. '70. Arthur Mitchell & the Dance Theater of Harlem. Olga Maynard.

Dance Magazine. 44:34-5+. My. '70. Agnes De Mille speaks to Congress on the state of the arts; address with excerpts from testimony, February 9, 1970. Agnes De Mille.

Dance Magazine. 44:72-8. My. '70. Sweet smell of money; schizophrenic saga of the Houston ballet. Doris Hering.

Dance Magazine. 44:70-3. S. '70. Opera today.

Dance Magazine. 44:47-62. O. '70. Kind of oneness: regional ballet and its festivals. Doris Hering.

Dance Magazine. 46:52-65. Ap. '72. Souvenir of a gala performance. Olga Maynard.

Dance Magazine. 46:84-9. My. '72. Give the public what sells, but ... [National Ballet]. Victoria Huckenpahler.

Dance Magazine. 46:26-9. Je. '72. Champions for modern dance. S. M. Schnessel.

Dance Magazine. 46:43-58. Je. '72. Balanchine and Stravinsky: glorious undertaking. Olga Maynard.

*Dance Magazine. 46:44-50. O. '72. Seeing ballet sideways [backstage with the City Center Joffrey Ballet]. Tobi Tobias.

Ebony. 27:151-4+. My. '72. Black cinema expo '72. B. J. Mason.

*Editorial Research Reports. v 1, no 21:413-19+. Je. 4, '69. Movies as an art. R. L. Worsnop.

*Editorial Research Reports. v 2, no 24:961-78. D. 25, '70. Directions of the dance. Yorick Blumenfeld.

Esquire. 76:136-47. N. '71. Another version of the dream; Nashville Music City U.S.A.

Esquire. 76:152-5. N. '71. Last of the schlockmeisters; movies for the teen-age audience. Roger Ebert.

Film Quarterly. 25:10-18. Summer '72. Meaning is not the message. Robert Chappetta.

Fortune. 86:66-71. Mr. '72. Making the instruments that make music. Ernest Holsendolph.

*Fortune. 86:118-27. N. '72. Backstage at the [Metropolitan] Opera. Walter McQuade.

Harper's Magazine. 240:116-18+. Mr. '70. Johnny and Merv & David & Dick; or, talk is cheap and how it got that way. Richard Schickel.

*Harper's Magazine. 242:11-12. F. '71. Is anybody listening? [the concert business] H. C. Schonberg.

Harper's Magazine. 243:103-4. S. '71. Depressing uniformity of the avant-garde. H. C. Schonberg.

Harper's Magazine. 243:106-8+. N. '71. What movies try to sell us. Lewis Lapham.

Harper's Magazine. 244:104-5. Ap. '72. Balanchine: slaughtering a sacred cow. H. C. Schonberg.

Harper's Magazine. 244:87-90+. Je. '72. Video pioneers; from banality to beauty. Jonathan Price.

Harper's Magazine. 245:40+. Ja. '73. Ripping off black music; from Thomas "Daddy" Rice to Jimi Hendrix. Margo Jefferson.

HiFi. 22:42-8. Jl. '72. Birth of the American film musical. Miles Kreuger.

*High Fidelity. 22:26. O. '72. Newport in New York. Gene Lees.

*Image. 10:12-13. N. '72. Can public broadcasting survive? J. T. MacGregor.

Life. 69:10. S. 11, '70. Whatever became of the family movie. Richard Schickel.

Life. 69:12. N. 20, '70. Deadly decor for the lively arts. Walter McQuade.

Life. 71:155-6. D. 17, '71. Roar, lion, roar! Theater where children take over.

Look. 35:11-24+. Jl. 13, '71. Country music. C. S. Wren and others.

Nation. 210:329-32. Mr. 23, '70. Public channels and private censors. Nicholas Johnson.

*National Observer. p 24. N. 25, '72. The (snip) sday night (bleep) ie. Bill Marvel.

New Republic. 162:17-19. Je. 27, '70. Hollywood: shivering in the sun. William Fadiman.

New Republic. 166:22+. My. 6; 30-2. My. 13, '72. Freedom & constraint; excerpt from address. Robert Brustein.
    Same abridged with title: Toward complete freedom of expression. *Current.* 142:25-33. Jl. '72.

*New York. 5:50-1. Ag. 21, '71. The youth audience—who it is and who it isn't. Alan Rich.

New York. 5:66-7. Mr. 6, '72. The only thing we have to fear; new music and old. Alan Rich.

*New York. 5:54-5. Ap. 24, '72. Twenty years of off-Broadway: it's a good score. S. W. Little.

New York. 5:76. My. 15, '72. Museum as theater. Barbara Rose.

New York. 5:59-60. Je. 12, '72. Is there a Tweedle in your future: there is no one music of the future. Alan Rich.

*New York. 5:64. Je. 19, '72. Nothing for everyone. Alan Rich.

New York. 5:40-3. Jl. 3, '72. Jazz comes home. Albert Goldman.

New York. 5:30-2. Ag. 28, '72. How to redeem next year's jazz festival and thereby the whole city. Albert Goldman.

New York. 5:52-3. S. 4, '72. Goodbye, Mr. Tibbs: the selling of pseudo-soul. Sally Beauman.

New York Times. p 54. D. 7, '71. How Ford Fund's aid to arts grew. Howard Taubman.

New York Times. p 39. D. 21, '71. American Place Theater finds a cozy home under New York City code. A. L. Huxtable.

*New York Times. p 43+. Ja. 10, '72. Arts get more corporate help. Howard Taubman.

New York Times. p 50. Mr. 26, '72. State art grants; less money for more groups. McCandlish Phillips.

New York Times. p 44. Mr. 30, '72. Humanities goal: broader audience. Howard Taubman.

*New York Times. p 55+. Ap. 2, '72. Parkway arts center popularizes program. Robert Hanley.

New York Times. p 20. Ag. 9, '72. More blacks in theater? Yes and no. George Goodman, Jr.

New York Times. p 12. Ag. 11, '72. Rock festivals on upbeat again. Don Heckman.

New York Times. p 44. S. 11, '72. Theatrics sweeping pop music scene. Don Heckman.

New York Times. p 36. O. 17, '72. Film festival to cast a 'new mold.' McCandlish Phillips.

New York Times. p 29. D. 27, '72. Critics at a *Times* roundtable say New York is the place for trends in arts. Clive Barnes and others.

New York Times. p 28. Ja. 10, '73. Rockefeller to seek more aid for arts. M. A. Farber.

New York Times. p 21. Ja. 16, '73. Ford orchestra aid: success story. Donal Henahan.

*New York Times. p 26. Ja. 31, '73. Nixon's $80-million aid for arts is hailed. George Gent.

New York Times. p 1+. Mr. 7, '73. Papp's troupe to replace Lincoln repertory; producer will stress new U.S. plays in major policy shift. Mel Gussow.

New York Times. p 38. Mr. 7, '73. Papp's dream enriches a city. McCandlish Phillips.

New York Times. p 1+. Ap. 16, '73. Leaders in country music see chance to win the city. McCandlish Phillips.

New Yorker. 47:113-16. O. 30, '71. Current cinema; New York-made movies. Pauline Kael.

New Yorker. 48:92-101. Je. 3, '72. Cookie Oscar, Grover, Herry, Ernie, and Company. Renata Adler.

Newsweek. 75:66-7. F. 2, '70. Old Hollywood: they lost it at the movies.

Newsweek. 76:78-9. Jl. 27, '70. Very special place; Berkshire theatre festival.

Newsweek. 76:62-74. D. 7, '70. New movies; independent producers and directors.

Newsweek. 80:73-4. Jl. 3, '72. Festival of genius. Hubert Saal.

*Newsweek. 80:86-7. Ag. 28, '72. America onstage [Paul Green's historical spectaculars].

Opera News. 34:26-9. Ap. 18, '70. To be a dancer; Violette Verdy and Edward Villela talk about the art. S. J. Cohen.

Opera News. 36:6-9. O. '71. Marble hall: Chicago's civic opera house.

Opera News. 37:10-15. Ag. '72. Whither City Opera? Alan Rich.

*Opera News. 37:18-19. Ag. '72. Up in the Adirondacks; Lake George opera festival company.

Opera News. 37:9-10. N. '72. Oranges and Lemons. J. W. Freeman.

*Opera News. 37:12-15. D. 9, '72. The economics of recording. Martin Mayer.

*Opera News. 37:26-9. D. 16, '72. In the balance: U.S. opera survey, 1971-72. M. F. Rich.

PTA Magazine. 66:28-9. Ap. '72. Sorry state of TV kid shows.

Parents Magazine. 47:36-9. Je. '72. Total theater for teenagers. Bonnie Silverman and Ellen Stodolsky.

Performing Arts Review. v2, no 2:255-69. '71. Approaching business for support of the arts. Granville Meader.

Performing Arts Review. v2, no 3:407-38. '71. The state of American symphony orchestras: past, present, future. A. R. Johnson.

Ramparts Magazine. 10:60-6. N. '71. Hollywood's new wave.

*Saturday Review. 53:22-4+. F. 28, '70. Where the dollars go. Martin Mayer.

*Saturday Review. 53:81-3. F. 28, '70. The silent spring of our symphonies. Amyas Ames.

Saturday Review. 53:25-8+. Ap. 4, '70. Seismic moment in cinematic history. H. S. Resnick.

Saturday Review. 53:43-6+. Jl. 18, '70. Black arts for black youth; community arts movement in the ghetto. D. D. Bushnell.

Saturday Review. 53:59-60. O. 24, '70. Fantasy-violence syndrome; Bradley S. Greenberg and Thomas F. Gordon report findings.. R. L. Shayon.

Saturday Review. 54:56. My. 29, '71. Future after the Fillmores: rock and society. Ellen Sander.

Saturday Review. 55:14. F. 19, '72. The trouble with transplants: Sanford and son. R. L. Shayon.

Saturday Review. 55:21-2. F. 19, '72. The ballet scene. Walter Terry.

*Saturday Review. 55:40-4. F. 26, '72. Joe Papp seeks a bigger stage. S. W. Little.

Saturday Review. 55:38-42. My. 20, '72. A foresight saga in Cincinnati. Irving Kolodin.

*Saturday Review. 55:38-41. Je. 17, '72. Theater in '72; the best theater of the season was created by subsidy. Henry Hewes.

Saturday Review. 55:65. Jl. 29, '72. The New York jazz festival. Stanley Dance.

Saturday Review. 55:47-53. S. 9, '72. Great American moviemaking game. Gary Binnie.

*Saturday Review. 55:62-6. S. 9, '72. Children's theater: too good to be so scarce [International Association of Theater for Children and Youth conference]. M. B. Lobl. [abridged version]
  Reprinted in this volume: Original text supplied by author.

Saturday Review of the Arts. 1:25-9. F. '73. The first black movie stars. Donald Bogle.

Saturday Review of the Arts: 1:38-40. F. '73. The National Theater of the Deaf, flying fingers and terrific talent. Patricia Bosworth.

Senior Scholastic. 98:10-11. My. 3, '71. Festivals: rock moving indoors, to theatres and auditoriums.

Sunset. 149:24. Ag. '72. Mozart in Inverness: chamber music, opera, ballet.

*Television Quarterly. 10:49-53. Fall '72. In daytime TV, the golden age is now. A. E. Nixon.

Television/Radio Age. 20:28-9+. D. 11, '72. "Golden oldies," new MOR concept, are highlights of stations' shifting music, audiences. Tom Ratner.

Time. 95:59-60. F. 23, '70. Soul drama; Chicago's new series titled Bird of the Iron Feather.

Time. 95:55. Mr. 16, '70. Youth and sociology; youth-oriented shows.

Time. 99:49. Je. 19, '72. A day in the life [a Rolling Stones fan at a concert in San Francisco]. Tim Tyler.

Time. 100:42. Jl. 17, '72. Newport in New York: jazz festival.

*Time. 100:44-7. Jl. 17, '72. The Stones and the triumph of Marsyas.

*Time. 100:48-58. S. 25, '72. The team behind Archie Bunker & Co.

*Time. 100:94. O. 16, '72. A novice for public TV.

U.S. News & World Report. 68:80-4. My. 4, '70. New life in new places for the American theater; with interview with David Merrick.

*U.S. News & World Report. 73:38-40. Ag. 28, '72. Big success story, the Hollywood comeback.

UNESCO Courier. 23:21. Je. '70. Expanding arts in the U.S.A.

Vital Speeches of the Day. 36:658-9. Ag. 15, '70. U.S. broadcasting freedom; television's silent majority; address, June 23, 1970. Julian Goodman.

Vital Speeches of the Day. 37:186-90. Ja. 1, '71. TV: the worst of times or the best of times? address November 17, 1970. Don Durgin.

Vogue. 160:76-9+. Jl. '72. Excitement of the new physical theater. Barbara Rose.

*Wall Street Journal. p 16. N. 22, '72. Bringing the arts back to Flatbush Avenue. Phyllis Funke.

Wall Street Journal. p 1. Ja. 10, '73. Ancient art of mime revives in the U.S., often in the street. J. S. Lublin.

*Wilson Library Bulletin. 45:744-9. Ap. '71. Working with foundations: how to start a local arts council. D. J. Sager.

*World. 1:67-9. S. 12, '72. Black box-office is beautiful. Roger Ebert.

Writer. 85:22-7. Ja. '72. Writing for the theater today: practical advice on getting a play produced.